AS/A-LEVEL

16th Century
British & European
History

Geoff Woodward

Philip Allan Updates
Market Place
Deddington
Oxfordshire
OX15 0SE

tel: 01869 338652
fax: 01869 337590
e-mail: sales@philipallan.co.uk
www.philipallan.co.uk

ISBN-13: 978-0-86003-446-9
ISBN-10: 0-86003-446-1

Cover illustration by John Spencer
Printed by Raithby, Lawrence & Co Ltd, Leicester

Contents

Unit 11 *Calvin and Calvinism, 1536–72*

Unit 12 *France, 1498–1559*

Unit 13 *France, 1559–1610*

Unit 14 *The Catholic Reformation*

Introduction

About this book

Before you read this book you should already have read the recommended textbooks, made detailed notes and produced answers to examination questions. These revision notes comprise three important elements:

- **The main factual material** — this is organised in a way that will be easy to remember and revise from.
- **Glossaries of essential terms** — words that are explained in the glossaries are emboldened in the text. Make sure you learn and understand these terms.
- **Examiner's tips** — these offer advice about what to expect in examinations and how to use the factual material contained in the book.

About the AS and A2 examinations

These notes cover the major AS and A2 modules of the three main examination boards: AQA, Edexcel and OCR. Check with your teacher to find out which examination board specification you are studying. Also check which units you will be examined on.

From the specification you are studying you should find out the format the examination will take. Some modules/units require you to answer several questions based on **source material**. You might, for example, have to compare material from several sources, or assess the reliability, usefulness or value of a source to a historian, or explain why different historical interpretations appear in different sources.

Other modules/units require you to **explain a historical term** within the context of the topic you have studied. Most examination papers will require you to engage in **extended writing**. This could be a question based solely on your own knowledge. Other questions require you to combine source material and your own knowledge to produce an analytical answer.

Finally, you may have to **write an essay** based on your own knowledge. In AQA AS module 3 you will be required to write a course essay. You will be given the title beforehand but you will have to write the answer under examination conditions using your own notes.

The Advanced Subsidiary (AS) is meant to be between GCSE and A-level. You might be asked questions that require you to explain causation, e.g. 'Why did…occur?' You might also have to explain the degree of success or the main problems facing a politician or government.

The A2 examination is of a GCE A-level standard, requiring you to write balanced, analytical answers by evaluating evidence.

The AS and A2 examinations have some important new features:

- They all require you to demonstrate **knowledge and understanding** of history. This book of revision notes will assist you in remembering the main factual information required to answer both AS and A2 questions.
- You should be able to identify and explain **different historical interpretations**. Most of the chapters in this book cover topics that have encouraged considerable historical

debate. It is important to know why historians have differed. They might have based their judgements on different evidence, written at different times, or have a different philosophy or view on history.

- You will be asked to study and assess **sources in historical context**. To do this you will have to have a good factual knowledge of the topic.
- In the A2 examination you will be expected to engage in **synoptic assessment**. This will require you to draw together different aspects of history to make a historical judgement. You might have to identify different political, social, economic and cultural reasons why a historical event occurred. You will also be expected to assess the role of the individual. OCR Unit 5 modules such as France, 1498–1610, and the Catholic Reformation in the sixteenth century, require synoptic assessment.

How to prepare for the examinations

Effective planning of your revision will enable you to get the best out of the examination. Use a diary or calendar to plan the amount of time you intend to use for revision. It is much better to engage in revision over a period of time rather than all at the last minute. **Steady, methodical revision is always the best strategy.**

Examinations take place either in the morning or in the afternoon. Try to revise at a similar time. It is unwise to revise in the evening or late at night. You might eventually alter your body clock and, as a result, when you take an examination you might be mentally tired.

If you face a morning examination, give yourself plenty of time to get up and organise yourself. To prevent last-minute hitches, pack all you will need for the examination the night before. Use these revision notes as a last-minute memory prod to ensure that you have remembered the topics.

In the examination room

- Always take time to **read the examination paper carefully** to make sure that you answer the question on the paper.
- What are the **command instructions**? You may be required to explain 'why' or 'how' in an AS paper. In an A2 paper you might be asked to explain 'how far…?' or 'to what extent …?' You might also have to assess the validity of a statement.
- Are you being asked to cover a **particular period**? If the question states 1509–29, you will need to confine your answer to these years.
- Does the question contain any words or phrases that require **definition**? Make sure, for example, that you can define terms such as 'absolute', 'constitutional' and 'medieval'.
- If the question is on a social or economic topic, try to include **statistical data** to support your case.
- Take a short time to **plan your answer**. This might be little more than writing down, in list form, the points you wish to cover. This will stop you forgetting important points.
- **Pace yourself.** Allocate your time so you spend an appropriate amount of time on each question. If, for example, you are sitting a 1-hour examination and one question is worth 15 marks, a second question is worth 30 marks and a third question is worth 45 marks, spend one sixth of the time (10 minutes) on the first question, one third (20 minutes) on the second question and approximately 30 minutes on the last question.

UNIT 1 The reign of Henry VII, 1485–1509

KEY QUESTIONS

(1) What were Henry VII's aims at his accession?
(2) How far did Henry's character help him to achieve his aims?
(3) How serious a threat to Henry and his dynasty were Yorkist plots and pretenders?
(4) How effectively did Henry VII govern his kingdoms?
(5) How far did Henry VII achieve the aims of his foreign policy?
(6) Was Henry VII a 'modern' or a 'medieval' ruler?

1 What were Henry VII's aims at his accession?

1.1 Background

On 22 August 1485 Henry Tudor won the Battle of Bosworth and declared himself King of England and France, Prince of Wales and Lord of Ireland. Few expected this little-known 28-year-old Welshman to last long: since 1455, three out of four English kings had died unnaturally, and eight uprisings and rebellions had taken place between the Houses of York and Lancaster, in conflicts known as the **Wars of the Roses**.

1.2 Henry's problems in 1485

Henry's main problems were:
- his weak claim to the throne, with several Yorkists having better claims (see section 3.1 of this unit)
- that he had been out of the country for 14 years and had no administrative experience
- that he had no army, little money, and many nobles were more powerful (see section 4.6 of this unit)
- that Scotland and France were traditional enemies, and Ireland and Burgundy supported the rival House of York

1.3 Advantages

Henry's position, however, was not so bleak. He had in his favour:
- no rivals from within his own family and support for him in Wales
- the fact that foundations of effective government had been laid by the Yorkist kings, Edward IV (1461–83) and Richard III (1483–85)
- widespread popular fear of **civil war**
- the prospect of marrying Elizabeth of York, and so uniting the rival families of York and Lancaster (the Tudors were linked to the House of Lancaster)
- the support of the King of France, at least in 1485–87
- the fact that his years in exile in Brittany and France taught him how to survive

1.4 Aims

Henry's aims were:
- to secure his claim and overcome any challenges to the throne
- to establish effective government
- to acquire foreign allies and maintain peace wherever possible

It is important to realise that Henry's aims changed as his reign progressed. New and recurring problems, as well as changing circumstances, meant that he had to review his situation and adapt his aims accordingly. Thus, as he became more politically and financially secure, so he was able to pursue a more adventurous foreign policy. England was not a major European power, however, and rarely was Henry in a position to impose his will on others.

GLOSSARY

civil war: a war between people of the same country.

Wars of the Roses: the red rose was the emblem of the House of Lancaster and the white rose that of the House of York. Between 1455 and 1485 they had been intermittently at war.

EXAMINER'S TIP

This subject appears at AS for both the AQA (Alternative N) and OCR examination board specifications. You may be asked to consider how far Henry had consistent aims and which of his problems gave him the greatest difficulty. To do this you will need to look at the situations at the beginning and end of his reign, explain any differences due to fluctuating problems, and account for continuity as well as changes in his aims.

2 How far did Henry's character help him to achieve his aims?

2.1 Different views of Henry's character

Little is known about Henry's character. He commissioned no biography and few contemporaries wrote about him. Traditionally, historians have depended heavily on a few accounts written by ambassadors and chroniclers, on a portrait painted in his later years, and on a description written after his death by Polydore Vergil.

Main features
- Henry was well-built, strong and above average height.
- He had small blue eyes, few teeth, thin hair, a sallow complexion and a cheerful face.
- He was wise, prudent, cunning, resolute, shrewd, gracious and generous.
- He was dutiful, hard-working, pious, preferred peace to war, could be remote and, in later years, he became **avaricious**.

Revisionism

Vergil lived in England from 1502 and knew Henry well. His descriptions became the source material for later accounts, which tended to praise the king's character and condemn that of his predecessor, Richard III. This Tudor propaganda was endorsed in 1621 by Francis Bacon in his *History of the Reign of King Henry VII*. He saw Henry's character as the key factor in explaining his successful reign. He stressed the king's increasing love of money and exaggerated some of his accomplishments.

While much of the traditional picture of Henry has stood the test of time, at least two features have been questioned by modern **revisionist** historians. These are:
- Henry was not as miserly and nothing like as financially successful as Bacon claimed.
- Henry was more conservative than radical in temperament. He built upon the foundations laid by the Yorkist kings before him, and owed his success as much to

continuing their policies as he did to any distinctive features in his own character. These views will be considered further in section 6 of this unit.

2.2 The influence of Henry's character

The following list of traits are examples of how Henry's character helped him to achieve his aims:

- Hard-working — he devoted much time and effort to running the government, holding council meetings, making decisions, even **auditing** the royal accounts.
- Prudent — he avoided mistakes by rarely rushing decisions, and so skilfully outmanoeuvred his opponents.
- Avaricious — he understood the need to build up royal finances and to be independent of the nobility.
- Determined — he rewarded loyalty but relentlessly pursued anyone he distrusted.
- Wise — a quick learner, he soon compensated for any lack of political experience.
- Shrewd — he was flexible enough to modify his aims and methods as circumstances changed.
- Cunning — he predated the start of his reign to the eve of the Battle of Bosworth Field so that he could **attaint** lands and impose fines on his opponents.
- Statesman — he commanded respect and loyalty without relying on **factions** or favourites at the court who might have weakened his rule.

attaint: 'acts of attainder' were passed by Parliament on traitors, usually when they could not be found and brought to trial. This resulted in the attainted property passing to the Crown.

auditing: annual reviews of financial accounts.

avaricious: one who loves money.

factions: rival groups who sought to advance themselves, often through royal patronage.

revisionist: a revisionist view revises a traditional interpretation. Some historians, for example, began to revise the standard view of Henry VII in the second half of the twentieth century.

This topic appears at AS in the OCR specification. You would not be required to describe Henry VII's character but should instead consider how his aims, methods of ruling and successes or failures were influenced by his own virtues and (perhaps) vices. Examples are needed as evidence for your argument. Note that a 'how far' question requires you to consider additional factors (e.g. lack of opposition, or support from foreign powers) that may have helped Henry to achieve his aims. A balanced response is needed for a high grade.

3 How serious a threat to Henry and his dynasty were Yorkist plots and pretenders?

3.1 Background

Henry won his crown on the battlefield but his claim to the throne was not strong. He was descended from an illegitimate branch of the House of Lancaster, and in 1485 there were ten better claimants, i.e. Elizabeth of York and her four sisters and the sons of the Duke of Suffolk, as well as Edward, Earl of Warwick (see family tree overleaf).

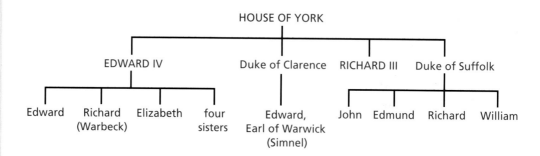

HOUSE OF YORK

EDWARD IV — Duke of Clarence — RICHARD III — Duke of Suffolk

Edward | Richard (Warbeck) | Elizabeth | four sisters

Edward, Earl of Warwick (Simnel)

John | Edmund | Richard | William

3.2 Action taken by Henry

To strengthen his position Henry was crowned king and then called Parliament, which only a king could do. He married Elizabeth of York in 1486, which took away her claim, and later that year she produced a son, Arthur, which helped to secure the **dynasty**. The remaining claimants were pursued and silenced.

Edward IV's daughters

Three of Elizabeth's sisters were married off to loyal supporters during Henry's reign; Bridget, the youngest girl, was sent to a nunnery.

Edward, Earl of Warwick

The 10-year-old son of Clarence was held in the **Tower of London** until 1499, when he was charged with attempting to escape, and executed.

House of Suffolk

The four sons of John de la Pole, Duke of Suffolk, were watched carefully. If they acted suspiciously Henry moved to arrest them. The eldest son, John, Earl of Lincoln, rejected Henry's trust and died at Stoke in 1487 fighting against the king. William, the youngest, was put in the Tower in 1501. His elder brother Edmund followed him in 1506, having eluded Henry for 5 years. Richard was never captured and fled to France.

3.3 Plots and pretenders

In some respects Henry was far more concerned about the plots and conspiracies backed by former supporters of Richard III.

Lord Lovel

In 1486 Francis, Lord Lovel (ex-Lord Chancellor) and two Stafford brothers plotted to kill the king. Henry sent troops to arrest them at Colchester but they escaped — Lovel travelled north and the Staffords went to Worcester and were caught. Henry executed the elder brother.

Lambert Simnel

Between 1486 and 1487 Simnel, a 10-year-old Oxfordshire boy, 'pretended' that he was Edward, Earl of Warwick who had escaped from the Tower. Supported by the Earl of Lincoln, Lovel and troops from Ireland and Germany (funded by Margaret of Burgundy, sister of Richard III), Simnel and his followers invaded England from Ireland in 1487 and marched to East Stoke. Earlier, Henry had tried to undermine the conspiracy by declaring the Pope's condemnation of it and by parading the real earl in London. Nevertheless, some 7,000 rebels lined up against Henry in the first really serious challenge to his throne. His nerve held, the **pretender**'s army lost, and Lincoln and Lovel were killed. Simnel was treated mercifully and became a royal servant.

Perkin Warbeck

Between 1491 and 1497 Warbeck pretended he was Richard, Duke of York, the younger of two princes who had disappeared in 1483 (allegedly murdered by Richard III). The Irish, French, Burgundians and Scots recognised him as Richard IV and promised to back his claim. Henry dealt with each challenge as best he could in the following ways:

- He threatened to dismiss the Earl of Kildare as the Lord Deputy of Ireland if he persisted in supporting Warbeck. The Irish proved loyal to the king and later disowned the pretender.
- At Etaples in 1492 the French agreed not to support Warbeck or any other claimant or pretender. They did not renege on this agreement.
- A 3-year **embargo** was imposed on trade with Burgundy, which was only lifted in 1496 (by the ***Magnus Intercursus***) when Warbeck was expelled from Flanders.
- Henry threatened to declare war on James IV of Scotland if he continued to support Warbeck in 1496–97. James backed down and was rewarded with marriage to Margaret, Henry's daughter.

In July 1497 Warbeck landed in Cornwall, gathered 6,000 supporters and marched to Taunton, where he was defeated by a royal army. He was captured, put in the Tower and, after trying to escape with the real Earl of Warwick, was hanged in 1499.

3.4 Additional problems

Warbeck's conspiracy brought Henry two more problems:

- In 1495 Sir William Stanley, Henry's step-uncle and **Lord Chamberlain**, was found to be plotting with Warbeck. Henry ordered his execution and seized his estates.
- In 1497 the Cornish protested at taxation imposed on them to pay for troops preparing to deal with Warbeck in Scotland. They claimed they should be exempt since the problem did not concern them. Fifteen thousand protesters marched to London but were dispersed by troops at Blackheath. At least 1,000 died and the ringleaders were hanged.

3.5 Further Yorkist threats, 1499–1506

In 1500 and 1502 two of Henry's three sons died. Only 10-year-old Prince Henry survived and the Tudor dynasty again seemed under threat. The king felt even more insecure when he learned that Edmund de la Pole had fled the country for Burgundy and there were rumours circulating in Calais that exiled Yorkists were discussing the succession. Henry reacted vindictively. Edmund's relatives in England were arrested, 51 estates were attainted and several 'conspirators' were hanged in 1504. Trade with Flanders was again suspended in an attempt to get Edmund deported. It was only restored in 1506 when an agreement was reached with the Archduke of Flanders to return Edmund to England. He stayed in the Tower until his execution in 1513.

3.6 How serious were the Yorkist threats?

The Yorkist claimants, plotters and pretenders presented Henry with many difficulties. Claimants could never be ignored and had to be dealt with quickly before they gathered support and slipped beyond Henry's control. His own weak claim opened the way for rivals to seek to remove him in the same way that he had removed Richard III. Henry's vulnerability, especially at the beginning of the reign, was exposed by Simnel, and both Simnel and Warbeck revealed that foreign powers were willing to exploit his domestic problems. His weak financial condition, absence of a regular army, and the difficulty of disproving the pretenders' claims, added to the seriousness of their threat.

The king's position, however, was not so bleak (although historians — unlike Henry — have the benefit of hindsight):

- None of the Yorkist plots and conspiracies received any significant support from the English nobility and gentry, who feared a return of the Wars of the Roses.
- Promises of foreign assistance did not materialise in Warbeck's case, and the armies of both pretenders were outnumbered when confronted by Henry's troops.
- The Church supported the king and discouraged potential opposition.
- Henry wisely kept genuine claimants alive so that they could be produced if required. (Not doing this had been Richard III's fatal mistake.) And Henry only executed Warwick when he was convinced it was no longer safe to keep him alive.
- Although the challengers were numerous, none received any support from London.

GLOSSARY

dynasty: family.

embargo: a trade restriction.

Lord Chamberlain: head of the king's household with direct access to the royal apartments.

Magnus Intercursus: the great treaty signed between Henry and Philip of Flanders. The agreement was given this title by Francis Bacon in 1621 to distinguish it from another trade agreement signed between England and Flanders in 1506.

pretender: someone who pretends to have a right to the throne but is a false claimant.

Tower of London: a palace where Henry resided, which also served as the state prison.

EXAMINER'S TIP

This topic is on the AS specification of the AQA (Alternative N), OCR and Edexcel examination boards. You may be asked to decide which pretender caused the greatest challenge to Henry and his dynasty. Try to make comparative points and consider the differences as well as the similarities between them. Arguably, each pretender in his own way presented a serious threat and at no time, even after the executions of Warbeck and Warwick, did Henry feel totally safe.

4 How effectively did Henry VII govern his kingdoms?

4.1 Background

Like earlier kings, Henry declared that he was ruler of England, Wales, Ireland and France. In practice his rule was more limited, both in terms of his jurisdiction and his authority.

Wales

The principality of Wales was left largely in the hands of the **Marcher Lords**, who were local landlords. Jasper Tudor, Henry's uncle, exercised considerable influence from his estates in Pembroke, and Wales as a whole benefited from increasing contacts with England.

Ireland

The Geraldine and Butler families continued to compete for the title of Henry's Lord Deputy, though their actual authority was only effective around Dublin and an area known as the **Pale**. Irish clans were notoriously unreliable: Kildare, head of the Geraldines, supported Simnel and Warbeck. In 1494 a new policy was tried. Sir Edward

Poynings was sent to conquer Ulster and to make the government of Ireland more effective. His only achievement was to pass a series of laws which in theory subjected Ireland to the English constitution. In 1496 Poynings returned to England and Kildare was reappointed Lord Deputy.

France

Calais was England's only continental possession. Henry relied upon a small garrison to protect and administer the town and surrounding lands near Guisnes. France did not attempt to recover Calais during this period.

England

England was at the heart of Henry's kingdoms. Though he travelled as far north as York and west to Bristol, the king preferred to stay near to London, his capital and centre of administration.

4.2 Councils

Henry administered his kingdoms through royal councils and the king's chamber. The king's council met regularly in London, usually with Henry in attendance, to discuss affairs of state, resolve problems and offer advice. Nobles, gentry and lawyers as well as clerics attended; loyalty and ability counted more to Henry than social status. After 1503 he held fewer meetings and relied increasingly on his chamber and household servants to implement his policies. At all times the king was at the centre of decision-making. There were three regional councils:

- The Council of the North, re-established in 1489, met at York to administer the six northern English counties.
- The Council of Wales, re-established in 1493, met at Ludlow to oversee the Welsh borders.
- The council in Ireland was based in Dublin.

4.3 Parliament

Henry called Parliament seven times to pass laws and gain money through taxation. It was not a regular part of government and was used to strengthen the king's authority. Generally supportive, granting him taxes in times of crisis, Henry was careful not to call Parliament too frequently: it only met once (1504) in the second half of his reign, when he was politically and financially more secure.

4.4 Local administration

Counties were run by a lord lieutenant, usually a royal councillor, and assisted by a sheriff, drawn from local noble and gentry families, whose prime duty was to uphold the law. The main administrators were JPs (Justices of the Peace), who sat in county law courts and were responsible for enforcing the king's laws.

4.5 Justice

A variety of law courts and kinds of justice existed in 1485:

- Church courts were subject to canon laws and were presided over by bishops.
- Common-law courts dealt with cases concerning the laity. Matters concerning the king and criminal cases were tried in London at the King's Bench, Common Pleas and Exchequer.
- **Prerogative** courts were extensions of the king's council and had been frequently used by the Yorkists. Star Chamber heard cases of rioting, **retaining** and robbery.

Requests (revived in 1493) tried cases brought by poorer people. The Council Learned in the Law (set up by Henry in 1495) dealt with royal tenants suspected of fraud and debt. These courts had no jury; instead councillors dispensed justice according to their will and the wishes of the king.

4.6 Nobility

Henry depended on the 60 or so noble families to maintain law and effective government in the counties. Members of some of the 20 aristocratic families were councillors and most served the king as lieutenants in their counties or as commissioners. A small number of peers and nobles, however, presented a military and political threat which Henry had to overcome if he was to rule effectively. For example Lord Abergavenny, the Earl of Northumberland and the Marquis of Dorset held vast estates, hundreds of retainers and castles, cannons and gunpowder.

Action taken to control the nobility

Henry overcame these challenges in the following ways:

- Gunpowder, cannons and castles were only permitted in strategic areas, e.g. on the coast.
- An Act of Livery and Maintenance (1487) tried to control retaining.
- An Act of Liveries (1504) imposed heavy fines on unlicensed retainers.
- Star Chamber and the Council Learned in the Law were used to try nobles and impose high fines (e.g. in 1506 Sir James Stanley was fined £245,000 for keeping retainers).
- The more powerful nobles were prevented from marrying heiresses.
- Two thirds of all nobles had **bonds and recognisances** imposed on them.
- Peerages were limited to a handful of nobles.
- Disobedience was punished by fines, loss of lands and (occasionally) death.

By 1509 most nobles had become obedient subjects, enjoying the benefits of a strong and stable government. Few had supported pretenders, joined rebellions or challenged Henry's right to rule. Many suffered financial losses and were 'at the king's mercy'. Nobles still exercised great influence in the counties but were less powerful in central government.

4.7 Royal finances

At his accession Henry found little money in the Treasury. Land rents were uncollected or pocketed by collectors, merchants avoided customs duties, and he was in debt to Breton and French moneylenders. The key to Henry's survival and future success lay in his building up the royal estate and in his careful management of revenue and expenditure.

Crown lands

- Crown lands were administered by the chamber system, which was flexible, efficient and watched over by the king.
- Lands lost in the Wars of the Roses were recovered by Acts of Resumption.
- Lands belonging to traitors were seized and very few (one third) were returned.
- Payments from **tenants-in-chief**, known as feudal dues, were rigorously collected.
- Cases of non-payment were investigated by Empson and Dudley, officials at the Council Learned in the Law.
- By 1509 revenue from land had increased by 50% to £42,000 a year.

Customs duties

- Henry was entitled to collect **tunnage and poundage** but, in spite of the growth in trade, merchants continued to smuggle and avoid paying duties to the king.
- The **Court of Exchequer** handled the money. There was an increase in revenue when the duties were revised in 1507.
- Customs duties were the second most valuable source of revenue, yielding about £40,000 in 1509.

Other sources of finance

- Bonds, recognisances and fines.
- **Forced loans** and benevolences (gifts).
- Parliamentary grants.

Conclusion

By prudent management of his household and by avoiding war for much of his reign, Henry left his finances in a strong condition. He was the last English king to die solvent:

- all his debts were repaid
- his revenue totalled £113,000 in 1509
- the crown jewels and plate were worth about £300,000
- the Treasury had a surplus of £225,000

EXAMINER'S TIP

This subject appears at AS in the OCR, AQA (Alternative N) and Edexcel specifications. At AS you may be asked to explain how Henry tried to improve the Crown's finances. A2 questions are more likely to want you to assess Henry's success in restoring order, controlling the nobility, handling finances and governing the country. The main issue in this question is how to measure success. You must avoid describing what happened and instead use examples to illustrate how far improvements occurred and explain why controlling the nobility was arguably the key to Henry's effective rule.

5 How far did Henry VII achieve the aims of his foreign policy?

5.1 Aims

Henry did not set down his aims but historians have offered several possibilities. They claim his aims were to:

- keep England out of war if at all possible (R. L. Storey)
- preserve the throne and the succession (P. Crowson)
- subordinate foreign relations to domestic affairs (S. B. Chrimes)

5.2 Methods

Henry managed foreign relations in a variety of ways. He used:

- diplomacy through political alliances and dynastic marriages
- economic pressure by suspending trade and negotiating agreements
- military activity that could lead to war

Henry was an opportunist, who reacted to events as they unfolded. He had little money, a small fleet, no standing army and many potential enemies.

5.3 France

In 1487 Charles VIII of France invaded Brittany. Henry had many friends there and had no wish to see France annex it. By 1492, however, Charles had forced the young Breton heiress to marry him and all that Henry could do was to attack Boulogne and negotiate a treaty. At Etaples (1492), France:

- recognised Henry as king
- paid a £10,000 pension and the costs of the English campaign
- expelled Warbeck
- kept Brittany

Good relations prevailed for the rest of Henry's reign. Indeed, when the Holy Roman Emperor (in 1498) and the King of Spain (1502) urged him to attack France, he refused.

5.4 Spain

To counter France's invasion of Brittany, Henry made an alliance with Spain at Medina del Campo in 1489. Ferdinand of Aragon agreed to:

- recognise Henry as King of England
- strengthen trade links
- try to expel France from Brittany
- consider a marriage between Arthur Tudor and Catherine of Aragon

In spite of their failure to save Brittany, Anglo–Spanish relations remained good, culminating in the marriage of Arthur and Catherine in 1501. Five months later, however, Arthur died and Henry tried in vain to wed Catherine to Prince Henry, his only surviving son.

5.5 Scotland

In 1486 a 3-year truce was signed with the Scots but relations were never stable. Trouble broke out in 1496 when Warbeck turned up in Edinburgh. He offered to recover Berwick if James IV would back his claim to Henry's throne. James agreed, although withdrew his support when an English army approached the border. At the Truce of Ayton (1497),

James agreed to:
- recognise Henry as King of England
- expel Warbeck from Scotland
- marry Henry's daughter, Margaret

Relations improved thereafter. Warbeck left Scotland (1497) and Margaret married James (1503).

5.6 Burgundy

Burgundy was a potential problem for Henry. Margaret of York, sister of Richard III, was the widow of the Duke of Burgundy. From her court in Brussels she planned to overthrow Henry and to use Burgundy as a haven for Yorkist claimants, pretenders and rebels.

Simnel

Margaret funded 2,000 German **mercenaries** to invade England in support of Simnel in 1487.

Warbeck

Margaret supported Warbeck in 1493, claiming he was Richard IV. To counter this, Henry imposed a trade embargo on English cloth exports to Flanders. Three years later Emperor Maximilian intervened in the dispute and agreed to the *Magnus Intercursus*. As a result:
- Warbeck was expelled from Flanders
- trade was restored and English merchants received improved terms

Edmund de la Pole

Edmund, Earl of Suffolk, fled to Flanders in 1503. He did not claim to be king but hoped to escape arrest in England. Henry's response was to impose another trade ban. This embargo did not bring the desired result. Edmund was eventually deported to England on the orders of Philip of Flanders (the emperor's son) since Philip was keen to secure Henry's alliance. Trade was restored by the *Malus Intercursus* (1506) but English merchants were no better off.

Burgundy had been a constant thorn in Henry's side, but by a mixture of skill, threats, persistence and luck he had been able to neutralise the damage it could potentially have caused to his throne.

5.7 Overseas trade and exploration

Henry was never strong enough to make much impact on European trade. The German Hanse company **monopolised** trade in northern and western Europe, and the Italian Levant company dominated the carrying trade around Italy and the Mediterranean. Attempts were made to expand overseas trade:
- The Treaty of Riga (1489) with Denmark secured fishing rights in the North Sea.
- The Treaty of Pisa (1494) with Florence set up a commercial base in Italy.
- The Navigation Acts (1485, 1486, 1489) required French wine to be imported in English ships.
- Henry backed John Cabot's expedition to North America (1497).

In practice, none of these developments brought much benefit to Henry and English merchants. The Hanse and Levant companies were too well established and there were insufficient native ships to challenge the Italian and French carrying trade.

GLOSSARY

mercenaries: hired troops.
monopolised: had exclusive control.

EXAMINER'S TIP

This topic appears at AS in the AQA (Alternative N), OCR and Edexcel specifications. You may be asked: 'Examine the claim that the *most* important achievement of Henry VII's foreign policy was to defeat any threat to a Tudor succession.' You might start by discussing what Henry's aims were and whether they changed in the course of his reign. An evaluation of his most important successes, with appropriate explanations and an awareness of his limitations, needs to be given. Overseas trade is also relevant and should be included.

6 Was Henry VII a 'modern' or a 'medieval' ruler?

6.1 Background

In the late nineteenth century historians suggested that Henry VII's reign marked the beginning of a new, modern era. (Similar claims were also put forward on behalf of Isabella and Ferdinand of Spain, Louis XI of France and the Italian Renaissance.) In the late twentieth century, revisionist historians countered this argument by claiming that Henry's reign saw more continuity than change; that he was really a medieval rather than a modern ruler.

6.2 Arguments in favour of 'modern'

- Henry began a new dynasty.
- He ended the Wars of the Roses.
- He established a strong, efficient, 'absolute' monarchy.
- He employed new, middle-class men instead of the nobility in central administration.
- He used innovative ways to restore royal finances, law and order and to regain control over the nobles.
- He established peace with England's traditional enemies — Scotland and France — and secured a dynastic alliance with Spain.
- He used art and architecture to enhance the status of the Tudors.

6.3 Arguments in favour of 'medieval'

- The Yorkists established a **conciliar** system of administration, which Henry used and modified.
- The chamber system of financial administration and all sources of revenue were in place at Henry's accession.
- Henry did not seek to destroy or exclude the nobility. In fact he consulted and relied upon them to make his government more effective.
- He developed existing common-law and prerogative courts.

6.4 Conclusion

Modern historians no longer accept the view that Henry was a 'new' king or that his reign marked the beginning of the 'modern' age. The manner in which his policies were pursued — his professionalism, determination and personal commitment — appeared 'modern' and his financial solvency, autocratic rule and increasing use of gentry and lawyers contrasted with earlier rulers, but his policies were essentially the same as his Yorkist predecessors. Continuity in administration, finance and justice characterised his rule. Some historians have further claimed that fundamental changes in government and administration did not occur until the 1530s (see Unit 2). Although Henry's rule did contain some new features, he was essentially a medieval king.

GLOSSARY

conciliar: government by councils, e.g. the king's council, the Council of the North, the Council Learned in the Law.

EXAMINER'S TIP

This subject appears at AS in the OCR specification. If you are asked: 'Assess the view that Henry VII was more a "medieval" than a "modern" ruler', you should begin by defining these terms and focusing on those aspects of Henry's reign that demonstrate continuity and those that show change. You would not be expected to write in depth about the preceding and succeeding periods, but knowledge of relevant events would certainly give you the perspective to write with greater conviction about Henry VII.

UNIT 2 The reign of Henry VIII, 1509–47

KEY QUESTIONS

(1) How far did Henry VIII continue the work of his father, 1509–14?
(2) How successful was Wolsey's management of the government, 1515–29?
(3) How effectively did Wolsey administer the Church, 1515–29?
(4) Who controlled English foreign affairs, 1515–29?
(5) Why did Wolsey stay in power so long, but fall in 1529?
(6) How significant was the work of Thomas Cromwell in the 1530s?
(7) How far did factions at court threaten the stability of the throne, 1529–47?
(8) What was the impact of foreign relations on domestic affairs, 1529–47?

1 How far did Henry VIII continue the work of his father, 1509–14?

1.1 The character of the king

Henry VIII's childhood and upbringing were quite different from his father's. Educated in a climate of Renaissance culture, he developed an interest in music, dance, painting, sport and theology, which stayed with him for the rest of his life. Whereas Henry VII had devoted his reign to accumulating money, Henry VIII enjoyed spending it. Unlike his father, the young king also took a keen interest in women and warfare. As soon as he had attended his father's funeral the 17-year-old king married Catherine of Aragon and prepared for war against France.

1.2 Changes

Between 1509 and 1514 Henry continued to be advised by clergymen like Archbishop Morton and Bishop Fox and by nobles such as Lord Darcy and the Earls of Surrey and Shrewsbury. Henry also instigated several changes in policy and personnel:

- Two of Henry VII's most loyal servants, Empson and Dudley, were executed.
- The Council Learned in the Law, where Empson and Dudley had worked, was abolished, as was the **Court of General Surveyors**.
- The Court of Exchequer began to handle more royal revenue since Henry showed less interest in overseeing chamber finances.
- Hundreds of bonds and recognisances were abolished; and investigations into the non-payment of crown rents and dues were cancelled.
- The **Gentlemen of the Privy Chamber** acquired greater prominence at court.
- Measures were taken to increase the size of the navy, develop new artillery and refortify Calais Castle.
- In 1511 Henry joined the Holy League against France and prepared for war.

1.3 War with France and Scotland

Motives

Henry went to war with France and its ally Scotland for a number of reasons:

- Henry was keen to make a mark in Europe as a new king.
- He wished to emulate Henry V, who had conquered much of western France.
- Louis XII of France had stopped paying the annual pension to England.

- The council and nobles at court supported war as a way of gaining lands, titles and royal patronage.
- Henry had sufficient finances to begin military preparations.
- Pope Julius II and Ferdinand of Spain, Henry's father-in-law, encouraged him.

Preparations

Between 1510 and 1512 Henry VII's legacy was spent, and a new way of raising money — the subsidy — was introduced. For the first time taxpayers were assessed on the value of their lands and goods rather than on where they lived. As a result, £170,000 was collected. The idea probably came from Thomas Wolsey, who had become a royal councillor in 1510. He also organised the transport of men and supplies, and escorted the king on the 1513 expedition to France.

Events

1512   A fleet attacked Brest and an army invaded Aquitaine in western France but inflicted little damage and returned home.

1513   Henry and 30,000 troops invaded Normandy and Picardy, defeated a small French cavalry at the Battle of the Spurs and captured Tournai and Therouanne. Unwisely, King James IV of Scotland declared war. An English army, led by Surrey, won the Battle of Flodden, killing 10,000 Scots, including the king.

1514   Henry heard that his Spanish and German allies had made a truce with France, which left England alone and at war. With debts mounting (war costs were over £1 million), Henry ordered Wolsey to negotiate a treaty. Accordingly Henry retained Tournai, Henry's sister Mary married Louis XII, and the Scots agreed to a ceasefire.

1.4 Wolsey's rise to power

Wolsey was born in Ipswich in 1473, the son of a butcher. His rise to power was meteoric. Having gained a theology degree at Oxford he became a client of Richard Fox, the Lord Privy Seal, and served Henry VII as an **almoner**, before entering the new king's council in 1510. War gave him his chance. His willingness to work hard, to solve the king's financial difficulties and to organise the French expedition successfully brought rewards from Henry and the Pope. Wolsey became Bishop of Lincoln (1513), Bishop of Tournai (1513) and Archbishop of York (1514). Finally, Henry made him Lord Chancellor and the Pope made him a cardinal in 1515.

almoner: a chaplain who said prayers for the king and handed out charity to the poor.
Court of General Surveyors: a council founded by Henry VII to manage crown lands.
Gentlemen of the Privy Chamber: some 45 drinking and riding companions of Henry VIII who had access to the king's private rooms and consequently enjoyed privileged status at court.

This subject appears at AS for Edexcel and OCR, and at A2 for AQA (Alternative N). At AS you will need to understand the legacy of Henry VII and explain why his son introduced changes in domestic and foreign affairs. A typical question is: 'How successful a king was Henry VIII during the period 1509–14?' At A2 you may have to assess how far the changes in these years can be attributed to the new king's character.

2 How successful was Wolsey's management of the government, 1515–29?

2.1 Background

As Lord Chancellor, Wolsey advised the king, administered the government to ensure laws were upheld, and implemented royal policies. It should be remembered that Wolsey kept Henry informed as much and as often as he thought appropriate and, though the servant appeared to some to be the *alter rex* (other king), Henry remained the master.

2.2 Administration

From his town house at York Place and his country residence at Hampton Court, Wolsey apparently worked 15 hours a day. Councils still met but he preferred to see the king privately and increasingly delegated authority to his own servants, whom he appointed to the court, council and Church. The nobility and gentry continued to attend court and to control county administration but many found themselves excluded from central government and decision-making.

Parliament

Wolsey, like Henry VII, called Parliament when necessary and dissolved it as soon as he had got what he wanted. In 1515 he successfully defended clerical privileges from a hostile House of Commons. In 1523 he called Parliament to raise money for Henry's war with France. Over £130,000 was awarded, the largest-ever grant. Some historians claim this showed considerable skill but others point out that Wolsey actually requested £800,000, which was a sum much closer to the king's needs, and he had to settle for a much lower figure. Wolsey resented MPs who criticised his power and administration and he did not call another parliament.

Finance

The wars of 1512–14 had emptied the king's coffers. Raising sufficient money to meet the needs of the government and Henry's indulgent tastes kept Wolsey very busy. Reforms in 1518–19 to various royal departments (e.g. the Council of the North, the Council of Wales and the Navy) and a reduction in the number of the Gentlemen of the Privy Chamber made extensive savings but in the 1520s Henry was again eager to join Spain in the war against France. Wolsey had to resort to a number of fundraising devices:
- A forced loan in 1522 raised £120,000.
- A parliamentary subsidy (1523) produced £136,000.
- A benevolence, known as the Amicable Grant, was demanded in 1525. This non-parliamentary tax was so strongly opposed that the king intervened and cancelled it, and then blamed Wolsey for not keeping him informed.

On balance, Wolsey fulfilled a very difficult task in raising revenue for the king.

Justice

Wolsey had no legal training but it was his proud boast that he had 'used the law to keep order'. He made extensive use of the prerogative courts:
- In Chancery, he applied his common sense to resolve cases that the common-law courts failed to settle (e.g. he tackled the serious problem of illegal **enclosures** by personally investigating nearly 200 cases in 1518).
- He ensured the Court of Requests had regular sittings and a fixed location, and that it kept records from 1517.

- He sat in Star Chamber and heard cases of rioting, retaining and robbery, and disputes involving the nobility.

Apart from his attempt to impose the Amicable Grant, which led to 10,000 rebels protesting in Suffolk, there were no disturbances during Wolsey's period in office. He avoided levying high or frequent taxation, made it possible for people to have their grievances heard locally and made sure that the king's laws were not abused by the more powerful subjects.

GLOSSARY

enclosures: fields that had been surrounded with a hedge, fence or line of trees. Landowners broke the law if the land was common land, since all commoners had right of access to it.

EXAMINER'S TIP

This subject appears at AS in the OCR and Edexcel specifications, and at A2 in the AQA (Alternative N) specification. If you are asked at AS: 'How effectively did Wolsey govern England between 1515 and 1529?', you should consider the problems facing Wolsey in serving the king over this 14-year period and explain why he was more successful in some areas of administration (e.g. keeping order) than in others (e.g. raising revenue).

3 How effectively did Wolsey administer the Church, 1515–29?

3.1 Background

The responsibility for administering the Roman Catholic Church in England lay with the Archbishop of Canterbury, William Warham (1515–32). His authority, however, was curtailed in 1518 when Wolsey was appointed papal legate. This gave him the power to intervene in Church affairs throughout England. Wolsey claimed that he wished to reform the Church, which seemed plausible: there was widespread **nepotism**, **pluralism**, absenteeism and **simony**. Some clerics kept mistresses and had illegitimate children; some seemed more interested in managing their lands than serving the people; and all agreed that the Church was exceedingly wealthy.

3.2 Wolsey's work

Historians generally see Wolsey as a hard-working servant of the Church. He was aware of its faults but only scratched the surface of reform. Perhaps he was mindful of his own position and, as Henry's servant, only did as much as the king demanded of him. Among Wolsey's 'achievements' were:

- his defence of Bishop Fitzjames, who was accused of complicity in the murder of Richard Hunne, and his defence of Fitzjames's right to **benefit of clergy** (1515)
- the **triennial visitations**, which began in 1518 and reported on the condition of the clergy
- his attack on Lutherans and **Lollards**. Their books were burned publicly (1521) and leading Lutherans, such as Barnes, Frith and Tyndale, were arrested
- the closure of 27 small monasteries. Ipswich School and Cardinal College, Oxford, were endowed with their lands. Further monastic closures were under consideration at Wolsey's fall in 1529

benefit of clergy: clerics in holy orders had the privilege of being tried in Church courts. These gave more lenient sentences than cases heard in the common-law courts.

Lollards: followers of John Wyclif, a fourteenth-century critic of the Roman Catholic Church.

nepotism: favouring one's relatives by procuring them clerical offices.

pluralism: holding more than one clerical office without a licence.

simony: selling a Church office.

triennial visitations: diocesan surveys held every 3 years.

This topic is in the AS specification for OCR and Edexcel, and A2 (Alternative N) for AQA. Any assessment of Wolsey's work in the Church must take into account his prime duty to serve the king. Henry saw Church reform as a low priority. Avoid being judgemental about Wolsey's apparent inactivity or accepting at face value criticism from Protestant historians.

4   Who controlled English foreign affairs, 1515–29?

4.1 Background

For many years historians have debated who was responsible for directing English foreign policy: Wolsey or the king? Some historians have argued that Wolsey suggested policies to Henry and then directed affairs, with the intention of serving the Pope. Some believe that Wolsey was nothing more than an enforcer of the king's policies. State documents do not reveal Wolsey's precise role or that of the king. That there was tension between them — Henry enjoyed war and Wolsey saw the virtues of peace — adds to the uncertainty of their relationship.

4.2 Wolsey's aims

Historians have suggested a variety of interpretations of Wolsey's aims:

* Wolsey pursued any policy that would endear him to the papacy. His ultimate aim was to become Pope (the view of A. F. Pollard).
* Wolsey was a **humanist** who wanted to bring peace to Europe and advised Henry to use diplomacy rather than war (the view of Jack Scarisbrick).
* Wolsey and Henry wished to raise their own and their country's prestige internationally, preferably by peace, but by war if necessary (the view of Peter Gwyn).
* Wolsey adopted a pro-papal policy, though becoming pope may not have been his ultimate goal.

4.3 Main events

1516   The Treaty of Noyon ended the war in Italy. France, Spain, the emperor and the papacy made peace without consulting Wolsey.

1518   Wolsey, encouraged by Pope Leo X, organised the Congress of London to achieve universal peace in Europe.

1519   Henry stood as a candidate for the imperial throne, but lost.

1520   The 'Field of the Cloth of Gold': Henry and Wolsey entertained Francis I and the French court near Calais in a show of diplomatic friendship.

1521 Wolsey signed the Treaty of Bruges with Charles V (King of Spain and Holy Roman Emperor) against France. Wolsey stood as a candidate for the papacy, but lost.

1522 Henry and Charles signed the Treaty of Windsor, pledging a marriage between Charles V and Mary Tudor. English troops invaded France.

1523 English troops invaded France and Scotland but with little success. The death of the Pope saw Wolsey stand again as a candidate — and again he lost.

1524 English troops invaded France.

1525 Charles V defeated Francis I in Italy; Charles revoked his agreement to marry Mary.

1526 Wolsey supported Francis I and the papal League of Cognac against Charles.

1527 The Sack of Rome by imperial troops convinced Wolsey and Henry that a French alliance was in England's best interests.

1528 Wolsey had to make a truce with Spain when English merchants complained about the loss of trade.

1529 Spanish victory over France in Italy brought peace at Cambrai; Henry and Wolsey were again ignored by the two protagonists.

4.4 The divorce

In 1527 Henry asked Wolsey to arrange a divorce. The king alleged that he had been living in sin with Catherine of Aragon as their marriage, though permitted by Pope Julius II, was illegal. Catherine was the wife of Henry's deceased brother (marrying one's brother's wife went against the Book of Leviticus) and she had not been a virgin when Henry had married her (which was contrary to Julius' Bull of 1503). God had therefore punished the king by denying him a son.

Wolsey advised Henry not to press these claims. The Book of Deuteronomy did permit a man to marry his brother's widow; Catherine claimed that she had been a virgin; and Pope Clement VII was unlikely to admit that an earlier pope had made a mistake. Wolsey argued that a more sensible strategy would be to request a divorce on the grounds of incompatibility. Henry was not convinced.

When Spanish and imperial troops overran the **Vatican** in May 1527, Clement VII was compromised into following the emperor's lead — and the emperor was Catherine's nephew and no friend of Wolsey's. The Pope did not allow a divorce court to meet in England until 1529, and within 3 weeks of its opening he adjourned it to meet in Rome. No divorce was granted. Wolsey had failed and, 3 months later, the king dismissed him.

4.5 Was Wolsey a success or a failure?

Wolsey tried to serve two masters — Henry VIII and the Pope — and to stay in office as long as possible. He achieved a mixture of successes and failures.

Wolsey's successes
- England remained at peace for most of Wolsey's time in power and, when it was engaged in war, there were no major military campaigns.
- England's international standing was much enhanced by the Congress of London, Henry's candidature for the imperial throne, Wolsey's candidature for the papacy, and by the magnificence of the Field of the Cloth of Gold.

Wolsey's failures
- Henry did not become emperor and Wolsey did not become pope.
- In 1516, 1526 and 1529 England was diplomatically outmanoeuvred and excluded from peace talks.

- Henry gained nothing from his 1522–24 war against France and Scotland.
- Between 1527 and 1529, Wolsey failed to secure a divorce; the emperor would not allow it and the Pope dared not grant it.

EXAMINER'S TIP

This subject appears at AS in the OCR and Edexcel specifications, and at A2 in the AQA (Alternative N) specification. At A2 you will be expected to offer several interpretations of who was more responsible for foreign relations — Wolsey, Henry or both of them — and you will need supporting evidence. Very little of this is conclusive, so a balanced argument and an open verdict would be a sensible approach. A typical AS question is: 'Who was more important in directing foreign affairs from 1515 to 1529, Henry VIII or Wolsey?'

5 Why did Wolsey stay in power so long, but fall in 1529?

5.1 Why was Wolsey in power for so long?

Wolsey was Henry VIII's principal minister for more than 14 years. Several factors account for his long stay in office:

- He assumed total responsibility for daily administration, which created the impression that he was indispensable.
- He was trusted by the king.
- He silenced his rivals and critics, such as **Buckingham**, **Compton** and **Surrey**.
- He oversaw an effective government: the nobles were subdued and popular complaints were minimal.
- He controlled royal patronage and promoted his own clients to the court and council.

5.2 Why did Wolsey fall?

As long as Henry was satisfied with Wolsey, the latter remained in power. In 1529, however, he was dismissed. Though his fall appears to have been sudden, the origins went back several years:

- In spite of being a cardinal and papal legate, Wolsey failed to secure Henry's divorce. Henry held Wolsey responsible. He had advised the king to change allies from Spain to France after the Sack of Rome, and this had encouraged Charles to pressurise the Pope into not granting the divorce.
- Wolsey was despised by Anne Boleyn. She was convinced that in the early 1520s he sent her lover away from court and was opposed to her relationship with the king. Anne may have persuaded Henry that Wolsey would never help them get a divorce. Her father, Thomas, was a councillor who also disliked Wolsey.
- Wolsey was 'universally hated', as declared by the Spanish ambassador in 1527. Nobles, like Norfolk and Suffolk, despised his influence, wealth and personal corruption; lawyers resented his regular use of prerogative courts; the gentry disliked his support for commoners; merchants blamed him for trade losses in 1527–28. No one spoke up for him in 1529.

- Henry and Wolsey had a series of disagreements which slowly undermined the king's confidence in him, e.g. the Amicable Grant (1524–25), how best to get a divorce (1527–28), the appointment of a new abbess of Wilton (1528) and misappropriation of crown revenue for Ipswich School (1528).

GLOSSARY

Buckingham: in 1521 the Duke of Buckingham was found guilty of treason and executed. He was seen as a potential threat to Wolsey at court and, as Wolsey presided over his case in the Lords, historians have argued over his complicity in the trial.

Compton: he criticised Wolsey and was sent to York to preside over the Council of the North.

Surrey: a successful soldier and advocate of a more adventurous foreign policy, Surrey was despatched to Ireland in 1520.

EXAMINER'S TIP

This subject appears at AS in the OCR specification and at A2 in the AQA (Alternative N) specification. You may be required to explain Wolsey's long stay in office or his fall. Each type of question needs several explanations. Start with the most important, which may well be his retaining/losing Henry VIII's support. Show how other factors were interconnected and contributed to his long stay/eventual fall.

6 How significant was the work of Thomas Cromwell in the 1530s?

6.1 Background

Little is known about Cromwell's early life. Born in London in 1485, he appears to have had no formal education. After a career as a soldier, merchant and lawyer he became an MP (1523), royal councillor (1531), principal secretary to the king (1532) and vicegerent (1535), i.e. a deputy responsible for administering the Church.

6.2 What did Cromwell do?

As Henry's principal secretary (1532–40) Cromwell was one of the king's most important advisers and administrators. His speciality appears to have been drafting parliamentary bills, overcoming opposition and bringing a more legalistic approach to the king's business.

The divorce

In 1530 a collection of documents known as the *Collectanea* was presented to the king. It claimed that Henry possessed '*imperium*' (the absolute power of an emperor) and, since he was an emperor, that he was subject only to God. The principle of royal sovereignty ran through various parliamentary bills written by Cromwell between 1531 and 1533. Each bill reminded the Pope what would happen if he did not grant the divorce:

- The English clergy had to submit to the authority of the king (1532).
- Papal **annates** were no longer paid to the Pope (1532–33).
- English subjects were denied the right of appeal to the Pope (1533).

Anne Boleyn's pregnancy, however, brought matters to a head. In the absence of any papal reaction, Cromwell convinced Henry that he had the authority to set up his own

divorce court and that Parliament would deny the Pope the right to intervene. Henry divorced Catherine and married Anne in 1533. The Act of Supremacy (1534) confirmed that Henry had displaced the Pope as 'supreme Head of the Church of England'.

Church reform

As vicegerent (1535–40), Cromwell was the king's secular officer in Church affairs and an active reformer. Cromwell:

- supervised the *Valor Ecclesiasticus*, a survey of Church property
- drafted a bill to dissolve the smaller monasteries and set up the Court of Augmentations to administer them
- supported the Act of Ten Articles, the first piece of Protestant reform
- supported injunctions that abolished saints' days, **shrines** and pilgrimages
- organised the dissolution of the larger monasteries
- arranged for an English Bible to be published and made available in every parish

Administrative reform

As principal secretary, Cromwell introduced several changes to central and regional administration:

- He took financial administration away from the royal household and gave it to six departments of state — Augmentations, Wards, General Surveyors, First Fruits and Tenths, Exchequer, Duchy of Lancaster.
- The offices of Lord Chancellor and Lord Privy Seal, and officers in the household (e.g. Lord Chamberlain), declined in influence.
- The privy council emerged in the 1530s as a small select group of royal advisers.
- Royal power was extended over regions and counties: Wales was divided into counties and made subject to English law (1536); the Council of the North was reorganised (1537); Calais sent MPs to London; and areas lost their **franchises** (e.g. the Palatine of Chester, Durham and Ripon).

Social reform

Cromwell may well have supported a group of scholars, poets and clerics, known as the Commonweal. They wanted the state to protect the victims of exploitation by landlords, to help the genuine poor and preserve towns in size. The following legislation occurred:

- An act of 1534 restricted the size of sheep farms to ensure more grain was grown.
- The Enclosure Act (1536) was designed to maintain arable land and prevent rising prices.
- The Poor Law (1536) required the parish to provide relief for the old and sick, and work for the unemployed.
- Towns were allowed to rebuild houses to prevent urban decay.

6.3 The significance of Cromwell's work

Elton's thesis

In the 1950s the historian Geoffrey Elton made great claims on behalf of Cromwell: that the king's minister developed a sovereign national state, demonstrated how effective the king in Parliament could be, and that he brought about changes in central administration so fundamental that they amounted to a 'revolution in government'.

Revisionism

More recently, historians have revised much of Elton's thesis. They have suggested that:

- Cromwell had no coherent plan but drafted legislation as and when required
- the idea of '*imperium*', which lay behind the Acts of Appeals and Supremacy, did not originate with Cromwell

- there was no 'revolution in government'. The decentralisation of financial departments was a reversion to Lancastrian practices; the reforms only lasted until the 1550s, when further changes took place
- no evidence has survived that Cromwell invented the privy council. Its records only begin in 1540

Conclusion

In spite of these criticisms, historians still accept the following parts of Elton's thesis:

- Cromwell did draft much of the parliamentary legislation in the 1530s. As a result Henry obtained his divorce, England broke away from Rome, and Parliament became a regular partner that expected to be consulted on religious affairs.
- As a Protestant sympathiser, Cromwell, together with Cranmer (see Unit 4), carried through several reforms in the 1530s, of which the most notable were the dissolution of the monasteries and the publication of an English Bible.
- If there was no revolution in government, the 1530s at least saw several important changes: royal power became more effective in the north, west and Wales; the role of the secretary continued to grow and the Yorkist chamber administration declined.

GLOSSARY

annates: annual payments made by new bishops to the Pope; usually worth one third of their salary.
franchises: liberties and jurisdictions previously outside the reach of the king.
shrines: burial places of saints that became centres of pilgrimage.

EXAMINER'S TIP

This subject appears at AS in the OCR specification, and at A2 in the AQA (Alternative N) specification. Although the historical debate centred upon Elton's thesis is no longer controversial, examiners do expect candidates to be aware of the competing views on the importance of Cromwell. The 1530s may not have seen a 'revolution in government', but in A2 synoptic papers in particular you are required to assess what continued and what changed during this decade. A typical AS question is: 'Explain any two factors that made Thomas Cromwell an important minister of Henry VIII.'

7 | How far did factions at court threaten the stability of the throne, 1529–47?

7.1 Background

The fall of Wolsey in 1529 left a power vacuum, which nobles, courtiers and their clients soon filled. Henry encouraged rival groups or factions, most of which came to be centred around the women in his life. As a result, court factions competed for royal favours. The majority sided with those in power; only the brave or reckless dared to challenge the king.

7.2 Factions in the 1530s

Aragon vs Boleyn

The question of the king's divorce split the court and council into three main factions:

- The Aragon faction had the support of More (Lord Chancellor 1529–32), Warham (Archbishop of Canterbury 1515–32), Bishops Fisher and Tunstall, the Earl of Shrewsbury and many MPs. These were devout Catholics who put their careers (and, in the cases of More and Fisher, their lives) on the line by backing Catherine.
- The Boleyn faction had the support of Cromwell, Cranmer (Archbishop of Canterbury 1532–54), Bishop Fox, Lord Audley (Lord Chancellor 1532–40) and several MPs. Some favoured Protestant reforms and most saw the advantages of backing a royal divorce.
- A third group remained undecided. The Dukes of Norfolk and Suffolk, the Earl of Sussex, Lord Darcy and Bishop Gardiner all supported the king but waited for him to make up his mind before taking sides.

The main beneficiaries of this power struggle were the Boleyn family, Cromwell, Cranmer, Norfolk, Suffolk and Audley. More and Fisher were executed for refusing to accept the divorce, and Catherine spent her remaining years in a nunnery.

The fall of Boleyn

In 1536 Anne Boleyn was executed for treason and incest. Though she proclaimed her innocence, ranged against her were powerful enemies consisting of Catholics loyal to Princess Mary and supporters of Henry's new mistress Jane Seymour. Cromwell was the decisive factor. He wanted to remove his opponents in the privy chamber (e.g. Norris and Brereton) and in the royal council (e.g. Wiltshire and Rochford). Having encouraged rumours of Anne's infidelity, Cromwell then switched allegiance to Jane. She became Henry's third wife and her brother, Edward, became a royal councillor.

Seymour vs Howard

Two main factions emerged in the late 1530s:
- The Seymour faction was initially centred around the queen but the birth of a son, Edward, in 1537, followed by her death, saw prominence pass to the prince's uncles, Edward and Thomas. Both were Protestant and supported Cromwell, Cranmer and bishops who were more active in the reformation of the Church.
- The Howard faction opposed the Seymours. Thomas Howard, Duke of Norfolk, was supported by the more conservative bishops and those courtiers who resented Cromwell. In 1540 they got their revenge. Cromwell arranged the marriage between Henry and Anne of Cleves, daughter of a German Lutheran. When the marriage began to fail, Norfolk introduced his young niece, Catherine, to the king. Henry fell in love and divorced Anne. In 1540 he married Catherine and executed Cromwell.

Throughout the 1540s the Howard family exercised great influence at court. Norfolk was one of Henry's closest advisers and his son, the Earl of Surrey, became a leading soldier. Backed by Gardiner and other Catholic bishops, they opposed any further Protestant reforms and even tried to get Cranmer dismissed. The discovery in 1541 that Catherine had committed adultery shocked the king, however, and undermined the Howard faction. Catherine was executed in 1542 and Henry married Katherine Parr, a twice-widowed Protestant. Crucially, she took charge of Prince Edward's education and kept clear of political and religious factions.

In December 1546 the Earl of Surrey was charged with treason (displaying the royal coat of arms) and he and his father were arrested. Surrey was executed in January 1547. Gardiner had also quarrelled with the king. When Henry died, the Howard faction was in disarray and the Seymour family was ready to assume control.

Conclusion

Court factions had long existed. They were not fixed groups with settled beliefs; clients changed patrons and factions shifted their viewpoints. What mattered was how the king channelled rival groups and whether factions actually weakened his throne. Some historians see Henry as a victim of factions, manipulated by groups competing for his favour. Such factions, if they became too powerful, could cause disunity in the council and at court. Other historians believe Henry kept a firm grip of politics and argue that conflicting groups were a useful way of maintaining lively competition for patronage. Because of Henry's unpredictable temperament his advisers could never become complacent, royal patronage was not monopolised by one faction (unlike in Wolsey's days), and the king ruled supreme.

This subject appears at AS in the OCR specification and at A2 in the AQA (Alternative N) specification. Questions on factions require you to show how Henry dealt with competing families and to understand the important role played by his queens and mistresses in court politics. If you can, avoid giving the impression that factions were immutable and principled. They were not. 'Why did court factions remain important throughout the period?' is a typical AS question.

8 | What was the impact of foreign relations on domestic affairs, 1529–47?

8.1 Background

For much of the 1530s Henry feared that his divorce and break from Rome would evoke a Catholic reaction from continental powers. Emperor Charles V, nephew of Catherine of Aragon, was a devout Catholic but he was also preoccupied with more pressing problems in the Netherlands, Italy, Germany and Austria. His rivalry with Francis, King of France, proved to be England's salvation throughout Henry's reign and presented Henry with the opportunity in the 1540s to indulge himself in war.

8.2 Events, 1535–40

Between 1535 and 1540 Cromwell believed England was likely to be invaded. Preparations began to improve coastal defences, ships were built, border towns strengthened and **musters** held. In 1538 Cromwell convinced the king that a continental ally was also needed. An ally was found in Cleves, a German state that was a member of the Lutheran **Schmalkaldic League**. In fact, Cromwell overestimated the Catholic threat to England's security and, when this became clear to Henry, Cromwell was executed.

8.3 Events, 1540–47

Free from the controlling hand of Cromwell and aware of his full Treasury, Henry devoted most of the 1540s to spending his monastic wealth on military campaigns against Scotland and France.

Scotland

Causes

- Henry was spoiling for a war and was supported by Seymour and Norfolk.

- James V of Scotland had married Mary of Guise, and France's influence on Scotland appeared to be threatening England's future security.
- The renewal of Franco–Spanish wars in 1542 gave Henry his chance to attack Scotland.

Events

- The Battle of Solway Moss (1542) resulted in an English victory; James V died shortly after.
- The Scots would not surrender. English troops burned crofts and overran Edinburgh but failed to take the castle where the French court survived.
- An act of 1544 excluded the Stuart family from the English throne.

France

Events

- In 1544 Henry joined Norfolk, Suffolk and Surrey at Calais and captured Boulogne.
- In 1545 the English south coast was threatened by a French fleet; the *Mary Rose* warship sank on its launch at Southsea.
- English troops sustained heavy losses in France in 1546.

Results

- The Peace of Ardres (1546) ended the French war; both countries ignored the Scots. England kept Boulogne (although it was returned in 1550) and France paid a pension and arrears of 2 million crowns.
- The wars cost £2 million. Henry resorted to the following expedients to pay for them: parliamentary subsidies (£450,000); sale of crown land (£800,000); loans (£128,000); benevolence (£119,000); and **debasement** of the coinage (£365,000). The wars left serious financial problems — a debt of £150,000, inflation and a debased currency.

EXAMINER'S TIP

This subject appears at AS in the OCR specification. The full impact of foreign relations upon domestic affairs was not felt until after Henry's death but you should be aware of the political, economic and religious effects in the 1530s and 1540s. Look for and explain any patterns of continuity (e.g. worsening of financial problems) and patterns of change (e.g. the fall of Cromwell due to the Lutheran alliance).

(1) How effectively did Somerset deal with his problems between 1547 and 1549?
(2) How effectively did Northumberland govern the country between 1549 and 1553?
(3) How effective was Mary Tudor as Queen of England, 1553–58?
(4) Was there a mid-Tudor crisis?

1 How effectively did Somerset deal with his problems between 1547 and 1549?

1.1 Background

Edward was 9 years old when his father died. For the next 6 years he ruled England while a council of regency governed in his name. Until 1549 his uncle, Edward Seymour (later titled the Duke of Somerset), acted as the Lord Protector; from 1550 to 1553 John Dudley (later titled the Duke of Northumberland) presided over the council.

1.2 Political problems

Henry VIII's will

Henry's will was kept secret for several weeks following his death, to allow Seymour to secure control of the council and reward himself and his colleagues with lands and titles. Seymour became the Duke of Somerset; Dudley became Earl of Warwick; Charles Wriothesley became Earl of Southampton. William Paget, royal secretary and fellow privy councillor, arranged these and other changes to the will.

The privy council

The privy council comprised 16 (later 22) members, mainly Protestant, and was headed by Somerset. His brother Thomas was appointed Lord Admiral. Religious factions persisted as Catholic councillors, such as Arundel and Southampton, vied with more radical members like Warwick and Northampton.

The privy chamber

Somerset's relationship with the king was vital. The boy rarely attended meetings of the council so Somerset needed to visit Edward and monitor political affairs at the court. In 1549 Somerset seems to have paid less attention to those who attended the king; and his enemies took full advantage. In October Edward agreed that his uncle should be dismissed.

Parliament

Somerset called Parliament in 1547–48 and 1548–49. He also made increasing use of royal **proclamations**, issuing 77 in all. Historians no longer believe that Somerset was deliberately seeking to bypass Parliament and the privy council. Most proclamations dealt with problems of public disorder which could not wait for Parliament to convene.

1.3 Economic and social problems

(For more information on this subject see also Unit 6.)

Between 1547 and 1549 Somerset faced a number of economic and social problems. Some were a legacy from Henry VIII's last years; some were the fault of Edward's administration. Most problems were interrelated. They included:

- a 50% price inflation coupled with falling wages
- debasement of the coinage, which stimulated the sale of goods but weakened the currency
- inherited debts and lack of Crown revenue
- limited food supplies due to poor harvests and a rising population
- unemployment, poverty and vagrancy
- tension between landlords and tenants

Policies

Somerset has traditionally been regarded as the 'good duke'. Historians once claimed that he sympathised with the poor and oppressed. This was partly because he shared the views of men like John Hales and Robert Crowley, who belonged to the **Commonwealth movement** and believed that governments had a Christian duty to help the common people. Revisionist historians, on the other hand, have questioned Somerset's genuine concern for the poor, suggesting that he was more interested in preventing internal disorder while at war with Scotland. Economic hardship caused popular rioting and poverty made the peasantry unfit for effective military service.

Revenue

To meet the shortage of revenue the government introduced taxation, borrowed money from foreign merchants, sold crown land and debased the coinage by a further 25% in 1549. War costs continued to rise, however, and totalled £1.3 million. To increase arable farming and tax the lucrative cloth industry, a Subsidy Act (1549) put a tax on wool and on the size of flocks. In 1549–50, £100,000 was raised.

Enclosures

The country was surveyed in 1548–49 to see which lands had been illegally enclosed since 1489. There was much resistance from landowners and the surveys were never completed.

Vagrants

The Vagrancy Act (1547) ordered able-bodied people to find work or to be branded and sold into slavery. Children of vagrants were to be taken away to become apprentices. It is not known how far local authorities enforced this law but it seems to have been widely disliked and was probably ignored.

Kett's rebellion

Disturbances occurred in several counties — most notably Norfolk and Suffolk — in the summer of 1549. Robert Kett led rebels protesting against **engrossed** farms, illegal enclosures, high prices, **rack-renting**, low wages and landowners who denied tenants their customary rights. The failure of JPs and local gentry to redress the rebels' complaints led to 16,000 peasants converging on Norwich, the region's capital. The Duke of Somerset was reluctant to act harshly or speedily, but other councillors felt force was essential and supported the Earl of Warwick and an army of mercenaries that set out to crush the rebellion. This they did, killing 3,000 at the Battle of Dussindale.

1.4 Religious problems

The religious problems that faced Somerset are dealt with in Unit 4, section 3.2.

1.5 Foreign relations

Somerset had been in charge of Henry VIII's army of occupation in Scotland in the early 1540s and was keen to end the war. He was aware that France had a new king,

Henry II, who was likely to renew hostilities. A pre-emptive strike against Scotland might secure Somerset a quick victory. War was also welcomed by the political élites: it would uphold English pride and enable the nobles to gain lands and rewards. Therefore, once Somerset had secured his position in the council he marched north, in September 1547.

War against Scotland and France

English troops quickly defeated a large Scottish army at Pinkie (1547) and went on to capture many lowland castles. Somerset returned to London but his troops never captured Edinburgh and the Scots refused to make peace. In 1548 French troops arrived to counterattack and gradually English-held garrisons fell due to insufficient financial and military resources. In 1549 the last English troops withdrew from Scotland, and France formally declared war on England and began to besiege Boulogne.

1.6 The fall of Somerset

In October 1549 Somerset fell from power. He had lost the support of the council through his indecisiveness and apparent betrayal of what the politically important groups expected. He was held responsible for widespread unrest, financial mismanagement and a disastrous foreign policy. Somerset further revealed his political naïvety by failing to secure his position in the council and allowing his enemies to convince the king that he should be removed. In a bloodless **coup** he was arrested and sent to the Tower. Three years later he was executed on charges of treason.

Commonwealth movement: a group of preachers and writers who wanted to improve the welfare of the common people.

coup: a sudden uprising.

engrossed: two or more farms forcibly joined together, which often resulted in surplus farm buildings becoming derelict.

proclamations: laws issued by the privy council, regent or monarch in the absence of Parliament. Such laws were expected to be confirmed at the next parliamentary sitting.

rack-renting: increasing rents to such a level that tenants felt as though they were being tortured on the rack.

This topic appears at AS in the OCR specification and at A2 in the AQA (Alternative N) and Edexcel specifications. Examiners are most likely to be interested in the reasons for Somerset's failure and whether his difficulties were largely of his own making. If you have to compare his administration with that of Northumberland or Mary, focus on those problems, policies and results that were common to them all.

2 How effectively did Northumberland govern the country between 1549 and 1553?

2.1 Political issues

John Dudley, Earl of Warwick, assumed control of the council and later gave himself the title of Duke of Northumberland. He was politically much more skilful than Somerset, keeping a careful watch over the Gentlemen of the Privy Chamber and holding the

crucial offices of Great Master of the Household and Lord President of the Council. He also regularly attended the king, called Parliament rather than governing through proclamations, built up his own following in the privy council, removed potential rivals and appointed 12 new councillors with special responsibility for keeping control in the counties. As a result there were no rebellions or political coups during his administration, despite his pursuit of radical policies.

2.2 Economic and social policies

(For more information on this subject see also Unit 6.)

As a major landowner, Northumberland sided with the politically powerful classes and reversed most of Somerset's policies. The Subsidy Act and enclosure commissions were repealed and a Treason Act made it unlawful for 12 or more persons to gather together. He borrowed £243,000 from continental bankers and debased the currency by 50%, but made the mistake of informing merchants in advance. They bought as much wool and cloth as possible, which led to a boom and then a collapse in exports.

The resulting economic crisis of 1550–51 forced the government to take urgent measures, which proved effective:

- The coinage was rebased, which reduced inflation and restored confidence.
- **Chantry lands** were sold to raise revenue.
- Financial departments were scrutinised and savings made by amalgamating them.
- The Keeper of the Privy Purse was revived to handle revenue and investigate debtors.
- Seven-year apprenticeships were introduced to improve the quality of cloth production.
- A Poor Law made the parish responsible for helping the infirm, old and crippled.

2.3 Church reforms

The Church reforms instigated by Northumberland are dealt with in Unit 4, section 3.3.

2.4 Foreign relations

Serious financial difficulties made a long war with France and Scotland unlikely. Indeed, Northumberland, who had considerable military experience, saw the importance of peace. At the Treaty of Boulogne (1550) he agreed to hand back Boulogne in return for 400,000 crowns and peace with France and Scotland.

He tried unsuccessfully to secure a marriage between Edward and Elizabeth Valois, daughter of the French king. Nevertheless, Anglo–French relations remained cordial whereas those with Emperor Charles V declined. He complained about the government's treatment of Princess Mary; Northumberland complained about the Inquisition's rough treatment of English merchants. Both Charles and Henry II of France looked for English support when war broke out in 1552 but Northumberland had to remain neutral.

Relations with Scotland became more stable. English troops completed their withdrawal and there was no further serious trouble on the borders. The French Guise family still exercised a commanding presence at the Scottish court, however, and would be a source of future trouble for England.

2.5 The fall of Northumberland, 1553

Northumberland only governed the country as long as Edward was a minor and incapable of assuming authority. In 1553 it was clear that the boy-king was dying. The duke may have acted alone but it seems likely that his subsequent attempt to exclude

Mary from the succession was willingly supported by Edward, who had no desire to see the country become Catholic again. Northumberland prepared to seize control of the throne in three stages:

- In May 1553 his son married Lady Jane Grey, the 15-year-old daughter of the Duke of Suffolk and great-granddaughter of Henry VII.
- In June the princesses Mary and Elizabeth were declared bastards and barred from the throne.
- In July, at Edward's death, his will was read and Jane was proclaimed queen.

For 9 days Northumberland retained control, ruling in the name of Jane. The council only backed him as long as he remained in London and when he left to confront Mary and her supporters gathering in Suffolk, they defected to her. Northumberland was arrested, imprisoned and, in August 1553, executed.

chantry lands: lands endowed to a chantry chapel or altar in a church, where prayers for the dead were sung by a chantry priest.

This topic appears at AS in the OCR specification and at A2 in the Edexcel and AQA (Alternative N) specifications. Northumberland is usually contrasted with Somerset and you should think in terms of explaining their differing methods of administration. Both men ultimately failed but Northumberland was altogether more successful.

3 How effective was Mary Tudor as Queen of England, 1553–58?

3.1 Mary's character

Mary's character and early life are the key to understanding her reign. Devoted to her mother, Catherine of Aragon, she always had a strong attachment to Catholicism and Spain. Henry VIII's divorce from Catherine separated Mary from her mother and removed Mary's right to the throne (Parliament reinstated it in 1543). She had few close friends and became estranged from Edward when he turned the country Protestant. Inexperienced in politics and administration, determined and inflexible in equal measure, Mary knew what she wanted to accomplish; but did England's first queen, at the age of 37, have the ability and time to succeed?

3.2 Political affairs

Mary took a keen interest in political affairs. Most offices in the privy chamber went to women but male courtiers in her household still exercised considerable influence. Rochester (Controller), Jerningham (Vice Chamberlain) and Hastings (Master of the Horse) became close advisers and James Basset, her private secretary, provided a vital link between herself and the household of Philip, her Spanish husband.

The privy council

The privy council again became the main arena of political importance. At first it

comprised a small number of moderate Protestants, like Paget, Petre, Pembroke and Winchester, who had served Edward VI, and a larger group of less experienced Catholics, such as Rochester, Englefield, Gardiner and Bonner. In fact with 43 members, the council was too large and factions soon centred around Paget and Gardiner. Paget in turn attached himself to the imperial ambassador, Renard, a man Mary felt she could trust, and from 1554 to Philip II of Spain. Gardiner sided with Rochester and — from 1554 — Cardinal Pole. Mary's marriage to Philip blurred the lines of patronage and influence even more. Moreover, Mary generally preferred to consult a handful of trusted Catholics rather than seek the advice of her council.

Parliament

Parliament met five times in the course of Mary's reign and was generally supportive of her policies, due to the presence in the Lords of Catholic bishops and peers. On three occasions, however, the Commons stood its ground and refused to support the queen. It would not:

- return monastic and chantry lands to the Church
- exclude Elizabeth from the succession
- allow Philip to be crowned king

3.3 Marriage and rebellion

In October 1553 Mary declared her intention to marry Philip II of Spain. There was opposition from her council, Parliament and some of her subjects. Some suggested she should marry Edward Courtenay, the great-grandson of Edward IV; a few hoped that she would stay single, but Mary was adamant. The best that her council and Parliament could do was to limit Philip's influence. It was agreed that:

- Philip could attend but not vote in the council
- he would not be crowned king
- he must not involve England in Spanish wars
- Spaniards could not be appointed to Church and state offices

Wyatt's rebellion

Thomas Wyatt, a courtier and wealthy landowner from Kent, was not satisfied. In January 1554 he raised the gentry and commoners to march on London and prevent the marriage from occurring. He wanted Courtenay to marry Princess Elizabeth and for them then to overthrow Mary. Risings were also planned in Devon, Wales and the Midlands but failed to take off when Courtenay revealed the conspiracy to the council. Wyatt persisted and advanced with some 3,000 troops to within 2 miles of the Tower. London, however, did not support him. Loyal troops halted Wyatt's rebels and Wyatt was arrested and executed. Mary showed leniency towards most of the rebels, even though they were traitors; only the ringleaders were hanged. Lady Jane Grey and her husband were also executed. Had Mary fallen, they might well have benefited and, in any case, Jane's father was implicated in the rebellion. Mary's marriage went ahead. In the opinion of most historians it was a serious mistake. Philip was unpopular in England, he never loved the queen and they had no children.

3.4 Social and economic policies

(For more information on this subject see also Unit 6.)

In recent years historians have presented a positive image of social and economic developments in Mary's reign. Several important measures were taken that laid the foundations for future success.

Commerce

Trade in the Baltic was developed, relations with the German Hanse company improved and an agreement with Danish merchants was signed. To open up new overseas markets away from the continent, explorers were encouraged to make contact with Russia and West Africa and trading companies were set up.

Finance

To increase revenue and reduce the state debt the following strategies were successfully employed:

- Revenue courts were amalgamated into the Exchequer (1554) and accounts were audited. This saved money and eliminated some corruption.
- Court and household expenditure was reduced.
- Crown lands were reassessed (1555).
- Customs duties were revised to include over 400 new rates and existing duties were revalued (1558).
- Coinage was re-minted (1556–58).

Industry

Most trades were associated with the wool and cloth industry. To make them more competitive the following acts were passed:

- the Weavers Act (1555), which obliged weavers to join town **guilds**
- the Woollen Cloth Act (1557), which imposed heavy fines on non-approved manufactures
- the Retail Trades Act (1557), which supported traders who had been chartered and licensed

Towns

There were serious social problems in the early 1550s. The poor, sick, homeless and unemployed went to the towns in search of relief and shelter. Partly to prevent urban unrest and partly because Mary genuinely cared for the welfare of her subjects, the government launched several initiatives:

- An act in 1555 was designed to stop enclosures and increase grain supplies.
- Larger towns, like Norwich, Exeter and York, were encouraged to stock-pile food, keep prices low and arrange their own poor relief.
- Five London hospitals were supported with grants: Christ's (which took in orphans), Bridewell (for paupers), St Thomas's (for sick children), St Bartholomew's (for sick adults) and Bedlam (for the insane).

3.5 The Marian Church

The Marian Reformation is dealt with in Unit 4, section 4.

3.6 Foreign affairs

Mary's marriage to Philip confirmed her personal wish to renew friendly relations with the Habsburgs. This was a sensible move as it attached her to the major Catholic European dynasty, strengthened trade with the Netherlands, Spain and Germany, and gave England a much-needed ally. But this alliance came at a price. Philip expected England to assist him in war against France. In 1557 he and Mary persuaded the privy council to do so, by:

- Philip offering to provide most of the money, men and resources
- reminding the privy council that Henry II, King of France, had made it known that he was going to attack Calais

- pointing out that France had harboured English Protestants, threatened merchants and supported a plot to start an uprising in Yorkshire

In 1557 a mainly Spanish army, supported by a small number of English troops, won the battle of St Quentin; but when Philip halted his campaign for the winter a large French force attacked and captured Calais (1558). The English council blamed Philip for not defending or recovering it; he blamed the English garrison for surrendering too soon; and the captain blamed the council for not providing him with sufficient troops or supplies. Mary was mortified. She fell into a state of depression, pining for her husband, but he never returned. In November 1558 Mary died; later that day Cardinal Pole died as well.

GLOSSARY

guilds: trade organisations that protected the interests of their members.

EXAMINER'S TIP

This topic appears at AS in the OCR specification and at A2 in the AQA (Alternative N) and Edexcel specifications. Questions usually either focus on Mary's religious policy (see Unit 4) or require a general assessment of her reign. In assessing Mary's administration do not forget to include her social and economic achievements: they can easily be ignored amid the political, religious and foreign developments.

4 Was there a mid-Tudor crisis?

4.1 Background

Historians have often viewed the reigns of Henry VIII and Elizabeth as periods of strong leadership, political stability and glorious deeds. In contrast, the reigns of Edward and Mary have been regarded as minor episodes characterised by weak rulers, political instability and national failure. It was, they contend, a time of crisis. Other historians, however, have questioned whether there really was a mid-Tudor crisis. They accept that there were difficulties but consider them to have been minor and temporary.

4.2 Arguments in favour of a crisis

- A boy-king and a woman married to a foreign prince were unable to command respect and obedience from their subjects.
- Noble factions exploited the Crown's weaknesses, especially between 1547 and 1553.
- Bankruptcy brought the royal administration to the brink of collapse.
- Unwise economic policies from 1547 to 1551 led to inflation and the collapse of the cloth trade.
- Religious reforms led to rebellions in 1549 and disquiet at the burnings in 1555–58.
- The threat of civil war was revived in 1553 when Northumberland tried to hold on to power.
- France and Scotland threatened invasion in 1549–50.
- Discontent between landlords and tenants threatened social stability.

4.3 Arguments against a crisis

- Several problems existed before Edward's reign and remained after Mary's reign, when they did not present a crisis (e.g. urban poor and unemployed).
- Many difficulties facing Somerset's administration were redressed by Northumberland (e.g. the French and Scottish wars).
- The administrative machinery constructed by the Yorkists, strengthened by the early Tudors and reformed by Cromwell, withstood a period of weak rule.
- The threat of foreign invasion proved unfounded.
- Popular rebellions only took place in 1549 and these were localised.
- The threat of civil war lasted only a few days in 1553.

EXAMINER'S TIP

This topic appears at AS in the OCR specifications and at A2 in the Edexcel specification. It is important that you define the term 'crisis' before considering the evidence. When do problems become 'critical'? How serious were these problems in the mid-Tudor period? How long did the difficulties last? The year 1549 may be seen as the time when England and its people were most vulnerable; but other years (1553, for instance) also had their flash-points.

UNIT 4 Reform in the English Church, 1529–1603

KEY QUESTIONS

(1) How far was the Church in need of reform in 1529?
(2) What was the nature of the Henrician Reformation, 1529–47?
(3) How far was England a Protestant country by 1553?
(4) How popular was the Marian Reformation?
(5) What was the nature of the Elizabethan Church Settlement?
(6) How successfully did Elizabeth tackle the Puritan challenge to the religious settlement?
(7) How serious was the threat posed by Roman Catholics to the Elizabethan Church and state?
(8) What was the condition of the Church of England in 1603?

1 How far was the Church in need of reform in 1529?

1.1 Background

(For more information on this subject see also Unit 2, section 3.)

Two main schools of interpretation have dominated the historiography of the English Reformation:

- The Church was in urgent need of reform. Popular complaints against the clergy encouraged the king to carry this out.
- People were generally satisfied with the Church. Changes were brought about by a self-interested minority.

1.2 The clergy

Two archbishops, 21 bishops, 9,000 parish priests, some 40,000 chantry priests and an unknown number of assistant clergymen served the spiritual needs of the English people in 1529. Most **beneficed** clergy had low salaries, averaging £8 a year; few had university degrees and they were not expected to preach sermons. Instead they confined their duties to conducting services and ministering the essential sacraments of baptism, confirmation, communion, marriage and burial. Bishops were better educated and received very high salaries, averaging £2,000. Many fulfilled administrative and diplomatic duties, which took them away from their dioceses, but some, like Sherburne at Chichester, regularly visited their parishes and actively improved the quality of their clergy.

Some 9,000 monks, friars and nuns lived in over 820 abbeys, friaries and nunneries. Conditions varied considerably. Large monasteries like Glastonbury had revenue from their estates in excess of £4,000 and were managed as businesses. Smaller institutions often ran up high debts, had few inmates and were poorly run. Most religious orders, known as 'conventuals', had relaxed their rules but a few houses, notably the **Carthusians** and Franciscans, 'observed' the original conditions that governed their order. These houses received regular endowments and attracted increasing numbers of **novices** in the 1520s.

1.3 Anti-clericalism

Criticism of the Church was commonplace in the Middle Ages. The main complaints were as follows:

- The Church owned one third of all land and was more interested in collecting rents and **tithes** than serving the people. This was Simon Fish's main criticism in his 1529 book *The Supplication for the Beggars*.
- The Church charged high fees for reading wills and conducting burial services. In 1511 a case concerning Richard Hunne caused notoriety when he refused to pay a mortuary fee and was arrested by the Bishop of London. Hunne was later found hanging in his cell.
- The clergy enjoyed special legal privileges known as benefit of clergy. Common lawyers resented their right to be tried by canon law. It took business away from them and clerics were treated much more leniently.
- There was widespread pluralism. Most poorly paid clerics had to hold more than one office to supplement their low wages but the main targets for criticism were the wealthier members of the clergy, like Wolsey, who held a vast number of clerical offices.
- There was absenteeism. Many cathedral canons, bishops and abbots attended university or served as diplomats and were away for long periods of time. Wolsey, for instance, never visited York following his appointment as archbishop.
- Some clergy behaved improperly, living with mistresses and fathering illegitimate children. Wolsey had a mistress and a son. Allegations of sexual misconduct were also made against the regular clergy but only a few complaints seem to have been upheld.

1.4 Anti-papalism

Until Henry VIII's divorce England had enjoyed good relations with the papacy. Licences and dispensations were granted to the Tudors upon request. Henry VIII exercised effective control over clerical appointments and, though Wolsey had not spared the clergy heavy taxation, only £4,000 was sent to Rome each year. Unlike Germany, there was no sign of anti-papalism.

1.5 Who wanted Church reform?

Most historians now believe that only a minority of people was calling for reform in 1529. These critics had their own agenda and fell into four groups:
- Common lawyers, most of whom practised in London.
- Merchants who resented paying rents, tithes and other fees to an over-wealthy organisation.
- Humanists like John Colet, Dean of St Paul's, who condemned the Church's pre-occupation with money and called for a better-educated clergy. Similar criticisms appeared in Thomas More's *Utopia* (1516).
- English Lollards and Lutherans rejected the supreme authority of the Pope and challenged a number of Catholic beliefs. Anne Boleyn supported Lutheran ideas and gave Henry a copy of Tyndale's *Obedience of a Christian Man* in 1528. Tyndale denied the papacy's claims that he wanted to assume spiritual and temporal headship. Anne may have urged Henry to reform the Church.

1.6 What did people believe?

Most people were attached to traditional Catholic beliefs and ceremonies, attending feast days and celebrating the lives of saints. They regarded baptism, confession and communion as the most important sacraments; they believed in heaven and hell, and were convinced that time spent in **purgatory** could be reduced if they performed good works. Many, therefore, collected holy relics, went on pilgrimages, bought **indulgences** and left money to chantry priests to sing Masses for their soul. Candles and lamps burned in every parish church in memory of the dead.

There is little indication that continental reformist ideas were popular outside university and court circles. Lutheran ideas entered England in 1520 and Henry and his bishops were quick to condemn them. In 1521 the king received the title of 'Defender of the Faith' from Leo X for his attack on Luther. A minority of scholars at Cambridge were converted to Lutheranism. Both Luther and Wyclif, the fourteenth-century English founder of Lollardy, encouraged people to read the Bible. Copies of Lollard Bibles circulated illegally and followers were persecuted. Historians have noted that Lutheranism became more firmly established in areas where Lollardy originally existed, but that levels of literacy in England were quite low and the speed and extent with which the new ideas could spread were limited.

1.7 Conclusion

The English Church was not in as poor a condition as its critics claimed. It was not perfect but was seen as indispensable in enabling people to enter heaven. Most people accepted what they saw and heard, even if they could not understand Church doctrine. By their own standards, they were devout and religious people. Only a minority was calling for reform.

GLOSSARY

beneficed: earning a living from a Church office.
Carthusians: monks belonging to the Charterhouse order.
indulgences: pieces of paper, authorised by the papacy, which guaranteed purchasers that their souls would spend less time in purgatory.
novices: trainee monks and nuns.
purgatory: a place where souls were purged of their sins.
tithes: a 10% tax on property and goods, levied by the Church.

EXAMINER'S TIP

This subject appears at AS in both the OCR and Edexcel specifications and at A2 in the AQA (Alternative N) specification. In assessing the condition of the Church you need to use your evidence carefully and distinguish between different groups of complainants when explaining their viewpoints. Be aware that the Church has always had its critics and the evidence on which historians base their judgements is rarely complete or unbiased. It is therefore extremely difficult, if not impossible, to reach an accurate verdict.

2 | What was the nature of the Henrician Reformation, 1529–47?

2.1 Papal relations, 1529–34

In 1529 there was no indication that Henry VIII intended to separate England from the Roman Church. All he wanted was a divorce. By 1534, however, he had not only divorced Catherine but had broken from Rome and assumed the headship of the English Church. How did this come about?

Parliament

Henry called Parliament in November 1529 and, under Thomas Cromwell's management, proceeded to put pressure on the Pope.

1529   Wolsey was accused of **praemunire** and prosecuted. Bills were introduced to limit clerical fees on reading wills and conducting burials, and the clergy was accused of pluralism.

1530   Foxe, the Bishop of Hereford, and Cranmer, a Cambridge theologian, informed Henry that they had documentary proof that he had the power ('*imperium*') to obtain a divorce independently of the Pope.

1531   The House of Commons accused the English Church of *praemunire* and Archbishop Warham agreed to submit to royal authority, but on certain conditions.

1532   A new bill, drafted by Cromwell, forced the clergy to submit unconditionally.

1533   Anne Boleyn became pregnant. An Act of Appeals was hastily passed, which denied Catherine of Aragon and her supporters the right of appeal to the Pope. Cranmer presided over the divorce court. An Act of Annates stopped future clerical payments to Rome.

1534   The Treason Act condemned any criticism of Henry's marriage to Anne Boleyn. In November he was declared Supreme Head of the Church of England. He could elect bishops and abbots, control Church courts, pocket clerical taxes and determine religious beliefs.

Henry's advisers

The king received advice from three main groups:

- Anne Boleyn, Cranmer, Cromwell, Foxe and some MPs and lawyers urged Henry to work with Parliament to pressurise the Pope until he yielded.
- Catherine of Aragon, Warham, Fisher and More counselled patience, opposed divorce and warned Henry not to compromise papal relations.
- The Dukes of Norfolk and Suffolk, Bishop Gardiner and perhaps the majority of MPs sat on the fence and waited for Henry to decide.

The king was a reluctant reformer. His heart told him to follow Anne Boleyn, his head warned him of the serious consequences if he did; and his conscience worried him to the point of distraction. Anne's pregnancy, rather than any desire to break with Rome or reform the English Church, determined his course of action.

2.2 Doctrinal changes, 1536–39

The earliest reforms to Church doctrine took place in July 1536. They reflect the Protestant and **erastian** views of Cromwell, who acted as Henry's vicegerent, and the reformist ideas of Cranmer, who steadily moved away from orthodox Catholicism. The king had still to make his mind up but, for the moment, he did not stand in their way. Over the next 4 years the Church of England saw a number of important and, in some cases, irreversible reforms.

The Act of Ten Articles, 1536

- Three of the seven sacraments — baptism, penance and communion — were given precedence following Lutheran principles (see Unit 9, 2.2); this pleased the reformers.
- Traditional beliefs — such as chantries, the worship of saints and doing good works — were retained; this pleased the conservatives.

Injunctions, 1536 and 1538

- Over 100 holy days were removed from the Church calendar.

- Protestant preachers were licensed to spread reform.
- Shrines, holy relics and places of pilgrimage were destroyed. Becket's shrine at Canterbury was among the casualties.
- The burning of lights and candles in front of images was to cease.
- Letters were sent to JPs and sheriffs urging them to encourage bishops to denounce saints' days and superstitious practices.

The English Bible, 1539

- Tyndale's 1525 version of the Bible was revised, first by Rogers (1537) and finally by Coverdale (1538), to establish an authorised English Bible.
- Cromwell oversaw the publication of the new Bible in 1539, even paying an advance to French printers to ensure enough were available for every church to have its own copy.

2.3 Reaction, 1539–47

Conservative bishops had warned Henry in 1537 of the dangers to social order if traditional beliefs were undermined. By 1539 he agreed. Outbreaks of violence and **iconoclasm** were sweeping the country as militant reformers took matters into their own hands. They vandalised churches, interrupted services and threatened priests if they were reluctant or unwilling to consent to reform.

The Act of Six Articles, 1539

- The seven sacraments were re-established as the official doctrine.
- Anyone who denied the real presence of Christ at communion would be burned.

The King's Book, 1543

Henry and his more conservative bishops, led by Gardiner and Lee, issued the 'King's Book'. It justified the Six Articles and ordered that no woman or 'working-class man' was to own or read a Bible. In the bishops' opinion the book was being misread by illiterates, resulting in blasphemy.

Cranmer's work

Cranmer retained the king's support, even though the archbishop did not agree with the prevailing conservative reaction. Indeed, three developments suggested that reform was not entirely dormant:

- In 1544 Cranmer published the Litany, a book of prayers in English, designed to help priests conduct their services.
- In 1545 Cranmer issued the Primer, a book of religious instruction for children, which omitted saints' and feast days.
- Eighty chantry chapels were dissolved in 1545, but for financial reasons rather than because Henry had rejected purgatory.

2.4 The dissolution of the monasteries

In 1536 there were at least 825 monastic houses containing over 9,000 monks, nuns and friars. By 1540 every house had been seized by the Crown and the occupants forced to leave.

Motives

- An act of reform: according to a survey of 1535, many houses were corrupt and run inefficiently. As a result, all small houses with fewer than 12 occupants were to close.
- Financial necessity: the government needed money to strengthen its defences, pay for troops in Ireland and meet the rising costs of administration. Monastic rents would

yield £136,000 a year. The first Act of Dissolution (1536) closed monasteries with an income below £200; a second act (1539) dissolved the remainder.

- Political security: by closing the monasteries Henry ended the final enclave of papal power. All subjects in England were now under the king's control. (Most historians consider this to be a minor motive.)

Process

The monasteries were dissolved in a series of stages. As early as 1532 some heads of houses were encouraged to surrender their keys to the king. Those who cooperated received good pensions and conditions. The acts of 1536 and 1539 compelled submission: to refuse was tantamount to treason. Teams of commissioners carried out the dissolution and reported to Cromwell, who masterminded the operation. From 1536 a Court of Augmentations operated in London to handle land sales, the collection of rents, pension payments and to resolve disputes.

Results

- A revolt known as the Pilgrimage of Grace began in Lincolnshire and spread to Yorkshire in 1536. It was a serious protest against the recent changes, especially the closure of the smaller monasteries. At its height it numbered over 30,000 rebels.
- From 1539 most monks and nuns received pensions, but they were not inflation-proof.
- Land sales began in 1540 and brought the Crown £800,000 by 1547. Plate sales produced £80,000. Most purchasers were nobles, gentry and merchants.
- Henry founded a small number of grammar schools and **almshouses**.
- Trinity College, Cambridge was completed and Christ Church, Oxford founded.
- Eight cathedral churches (e.g. Ely and Wells) were re-endowed with lands.
- Six new dioceses (e.g. Chester and Westminster) were established.
- An unknown number of holy relics and ancient manuscripts were destroyed.

2.5 Opposition to the reformation

The following people opposed Henry's reformation:
- Supporters of Catherine of Aragon, notably Bishop Fisher, who was executed (1535) for accepting a cardinal's hat.
- Bishops loyal to the papacy, such as Warham and Longland.
- Elizabeth Barton, the nun of Kent, her confessor and four Canterbury monks. All of them condemned Henry's marriage to Anne and were executed.
- Twelve **Anabaptists**, burned at the stake for heresy (1535).
- Seven London Carthusian monks, executed (1535) for not taking the oath of supremacy.
- Thomas More, Lord Chancellor (1529–32), who was executed for denying the royal supremacy.
- Abbots who would not surrender their monastery (e.g. Reading and Glastonbury); they were executed.
- A small number of MPs in the 1533 parliamentary session.
- The 30,000 rebels in the 1536 Pilgrimage of Grace (the leaders and 300 of the rebels were executed).

2.6 Support for the reformation

The following people supported Henry's reformation:
- Bishops trained in civil law, such as Cranmer and Fox.
- Cromwell and his clients, notably Marshall and Morrison.

- Lutheran preachers like Jerome, Garrett and Barnes (though Henry had them burned for being too radical).
- Reform-minded bishops such as Latimer and Shaxton.
- Anne Boleyn, her father and brother.
- Katherine Parr, though she wisely avoided discussing religious reform with the king.
- MPs who stayed loyal to the king and benefited from the sale of monastic lands.

2.7 Conclusion

At his death in 1547 Henry ordered Masses to be said for his soul. There had been opposition to his political and religious reforms but also support from political opportunists and advocates of Protestantism. The Church was officially Catholic but rested now in the hands of a small group of men and a boy-king who were determined to make it Protestant.

GLOSSARY

almshouses: houses for the poor and homeless.
Anabaptists: those who rejected child baptism in favour of adult baptism.
erastian: the belief that the Church should be controlled by the state.
iconoclasm: the destruction of icons, or holy images and ornaments.
praemunire: owing allegiance to a foreign power, such as the papacy.

EXAMINER'S TIP

This subject appears at AS in the OCR and Edexcel specifications and at A2 in the AQA (Alternative N) specification. Questions are usually set on the nature of Henry's reformation. You could be asked: 'How far do the policies introduced by Henry VIII from 1529 to 1547 suggest that he wished to make England a Protestant country?' or: 'Why did opposition to Henry's changes fail?' or: 'Assess the aims, process and results of the dissolution of the monasteries.' The Henrician Reformation is a complex topic and each stage — 1529–34, 1534–39 and 1539–47 — needs to be studied carefully.

3 How far was England a Protestant country by 1553?

3.1 Factors affecting the Edwardian Reformation

In 1547 England was officially Catholic. Recent changes to traditional beliefs and customs had been well received in some counties, like Kent and Essex, but most people still enjoyed the local rituals and communal festivals, or were unwilling to break the law.

Political factors

Edward VI held strong Protestant views and his council was dominated by like-minded men. In contrast, the Catholics were in a weak condition: Norfolk, their leading peer, was in prison; Gardiner was no longer in the council; and Wriothesley was soon persuaded to retire.

Episcopal factors

Archbishop Cranmer held moderate, if not progressive, views but other bishops were radical, e.g. Latimer (Bishop of Worcester), Hooper (Bishop of Gloucester) and Ridley (Bishop of London).

Continental factors

Reformers from the continent arrived in England: Martin Bucer, a **Zwinglian**, was appointed to Cambridge; Peter Martyr, an Italian Protestant, lectured at Oxford; and Bernardino Ochino, a Strasbourg preacher, set up the first **stranger church** in London for foreign Protestants.

3.2 Changes under Somerset, 1547–49

- The government moved cautiously at first, partly due to its own political insecurity and partly to its desire not to stir up popular opposition.
- Cranmer published the *Book of Homilies* to improve levels of preaching.
- Parliament repealed the Act of Six Articles, the Treason Act and death by burning for heresy.
- The Chantry Act (1547) abolished Masses for the dead, and the government seized lands, cash and goods donated to chantry priests. Every church was affected in some way, yet there was very little open resistance. Those who opposed the reforms did so passively, by not cooperating with Crown servants, by confiscating Church goods and by concealing chantry property.
- In 1549 priests were allowed to marry. It was a popular piece of reform, since many had been living with their 'housekeepers' for years.
- In 1549 Cranmer published a prayer book containing a mixture of English and continental prayers. Several Catholic rituals continued (e.g. traditional clerical vestments) but there were some innovations: anointing at confirmation and the elevation of the **host** ended, and wine was now offered as well as bread at communion. This was declared an 'act of remembrance'.

The Act of Uniformity, 1549

The Act of Uniformity laid down punishments for anyone who refused to use the new prayer book or failed to attend services at least once a year (at Easter). The laity faced fines and the loss of possessions; the clergy faced the loss of earnings, dismissal and imprisonment. No one was to be burned. By the end of 1549 at least eight bishops had been dismissed or imprisoned.

The Western Rebellion, 1549

Opposition to the new prayer book occurred in several counties but was most vociferous in Cornwall and Devon. Six thousand protesters marched to Exeter and camped outside the city. It took Somerset and his council 11 weeks to raise an army large enough to kill or disperse the rebels. Small-scale protests in Oxfordshire, Hampshire and Buckinghamshire were also suppressed but Somerset faced growing criticism from fellow councillors about his handling of this problem.

3.3 Changes under Northumberland, 1549–53

Historians are undecided over how far Northumberland encouraged further Protestant reforms. Did he follow the lead of more radical councillors and preachers like St John, Latimer and Ridley, or did he set the pace of reform? Cranmer certainly supported a more Zwinglian English Church but was not willing to adopt **Calvinist ideas**, which were favoured by a minority of politicians and bishops.

Main changes, 1550–51

The 1550s saw a new ordinal, which ordered priests to preach the Gospel and to celebrate communion at a wooden table rather than at the stone altar. Bishops in favour of reform were appointed to London, Norwich, Gloucester and Worcester, and Catholic bishops were removed. A survey of church bells, plate, ornaments and goods identified those items that were surplus to requirement.

Second English Prayer Book, 1552

Among the main features of this prayer book were the following:

- Side altars and images were to be removed from churches.
- The high altar was to be replaced by a movable wooden table.
- Ministers had to wear a plain white surplice and none of the traditional vestments.
- Communion, using household bread and wine, was to be an act of remembrance.
- There was to be no signing of the cross at confirmation.
- There was to be no **exorcism** at baptism.

Some bishops, led by Knox, Hooper and Latimer, wanted to go further and persuaded **Convocation** to insert additional rules, known as the Black Rubric. For instance, communicants were not to kneel at communion and priests were not to bless the ring in marriage ceremonies. To Cranmer, such rituals were unimportant; to radicals, it was essential that they were removed.

The Act of Uniformity, 1552

The 1552 Act of Uniformity enforced stiffer penalties for non-compliance and non-attendance. There were no subsequent rebellions or executions but life imprisonment was given to Bishops Bonner, Tunstall, Day, Heath and Gardiner when they refused to use the new prayer book.

The Act of 42 Articles, 1553

This summarised the faith of the country, although it was never passed by Parliament.

3.4 How Protestant was England in 1553?

Historians are divided over the condition of the English Church in 1553. Geoffrey Elton and Geoffrey Dickens, for example, have suggested that England had become Protestant. Other historians, like John Guy and Patrick Collinson, have argued that the country only adopted Protestant views in the second half of Elizabeth's reign.

A major problem facing historians is how to interpret the fragmentary nature of the surviving evidence. Visitation records, which contain material concerning parish and diocesan affairs, often have more gaps than entries. Where evidence has survived, it is often biased towards Church and lay officials and is not necessarily typical of what ordinary people thought. Wills and Churchwardens' Accounts contain much useful material and state records reflect what officially happened, yet we can only guess as to how people felt about the Protestant reforms. The following conclusions, however, may be tentatively drawn:

- South and east England, especially London, Kent and Essex, welcomed Protestant reforms; the north and west of England, especially Lancashire, Durham and Cornwall, opposed reforms.
- Enthusiasm for purchasing chantry and monastic land reflected opportunists with money to spend rather than ideological reformists; in fact, both Catholics and Protestants bought Church land.
- Most people obeyed the law and, due to the Treason Act, avoided public displays of opposition after 1549. There was, however, considerable passive resistance in 1552–53.
- Most clergy went along with the changes. Many welcomed the freedom to marry but few shared the extreme views of the minority of radical and conservative bishops.

Calvinist ideas: the beliefs of John Calvin, a sixteenth-century Genevan reformer who believed in predestination.

Convocation: the governing body of the Church of England.

exorcism: a ritual of removing evil spirits.

host: bread consecrated in the Eucharist. It was then elevated, or lifted up, so that the whole congregation could see.

stranger church: a church where foreigners could hold their own services.

Zwinglian: a follower of Ulrich Zwingli, a sixteenth-century Zurich reformer who believed in sacramentarianism.

This topic appears at AS in the OCR specification and at A2 in the AQA (Alternative N) specification. AS questions are likely to require an explanation of the main religious changes and an understanding of the consequences. For instance, you might be asked: 'How far was England a more Protestant country at the death of Edward VI in 1553 than at his accession in 1547?' A2 questions may set this period of reform in a wider context. Candidates should therefore consider how far the Edwardian Reformation seriously impeded Mary's plans to restore Catholicism, and how far it influenced developments in Elizabeth's reign.

4 How popular was the Marian Reformation?

4.1 Background

Mary was a devout Roman Catholic. She believed that a minority of Protestants, backed by Edward VI's councillors, had led astray the vast majority of English people and, once these men had been removed, the country would quickly return to the true faith. Her advisers were not so sure. Some called for more direct action; others favoured a slow and moderate reformation. But was time on her side?

4.2 Mary's aims

Mary had three main aims, which were to:
- return the English Church and ex-monastic and chantry lands to the papacy
- remove heresy and enforce Catholic uniformity
- improve standards of preaching, **pastoral** care and clerical behaviour

4.3 Advisers

Mary was advised by a small group of Catholics, led by Cardinal Pole (Archbishop of Canterbury), Bishops Bonner (London) and Gardiner (Winchester; he was also her Lord Chancellor), Philip II and the Spanish clerics who accompanied him, such as Villagarcia and de Soto (Dominican monks appointed to Oxford) and Carranza (who became Mary's confessor).

4.4 Main changes

1553
- Catholic bishops (e.g. Gardiner, Bonner, Tunstall and Heath) were released from prison.
- Foreign preachers and refugees departed.

- Parliament repealed all of Edward's reforms.
- Latin services, orthodox Mass and the Act of Six Articles were restored.

1554

- Married clergymen had to give up their wives or their livings; 2,000 members of the clergy were dismissed.
- The Protestant bishops Cranmer, Latimer, Hooper and Coverdale were arrested.
- Marian 'exiles' began to emigrate; by 1558 they totalled 800.
- Pole, on behalf of the Pope, accepted Parliament's apology for the break from Rome.

1555

- Parliament refused to return Church lands; instead it offered £60,000 a year as compensation.
- Death by burning was reintroduced. By 1558 some 287 Protestants had died, including the 'Oxford Martyrs' — Cranmer, Latimer and Ridley. Eighty-five per cent of those burned came from London and southeast England, and most victims were urban workers, lower members of the clergy and scholars. Few held extreme Protestant views.
- Attempts were made to improve the moral and spiritual condition of the people. Colleges for priests were to be set up in every diocese and grammar schools in every town. Visitations were regularly held and Pole and Bonner wrote books to make Catholic rituals more relevant to the people.

4.5 Achievements by 1558

Most historians have argued that Pole was an unsuitable choice as Archbishop of Canterbury. He had been out of the country for over 20 years and had little conception as to how and why people had become Protestant. Moreover, he largely ignored the English laity, who controlled much of the Church patronage. As a result little was achieved by 1558. Historians claim that:

- the lack of money prevented the restoration of monasteries and chantries; priests' salaries remained low and, by excluding married clergymen, many parishes never had a resident priest
- no **seminary** was founded during Mary's reign and only a handful of schools were established
- relations with the papacy were restored but most people were disinterested
- the decision to burn heretics proved disastrous and compromised the entire reform programme

Revisionist viewpoints

Revisionist historians in recent years have taken a different stance. They have suggested that:

- real progress was made in re-establishing traditional prayers and doctrine. Inroads were even made in areas where Protestantism was well established (e.g. Kent)
- Bonner's 13 Homilies (prayers) were popular with the less-educated clergymen
- Churchwardens' Accounts indicate that genuine efforts were made by parishes to acquire vestments, copes, ornaments, bells, prayer books, images, lights and candles
- seminaries were established on the continent during Elizabeth's reign. They trained missionaries who helped keep English Catholicism alive
- the Catholic Reformation could have succeeded if Mary had produced a child, lived longer or burned fewer Protestants

4.6 Who was to blame for the burnings?

- The queen was ultimately responsible for restoring the death penalty and persisting with the burnings, in the face of growing doubts from her advisers.
- Philip initially supported her but later urged moderation.
- Some historians have held Bishops Bonner and Gardiner responsible.
- Others have suggested that Spanish clerics and Pole played a major role.

What is clear is that Mary failed to rid England of Protestantism.

GLOSSARY

pastoral: spiritual and personal guidance given to people by the clergy.
seminary: a college where Catholics are trained to be priests.

EXAMINER'S TIP

This subject appears at AS in the OCR specification and at A2 in the AQA (Alternative N) specification. At A2 you may be required to evaluate the impact of the burning of heretics and to assess the work of Mary, Bonner and Pole. Consider whether it was their aims and methods, or circumstances beyond their control, that led to their ultimate failure. A typical AS question is: 'To what extent was England a Catholic country by 1558?'

5 What was the nature of the Elizabethan Church Settlement?

5.1 Factors affecting the settlement

- Elizabeth wanted a Protestant Church and disliked the Catholic Mass. However, she did like some of the traditional ceremonies, believed that bishops should be unmarried, and was aware that many of her subjects wanted a Catholic Church.
- The privy council in 1558 contained a majority of Catholics.
- Many peers and the majority of existing bishops opposed changes to the Church.
- Spain and France would require careful handling as both were strong Catholic states and England was still at war with France.
- The Pope needed to be kept on side. In the eyes of most Roman Catholics, Elizabeth was illegitimate but the Pope could command them to accept her as the legitimate queen.
- The House of Commons contained a small number of outspoken Protestants, who required managing if religious bills were not to be blocked or defeated.

5.2 The Church Settlement, 1559

The Elizabethan Church Settlement consisted of two acts of Parliament passed in 1559:
- The Act of Supremacy declared Elizabeth the 'supreme Governor in all things ecclesiastical as well as temporal', which was a vague title that satisfied all religious groups.
- The Act of Uniformity established the doctrine based on the 1552 Prayer Book (communion in two kinds in remembrance of Christ and services said in English). Customary rituals, such as bowing at the name of Jesus and making the sign of the cross, were retained as prescribed in the 1549 Prayer Book.

The settlement was a compromise. For example, ministers could marry, which pleased Protestants; they were expected to wear traditional clerical robes, which pleased Catholics.

Injunctions, 1559

Further reforms were contained in royal orders issued later in 1559. All churches had to:
- remove images, lights, side altars and chantries
- possess the English Bible, Erasmus's *Paraphrases* and the Primer

All preachers had to:
- teach children the Ten Commandments and the Lord's Prayer
- possess an MA and hold a licence from the Archbishop
- preach 4 sermons on the royal supremacy and give 48 official sermons each year

The 39 Articles, 1563

In 1571 Parliament confirmed 39 articles produced in 1563. These embodied the Elizabethan Church Settlement and were the basis of the Church of England's faith.

5.3 Enforcement

Elizabeth declared that she would 'open windows into no man's soul'. She had no wish to persecute people for their religious beliefs, and bishops, councillors and JPs were instructed to tread softly in the early 1560s. Only those who deliberately and persistently flouted the laws were likely to be prosecuted.

Punishments

The heresy laws were repealed. A nominal fine of 1 shilling (5p) a week would be imposed on anyone who failed to attend services on Sundays and holy days, but payments were rarely collected. The queen was much more concerned about her clergy. Between 1559 and 1560 about 300 out of 9,000 beneficed members of the clergy resigned or were dismissed. Elizabeth appointed Matthew Parker, a moderate Protestant, as Archbishop of Canterbury and vacancies were gradually filled, some by bishops returning from continental centres of reform (e.g. John Jewel, who had been in Zurich, became Bishop of Salisbury).

EXAMINER'S TIP

This subject appears at AS in the OCR specification and at A2 in the OCR, Edexcel and AQA (Alternative N) specifications. AS questions usually want you to consider the factors that influenced the content of the Church Settlement. At A2 the most common themes are the nature of the settlement, its Protestant and Catholic features, and reactions to it in the early 1560s.

6 | *How successfully did Elizabeth tackle the Puritan challenge to the religious settlement?*

6.1 Who were the Puritans?

In the 1560s the term 'Puritan' was coined to describe the 'hotter sort of Protestant' who wanted to purify Elizabeth's Church of any remaining Catholic practices. The Puritans were a small group — about 3% of the population and 15% of the clergy — who came from all walks of life and from most areas of the country, though mainly from London and the southeast of England.

6.2 What did the Puritans believe?

Not all Puritans held the same beliefs. Most of them, however, believed that:
- the New Testament should be the basis of Christian teaching

- the Prayer Book was 'but half reformed' and should be replaced
- justification by faith was more important than doing good deeds
- the 'godly elect' were predestined to go to heaven
- Church rituals were totally unimportant
- the sermon was the best way to educate people in spiritual matters
- all church officials should be elected by their congregations
- all ministers should wear a black cloak, square cap and a plain white surplice; traditional vestments should be abolished

6.3 The Puritan challenge to the Church

In Elizabeth's reign Puritans sought to change the Church in so many different ways that their movement lacked unity, coherent leadership and widespread popular support. But several powerful patrons, such as Leicester and Walsingham, gave it a voice in the council and Parliament. The challenge of Puritanism seemed greater than it actually was, and never posed a serious threat to the Church Settlement.

The Vestiarian controversy, 1563

Members of the lower house of Convocation proposed the abolition of vestments, church music and holy days. The proposal was narrowly defeated and Archbishop Parker suspended 37 clerics, revoked all licences for preaching and issued 'Advertisements', which insisted on uniformity of clerical dress.

William Strickland, MP

In 1571 some Puritan MPs proposed moderate reforms to stop pluralism and absenteeism. William Strickland added extra clauses, however, which he lettered A–D and which became known as the Alphabet Bills. One bill advocated a new Genevan prayer book and so angered the queen that she insisted all the proposed reforms should be rejected.

Presbyterianism

In the 1570s a small number of MPs, led by John Field and Thomas Wilcox, proposed that bishops, deans and archdeacons should be replaced by elected assemblies. The idea was taken up by a Cambridge scholar, Thomas Cartwright, but was rejected by the master of his college, John Whitgift, who expelled him and effectively silenced the discussion. Presbyterianism survived but most Puritans believed their ideas were too extreme.

'Prophesyings'

Field and other Puritans encouraged the clergy to hold regular classes, at which clerics discussed the Bible, practised their sermons and convinced listeners of their views. Several bishops, like Grindal and Parkhurst, saw these meetings (known as 'prophesyings') as an effective way of raising the standards of preaching. Elizabeth saw things differently. In her opinion they were occasions for Puritans to spread their own views.

Elizabeth suspended Archbishop Grindal from office in 1576. Whitgift, his successor, used the Court of High Commission to root out supporters of the movement. Some MPs (e.g. Turner and Cope) organised petitions to replace the Prayer Book with Genevan services and others, like Peter Wentworth, insisted that they had the right to speak freely on religious topics. They were sent to the Tower to cool off.

Separatists

Separatists appeared in the 1580s in London (led by Barrow and Greenwood) and in Norwich (led by Browne and Harrison). They formed their own separate churches but were forced into hiding. The publication of nine satirical pamphlets in 1588–89 prompted Whitgift to round up Presbyterians and separatists and hang their leaders. By 1603 Puritanism had been effectively suppressed.

This topic appears at AS in the OCR specification and at A2 in the Edexcel specification. A2 questions are likely to require an assessment of the Puritan challenge to the Church, such as: 'Assess the nature and extent of Puritanism during the reign of Elizabeth.' Remember that the threat of Puritanism would have seemed greater to contemporaries than it does to modern historians. Nevertheless, its ultimate failure does not mean that it was bound to fail.

7 How serious was the threat posed by Roman Catholics to the Elizabethan Church and state?

7.1 Background

Between 1558 and 1570 most Catholics in England accepted the Church Settlement and continued to attend church. A few paid fines for non-attendance and some still celebrated Mass as if there had not been a Protestant reformation. Until 1566 the Pope gave no guidance as to whether Catholics should obey the laws and there was no English leader around whom opposition groups might form. The queen's view of Roman Catholics changed in 1568, however, with the arrival in England of Mary, Queen of Scots.

7.2 Mary, Queen of Scots

Mary presented Elizabeth with the following problems:
- Until Elizabeth married and had a child, Mary was heir to the throne of England. Some of her supporters wanted to kill Elizabeth.
- Mary was a Roman Catholic. This encouraged the Pope and other Catholic powers, such as Spain, to support plots and rebellions against Elizabeth.
- Mary was half French and half Scottish. Both France and Scotland could use her to further their own interests against England.
- Mary was a fugitive in England. Should Elizabeth return her to Scotland, send her back to France, keep her in England under house arrest or agree to her execution?

7.3 The Northern Earls' Rebellion, 1569

Over 5,000 rebels supported the Catholic Earls of Westmoreland and Northumberland, Lord Dacre and the Duke of Norfolk, to protest against Elizabeth's Church and her Protestant advisers. Their aim was to release Mary, Queen of Scots from captivity in Tutbury, marry her to Norfolk and put them on the throne instead of Elizabeth. In the event, apart from occupying Durham Cathedral, they achieved nothing. No foreign troops came to their aid and they were dispersed by a royal army. Parliament demanded Mary's execution; instead the queen imprisoned Norfolk and had Northumberland executed.

7.4 The Bull of Excommunication, 1570

Pope Pius V excommunicated Elizabeth in the hope that English Catholics would rise up and depose her. The bull, however, arrived after the rebellion of the Northern Earls had ended and most Catholics ignored it. Only a minority became **recusants**. These Roman Catholics faced fines, confiscation of goods and imprisonment. Parliament also declared that anyone found in possession of papal objects was guilty of treason.

7.5 The Ridolfi Plot, 1571

Ridolfi, an Italian banker working in London, acted as an agent to recruit Catholic support to release Mary, marry her to Norfolk and assassinate the queen. Ridolfi was deported, as was the Spanish ambassador, de Spes. Norfolk was executed in 1572.

7.6 Missionaries

In 1574 missionaries arrived from Douai College to train English priests and to persuade Catholics not to attend church services. Wherever they went they were followed by Elizabeth's secret service agents, and prosecuted from 1577. **Jesuits** arrived in 1580. Led by Campion and Parsons, they planned to restore the country to Roman Catholicism. Some of them plotted treason. Parliament reacted with heavy £20 fines and in 1581 they imprisoned anyone who said or heard a Mass or refused to attend church.

7.7 The Throckmorton Plot, 1583

Throckmorton confessed to plotting to free Mary, kill Elizabeth, enlist military support from France and Spain and foment a Catholic uprising. The council arrested the ringleaders before the plot could materialise. Mendoza, the Spanish ambassador, was deported, over 100 Jesuits were sent home and harsher penalties (exile or death for missionaries, loss of property and goods for landowners) were introduced.

7.8 The Babington Plot, 1586

Mary signed letters sent to her by Babington to enlist the help of Spain in freeing her from captivity. Elizabeth finally agreed to execute her and some 13 conspirators in 1587.

7.9 Reaction to war with Spain

Fear of a Catholic invasion after 1586 saw the execution of 123 missionaries and a 5-mile restriction imposed on all recusants in 1593. Parliament proposed a tougher bill to remove children from their Catholic parents, but Elizabeth sensibly vetoed it.

GLOSSARY

Jesuits: priests trained to serve the pope as teachers, preachers, confessors and missionaries.
recusants: those who refused to attend church.

EXAMINER'S TIP

This subject appears at AS and A2 in the OCR specification and at A2 in the Edexcel specification. A typical AS question might be: 'How great a threat to Elizabeth I's religious settlement was presented by English Catholics until the end of her reign?' Questions at A2 are usually centred upon the seriousness of the Catholic threat and whether or not Elizabeth and her council handled Mary's presence in England effectively. Avoid giving descriptions of the plots; instead comment on their significance.

---

8   What was the condition of the Church of England in 1603?

8.1 The condition of the laity

To be effective, Elizabeth believed that the Reformation must be a slow and gradual process. Well into the 1570s, reports from bishops and churchwardens suggest that there was little enthusiasm for Protestantism. Ministers frequently claimed that few attended weekday services, only children regularly learned **catechisms** and most chose to take communion only at Easter. If there was a surge of interest in more Calvinist ideas, it was due mainly to people's fear of Catholicism generated by the Spanish war. To be outwardly Protestant was to be patriotic. In contrast, many people kept their Catholic relics and priests hid their old chalices, 'looking for to have Mass again'. Some historians, such as John Bossy, believe the number of Catholic converts — particularly in the north — was rising in the 1590s, due mainly to the work of missionaries.

8.2 The condition of the clergy

The quality of Church of England ministers appears to have been very varied. There was a shortage of preachers; only one quarter of Oxfordshire parishes received regular sermons in 1586. A few towns, such as Coventry and Warwick, established lectureships to pay for visiting lecturers but there was little enthusiasm for Puritan preachers. In fact by 1603 most Catholic-educated clergymen had died and the more militant Puritans had been hounded out of office. Instead the Church had fallen under the iron grip of Archbishop Whitgift and John Bancroft, Bishop of London. They enforced religious uniformity and approved of Richard Hooker's *Of the Laws of Ecclesiastical Polity* (1594–97), which defended the importance of bishops, confirmed Elizabethan doctrine and emphasised salvation rather than preaching.

GLOSSARY

catechisms: books containing the principles of the Elizabethan Church doctrine.

EXAMINER'S TIP

This topic appears at AS in the OCR specification. You might be asked: 'How much support was there in England for the Church of England at the time of Elizabeth I's death in 1603?' To answer this kind of question you will need to consider what happened to the Puritans and Catholics in the 1580s and 1590s, how far people really were interested in Church doctrine and rituals, and who really cared about the Church of England in 1603.

1 How effective was the government of Elizabethan England?

1.1 The role of the queen

Elizabeth believed in the **divine right of kings**. Her rights or prerogatives were undefined and in theory unlimited. Matters of state that concerned her own welfare, such as her marriage and the succession, religion and foreign affairs, she regarded as her preserve. Politicians and administrators were expected to be her obedient servants; their function was to assist the queen in ruling the country. If she needed advice she might ask for it, but all decisions would be taken by her.

1.2 The privy council

The privy council comprised 18 members in 1558 and 12 by 1603. Councillors advised the queen and implemented her decisions. She did not usually attend but was kept informed of the discussions by her principal secretary, who drew up the daily agenda. He was the most important privy councillor as he supervised the work of all other secretaries. William Cecil, Lord Burghley was secretary until 1572 before becoming Lord Treasurer. Francis Walsingham served as secretary from 1573 to 1590, and Robert Cecil between 1596 and 1610.

The council was supportive but it clashed with the queen over three main issues:
- Marriage and succession — she would not discuss her marriage and was reluctant to name her successor.
- Roman Catholics — she refused to impose heavy punishments on recusants.
- Mary, Queen of Scots — she was unwilling to accept that Mary should be executed.

Between 1560 and 1580 the council was mainly Protestant, which gave it a degree of unity, but factions were always present. Clients and followers of William Cecil competed with those of Robert Dudley, Earl of Leicester in the 1570s and 1580s, and rivalry between Robert Cecil and Robert Devereux, Earl of Essex often divided the council in the 1590s. The main topic of disagreement was usually whether or not England should intervene in another country's affairs. In 1559 Catholic councillors (Winchester, Arundel and Petre) opposed the sending of an army to help Protestant rebels in Scotland. In 1565 Protestants like Leicester opposed the idea of the queen marrying a Catholic. In 1572 the Earl of Sussex opposed the sending of help to Protestant Dutch rebels. In 1585 Leicester, Walsingham, Warwick, Bedford and Knollys spoke in favour of declaring war on Spain but Burghley, Sussex, Bacon, Croft and Clinton were against it.

1.3 The court

Elizabethan government was personal and those courtiers who lived with and attended the queen became key figures in her administration. About 1,000 courtiers were in full-time attendance and a further 1,300 administrators worked at the court in the exchequer, council, finance and legal departments. Access to the queen was vital. She had daily meetings with her secretary and treasurer, gave public audiences to ambassadors and visitors, and held private discussions with her nobles and favourites. She could confer titles, appoint officers to Church and state, and grant gifts, fees, pensions, annuities, licences and patents to reward her subjects. To be absent from court, as Essex was in the late 1590s, could prove fatal.

1.4 Administration

Continuity was the keynote of Elizabeth's administration. Loyalty and ability were rewarded with long tenures in office — Winchester was Lord Treasurer between 1550 and 1572; Mildmay was Chancellor of the Exchequer 1559–89 — and the opportunity to gain titles, lands and fees. There were no reforms to the central and local government machinery. Existing practices were continued and extended. For instance, by 1585 lord lieutenants were appointed to every county. They supervised the musters, exercised the county militia, raised troops and supplied them with money and weapons. As the country became preoccupied with war the lord lieutenants became the link between central and local government, displacing the sheriff as the most important royal servant in the county.

Justice

Common-law courts (King's Bench, Common Pleas and Exchequer) and prerogative courts (Chancery, Requests and Star Chamber) continued as before. Staffed by legal experts, the law courts were less corrupt, though still slow in procedure.

JPs

The number of JPs in each county steadily increased to about 40 by 1603. Most were local gentry, nobles and merchants who served the Crown out of duty and self-advancement. As judges they resolved local disputes, and as administrators they enforced the law. Without their hard work government would not have been so effective. They could, however, be partisan: Catholic JPs, for example, often failed to enforce laws against recusants, and landowning JPs accepted their friends' ridiculously low tax assessments.

Finance

The Crown faced several financial problems, such as:

- an inherited debt of about £150,000 due to the war against France
- declining revenue from crown lands as sales continued
- a small increase in customs duties due to the trade depression in the Netherlands
- an increase in household costs
- the decline in real terms of parliamentary subsidies
- widespread corruption among court officials

From the 1580s the government also faced heavy war costs. An Irish rebellion in the 1590s worsened the situation so that, by 1603, government expenditure far exceeded revenue. How did Elizabeth manage her finances?

- She avoided heavy expenditure until the 1580s and had balanced her budget by 1578.
- She retained crown lands for much of her reign.
- She dispensed patronage sparingly, granting **reversions** and paying low salaries.

- She called Parliament ten times, requesting modest sums until the 1590s and large subsidies thereafter (£300,000 in 1589, £450,000 in 1593 and 1597 and £600,000 in 1601). Her requests were always met.
- She had very able treasurers — Winchester (1550–72) and Burghley (1572–98).
- She tried to make military and naval expeditions largely self-funding.

At her death Elizabeth only left a debt of £300,000.

1.5 How effective was the administration?

With no army or police force and only a small bureaucracy and revenue, the queen demonstrated considerable skill in managing her administration. Lord lieutenants, sheriffs and JPs kept the counties peaceful. The Church preached loyalty and obedience to the queen, and the nobility and gentry held the main offices of government. Her policies were noncontroversial and well received by most people. Wales was governed well and the northern counties, after the 1569 rebellion (see Unit 4, section 7.3), had their council reformed. Only Ireland presented continual problems — in 1569, 1579 and 1595–1603 there were rebellions against: English laws; the introduction of the shire system; Protestants; and **planters**.

divine right of kings: the view that monarchs held their power directly from God.

planters: English landowners who were given lands or plantations in Ireland, particularly in King's County and Queen's County; many preferred to live in England as absentee landlords.

reversions: offices or pieces of land that reverted to a person upon the expiry of a lease or death of an incumbent. Elizabeth increasingly used grants of reversion as a way of saving money.

This subject appears at AS in the OCR and AQA (Alternative N) specifications and at A2 in the OCR specification. Questions that ask 'How effective was…?' require you to think about successes and limitations, and to supply explanations for them. In the sixteenth century no government was totally effective, but Elizabeth was more successful than most.

2 How far did the nature and role of Parliament change?

2.1 The queen's view of Parliament

Elizabeth was an 'absolute' queen: she was to be obeyed and should not have to defend her policies or prerogatives. In 1566 she declared that 'it is monstrous that the foot [the House of Commons] should control the head [the monarch]'. She believed that Parliament had no rights, only privileges, and these could be withdrawn. Parliament was called for three main reasons:

- To vote taxes in emergencies.
- To pass laws in the interest of Elizabeth's subjects.
- To support royal policies.

2.2 Parliament's view of Parliament

Some MPs believed that the queen's 'absolute' authority rested in Parliament. Since Henry VIII's reign Parliament had been consulted over religious issues, and some of the most important political developments had been a result of the king and Parliament

working together. Moreover, in the course of the sixteenth century MPs had regularly enjoyed a number of practices, such as:

- amending parliamentary bills
- exercising freedom of speech
- avoiding arrest for debt during a parliamentary session
- determining the outcome of disputed elections

Some MPs wanted to turn these practices into rights that did not depend upon the favour of the Crown. Paul and Peter Wentworth claimed that 'free speech' entitled MPs to discuss any matter of state, such as royal finances or the succession. Most MPs did not agree, however; in their view, MPs had no rights, only privileges, and policy-making and matters concerning the queen's person were part of her prerogative.

2.3 Historians' views of Parliament

The traditional interpretation

In 1953 John Neale claimed that the House of Commons rose to prominence in Elizabeth's reign. Puritan MPs tried to reform the Church and discovered that they could hold the Crown to ransom by refusing financial requests until they had first discussed their own concerns. Neale believed that this 'choir' of MPs won control of committees that amended parliamentary bills and that, in the course of the seventeenth century, they began to draft legislation in their own interests.

Revisionism

More recent historians, like Geoffrey Elton and Conrad Russell, have challenged the above interpretation. They have argued that Elizabeth's reign saw no changes in the procedure, privileges and political role of Parliament. It was still essentially a medieval institution. The Commons, they believed, had no desire to challenge the Crown's prerogatives. Instead, most MPs were cooperative and the few who proved awkward, some of whom were Puritans, were not typical of the majority. In fact, the disputes that occurred in the Commons and between the Commons and the Lords were often orchestrated by privy councillors who encouraged their client MPs to raise issues that the queen had already disallowed in the Lords' chamber and in the privy council.

2.4 Parliament's function

Elizabeth's first parliament comprised 400 MPs and 80 peers. They met when summoned by the queen — on ten occasions in all between 1559 and 1601. Most representatives did not attend, since sessions were usually short, expenses were small and the journey to and from London was generally unpleasant. Parliamentary business, moreover, held little interest for most MPs. Once she had passed any government-initiated bills and gained her financial requests, the queen dissolved Parliament.

2.5 Management of Parliament

The Commons was managed by the Speaker, appointed by the queen, who drew up a daily agenda and determined which MPs could speak. Privy councillors sat in the Commons, usually near to the Speaker, and used their client MPs to express their views. The Lords were controlled by the Chancellor and, as a body, the peers could amend or reject a Commons' bill. Finally, the queen had several ways of controlling MPs. She could:

- send instructions to the Commons
- send MPs to the Tower
- lecture MPs and peers privately

- veto a bill (she did this on 66 occasions)
- adjourn or prorogue (suspend) a session
- dissolve Parliament with or without warning

2.6 Disputes

Historians acknowledge that disputes did occur in the Commons and that they became more frequent as Elizabeth's reign progressed. Neale believed that the disputes represented a worsening relationship between the Crown and Commons; Elton considered that they were exceptions that went against a generally harmonious trend. Some examples of disputes are as follows:

- Bishops in the Lords opposed the Bill of Uniformity (1559); Puritans in the Commons tried to introduce the Genevan prayer book (1571, 1584, 1587) and increase anti-Catholic punishments (1571, 1580, 1586, 1593).
- MPs urged the queen to marry (1559, 1563) and to name her successor (1566).
- Commons and Lords called for the death of Mary, Queen of Scots (1572, 1584, 1586).
- Paul Wentworth (1566) and Peter Wentworth (1571, 1576, 1587, 1593) demanded the right to have freedom of speech.
- MPs complained that the Crown's right to grant monopolies was being abused (1597, 1601).

2.7 The situation in 1603

In spite of occasional disputes, relations between the Crown and Parliament remained very sound. The Commons required skilful management and only a minority of MPs were persistent troublemakers. Most cooperated with the Crown, sessions ended amicably and over 400 acts were passed. By 1603 the Commons still had no rights, only privileges, which could be amended or withdrawn. The Crown had surrendered none of its prerogatives. Only on three occasions had Elizabeth yielded to parliamentary pressure:

- The Church Settlement (1559).
- The execution of Mary, Queen of Scots (1587).
- The cancellation of several monopolies (1601).

3 | *Why did the popularity of Elizabeth's government decline after 1588?*

3.1 Background

For much of Elizabeth's reign her government was held in high esteem. Unlike most continental countries, England did not experience religious wars, the economy was sound, there was little sign of popular unrest and the country had defeated the invincible Spanish Armada. Yet in the years following 1588 Elizabeth's government fell into decline.

3.2 Reasons for the decline in popularity

Death of advisers

Many of the queen's most able and experienced councillors died in the decade after 1588 (e.g. Mildmay, Walsingham, Leicester, Bedford, Huntingdon, Burghley). Elizabeth showed signs of ageing and a state of inertia characterised the administration. Factions centred upon Cecil and Essex further weakened the government.

War with Spain

As war continued into the 1590s, complaints increased about its cost, the presence of soldiers who were billeted on civilians, and whether the government had the desire and competence to end the war successfully.

Social problems

Unpaid soldiers and sailors, 'masterless' men and retainers preyed upon vulnerable towns and villages in the 1590s. JPs complained that they were unable to control them. Bad harvests (1594–97), enclosure riots (1596) and rising food prices added to the problem of the unemployed and starving poor moving to the towns.

Financial difficulties

The Spanish war cost £3.5 million, aid to the Netherlands was over £1 million, and the Irish rebellion £1.2 million. To meet these costs, parliamentary taxation doubled to £300,000 in 1589, trebled in 1593 and 1597 and quadrupled to £600,000 in 1601. Crown lands were sold, benevolences and forced loans imposed, and unpopular duties like **coat and conduct money**, **ship money** and **purveyance** were collected.

Rebellions

The Tyrone Rebellion in Ireland (1596–1603) required English armies and over £3 million before it was suppressed. Essex's attempt to seize the queen and take control of London in 1601 confirmed the government's uncertain grip on political affairs.

Monopolies

The Crown granted monopolies as a way of raising revenue and rewarding servants and favourites. Several merchants complained in Parliament that some monopolists were damaging trade. In 1601 Elizabeth reviewed recent grants and cancelled 11 monopolies, but allegations of abuse by government officials continued.

4

What were the aims and limitations of Elizabeth's foreign policies?

4.1 Background

Elizabeth did not write down the aims of her foreign policy and historians have even argued about whether she actually had a policy or whether she simply reacted to events as they developed. Most rulers adapted general guidelines and principles to suit their own circumstances; few were powerful enough to impose their will on other states.

4.2 Principles

Elizabeth's foreign policy principles were:
- to avoid war if at all possible
- to defend England from invasion
- to maintain and expand overseas trade

4.3 Limitations

Several factors limited Elizabeth's conduct of foreign affairs. Some of these were constant; other factors changed in the course of her long reign. It is important to recognise that as time passed and events unfolded, Elizabeth's relations with foreign powers also changed. In 1558 she was friendly with Spain and at war with France; by 1603 Spain was her enemy and France had become an ally.

The main factors that affected her foreign policies were as follows:
- The queen's personality: she disliked war yet acted provocatively; she could be dogmatic yet indecisive; she put her own country's interests first yet expected her allies to support her.
- Conflicting advice: some councillors, like Cecil and Mildmay, advocated peace and conciliation; others, like Walsingham and Leicester, wanted the queen to be more aggressive. She also held discussions with courtiers, ambassadors, household servants and royal favourites before making up her mind.
- The lack of permanent armed forces: the few troops with military and naval experience were no match for the enemy in an offensive war against Spain or France.
- Insufficient revenue: until the 1580s, limited revenue prevented the strengthening of military and naval defences or of Elizabeth pursuing an expansive foreign policy.
- Domestic issues: problems such as settling the Church and improving government finances were of greater importance in the 1560s and 1570s.
- The **Counter-Reformation**: as a Protestant country, England was a potential target for Catholic powers intent upon advancing the Counter-Reformation.
- Trade with the Netherlands: most English trade was conducted with the Spanish Netherlands, yet relations between Spain and the Netherlands steadily deteriorated until war erupted in 1572.

GLOSSARY

Counter-Reformation: the reaction by the Catholic Church and states to the Protestant Reformation, notably in the second half of the sixteenth century.

EXAMINER'S TIP

This subject appears at AS in the OCR specification and at A2 in the Edexcel specification. Learn the main principles behind Elizabeth's foreign policies and understand how they were shaped by internal and foreign influences. You may take the view that her strategy was to be defensive rather than aggressive and that only after 1580 was she able to become more adventurous. You might be asked: 'How far did the issues of marriage and succession to the throne affect Elizabeth's foreign policy from 1558 to 1587?'

5 Why did relations between England and Spain change in the course of Elizabeth's reign?

5.1 Background

England and Spain had been allies since Henry VII's reign (see Unit 1). They were linked by marriage, trade and a mutual enemy — France. Though their friendship had been occasionally tested during Henry VIII's reign and under Northumberland, Queen Mary's marriage to Philip II of Spain and their war against France once again drew the countries together.

5.2 Years of continuing friendship, 1558–67

Elizabeth and Philip II were on good personal terms. She was keen to retain his support to prevent France from building up its influence in Scotland and he befriended her as an ally against France. Philip demonstrated his friendship by proposing marriage, representing her at the peace talks with France, restraining the papacy from excommunicating her, and appointing likeable ambassadors to England. There were signs of trouble, however. A minor trade war with Flanders broke out in 1563–64 and trade was further disrupted by disturbances in the Netherlands in 1566–67.

5.3 Years of growing conflict, 1567–86

Historians generally acknowledge the fact that both Elizabeth and Philip were responsible for the breakdown in Anglo–Spanish relations. Each ruler acted in a manner designed to protect their country's best interests but, in so doing, they provoked one another into a spiralling pattern of action and reaction.

Acts of provocation by Elizabeth
The Netherlands and the Atlantic

In 1567 Philip sent 10,000 troops, under the command of Alva, to suppress the Dutch Protestants. Elizabeth and some of her advisers feared that once Alva had achieved his objectives he might use his army to invade England and force Catholicism on her. Elizabeth's aim was to prevent Spanish troops from succeeding, to stop France from interfering and to give the Dutch a measure of freedom under Spanish rule. Her strategy was to allow English volunteers to assist the Dutch rebels and to blockade the Channel to stop Spanish ships from reaching Dutch ports. She never openly admitted her responsibility for these activities.

Silver ships

In 1568, four Italian ships carrying silver bound for Alva's army were forced to take shelter in Plymouth. Elizabeth 'borrowed' the silver for her own use. Philip retaliated by

seizing English goods and shipping in Spanish ports. Elizabeth responded by confiscating Spanish assets in England.

Sea beggars

In 1572 Elizabeth expelled Dutch 'sea beggars' (pirates) from Dover but they sailed to the Dutch port of Brill and, on finding it undefended, seized it. Spain believed that England had acted wilfully but this was not true. Later that year, however, Sir Humphrey Gilbert and volunteer troops arrived to give 'unofficial' help to the nearby port of Flushing.

Foreign aid

In the 1570s Elizabeth offered to mediate in the on-going conflict in the Netherlands and at the same time she lent money to the rebels. Approaches were made to enlist mercenary leaders — Casimir of Poland (1578) and Alençon of France (1579) — but they achieved little in the face of the superior Spanish Army. By 1585 the Spanish Army had overrun all but two of the Dutch provinces and a treaty was signed between Spain and the French Catholic League (at Joinville) agreeing to a joint attack on all Protestants. Elizabeth now decided that she had to send her own troops to the Netherlands.

The Treaty of Nonsuch, 1585

- The Earl of Leicester and 7,000 men were sent to garrison Brill and Flushing.
- The earl was given £125,000 for the campaign.
- He was ordered not to accept any offer of sovereignty from the rebels.

If Elizabeth hoped to avoid responsibility for this expedition, Philip saw through her stratagem. He regarded Leicester's presence in the Spanish Netherlands in 1586–87 as an act of war.

The Atlantic

According to the Treaty of Tordesillas (1494), English merchants had no right to sail the Atlantic and trade with Spanish and Portuguese colonies. The Americas were forbidden lands. In the 1560s a Plymouth merchant, John Hawkins, began selling African slaves to the Caribbean but was attacked in 1567 by Spanish officials, who confiscated his goods. Francis Drake accompanied Hawkins on his last voyage and vowed revenge. His goal was not slave trading, but pirating Spanish silver ships.

Drake

1572–73	Drake captured the silver fleet at Nombre de Dios but the queen denied all knowledge.
1577–80	He circumnavigated the globe, seizing silver bullion. Elizabeth knighted him on his return.
1585–86	He plundered West Indian islands and captured Spanish and Portuguese bullion ships. The queen's support for Drake (which she still denied) was tantamount to war.

Acts of provocation by Philip

Philip used his resident ambassadors in London to coordinate Catholic activities in England and Ireland.

1569–70	Alva was urged to help the northern rebellion but he persuaded Philip to change his mind.
1569–73	Philip considered sending troops to assist the Geraldine Rebellion in Munster.

1571	Philip discussed the idea of sending troops to aid Ridolfi in his plot to kill the queen. De Spes, the Spanish ambassador, became involved and as a result was deported.
1580	Spanish troops landed at Munster but were quickly arrested.
1584	Mendoza, the new Spanish ambassador, was deported for his involvement in the Throckmorton plot to kill the queen.
1585	English ships were seized and plans drawn up to invade England.

Years of war, 1585–1604

Philip wanted to send his armada in 1587 but Drake attacked 30 ships in Cadiz and delayed the fleet's departure. In 1588, 130 ships set sail for Calais. English fireships scattered them before they could rendezvous with the Spanish Army of Flanders. The fleet sailed north and only two thirds of the fleet eventually returned home. In 1589 Drake and Norris launched a counter-armada against mainland Spain. They failed to capture Lisbon and made a loss on the voyage.

In the 1590s the war dragged on without either country gaining any decisive advantage. Philip sent two more invasion fleets in 1596 and 1597, but both were destroyed by storms. English privateers launched attacks on Cadiz and the Azores but with little success. Neither Elizabeth nor Philip could bring themselves to admit they could not win the war. Only in 1604 did it end when the new rulers, James I and Philip III, signed the Treaty of London.

EXAMINER'S TIP

This subject appears at AS in the OCR specification and at A2 in the OCR, Edexcel and AQA (Alternative N) specifications. A typical AS question is: 'Assess the influences that shaped Elizabeth I's policies towards Spain during the period to 1585.' A2 questions will require you to explain why Anglo–Spanish relations changed from friendship to war during Elizabeth's reign. You may be asked to assess her role in causing the war. Was she mainly responsible or just reacting to Spanish acts of provocation? Remember that a balanced argument will score the highest marks.

6 What were the main factors that influenced Anglo–Scottish relations, 1558–1603?

6.1 Background

Relations between England and Scotland fluctuated for much of the Tudor period. Wars had occurred in the reigns of Henry VII, Henry VIII and Edward VI and, even when there were periods of peace, conditions on the border suggested conflict was always near to the surface.

6.2 Why was Scotland a problem, 1559–60?

- Scotland was ruled by Mary Stuart, who in 1559 became Queen of France (she was married to Francis II). Her mother was Mary of Guise, who acted as the regent in Scotland. The French in Edinburgh therefore presented a security threat to England.
- Mary Stuart was heir to Elizabeth's throne. Some of Mary's followers hoped Elizabeth would not be ruling for a long time.

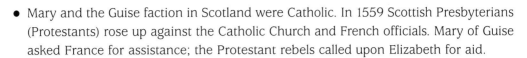

- Mary and the Guise faction in Scotland were Catholic. In 1559 Scottish Presbyterians (Protestants) rose up against the Catholic Church and French officials. Mary of Guise asked France for assistance; the Protestant rebels called upon Elizabeth for aid.

Elizabeth's dilemma

The council urged Elizabeth to send military assistance to the Presbyterian rebels. If they succeeded, Scotland might become Protestant and French influence would be ended; but such action could well incite France to attack England and send troops to strengthen Mary of Guise's control in Scotland. At first Elizabeth only permitted volunteers but in 1560 she agreed to 8,000 troops, led by Wilton, being sent to assist the Scots. Mary of Guise died in July and no French relief troops arrived, so the rebellion came to an end.

Treaty of Edinburgh, 1560

The Treaty of Edinburgh was negotiated by Cecil and Scottish lords and Presbyterians, and later presented to Mary, Queen of Scots for approval. According to its terms:
- all troops had to evacuate Scotland
- Mary had to recognise Elizabeth as the true Queen of England
- Presbyterianism was to become the official faith of Scotland

6.3 Mary in Scotland, 1561–67

Upon arriving in Scotland in 1561, Mary refused to sign the Treaty of Edinburgh. She wanted a Catholic Church and was hopeful that France would back her. Elizabeth hoped to neutralise Mary's potential threat by suggesting that she marry Robert Dudley. Mary married Lord Darnley, however, an Englishman with a distant claim to the throne, which alarmed Elizabeth even more.

Mary's marriage was a turbulent affair. A son, James, was born but Darnley accused Mary of adultery and killed her lover. She took revenge by arranging the murder of Darnley and then compounded her felony by eloping with Bothwell, a Protestant divorcee who was one of the murderers, in 1567. Outraged Scottish lords forced Mary to abdicate, seized her son and imprisoned her, but she escaped and fled to England.

6.4 Mary in England, 1568–87

Elizabeth had two main options when Mary arrived in England:
- to return her to Scotland or France
- to keep her under house arrest in England

Elizabeth took the second option. For the next 19 years Mary was moved from house to house but always kept at a safe distance from London. Nevertheless, she became the focus of Catholic plots and was the subject of parliamentary and council meetings as pressure was exerted on the queen to execute her (see Unit 4). Elizabeth was reluctant to execute her because this would set a precedent for regicide and encourage Catholic sympathisers to seek revenge.

In Scotland Elizabeth hoped to support the Protestant lords who were guarding James, but she was unable to keep control of events when civil war recurred in the 1570s. As he grew older, James realised that if he was going to succeed to the English throne then he must distance himself from any plot involving his mother. Therefore, when he heard of the Babington Plot and Mary's execution in 1587, he remained unmoved.

6.5 Conclusion

Elizabeth succeeded in keeping Scotland friendly towards England. France never recovered its influence at the Scottish court and James, eager to become King of England, was persuaded not to destabilise Anglo–Scottish relations in the 1590s.

EXAMINER'S TIP

This subject appears at AS in the OCR specification and at A2 in the OCR, Edexcel and AQA (Alternative N) specifications. Most questions are concerned with Mary, Queen of Scots. You need to be clear about the problems she posed and be able to assess whether Elizabeth's policies before and after 1568 were appropriate. Think of arguments for and against keeping Mary a prisoner in England.

7 How did relations with France affect Elizabeth's foreign policy, 1558–1603?

7.1 Background

In 1558 England and France were at war. Calais had been recovered by France but Elizabeth was unwilling to accept its loss, despite Philip formally handing it over at the Treaty of Câteau-Cambrésis in 1559. When civil war began in France in 1562, Elizabeth agreed to 3,000 troops sailing to Le Havre in support of Condé, a Protestant prince. He was captured and her plan failed. By the Treaty of Troyes (1564) Elizabeth renounced her right to rule Calais for ever.

7.2 French wars

For much of the period 1562–98 France was seriously affected by civil war. Disputes between nobles, towns and much of Catholic France on the one hand, and a minority of Protestants (known as Huguenots) on the other, underpinned the conflict. Political and social issues also kept France divided. Elizabeth chose not to exploit France's vulnerability. Instead she courted the friendship of the Queen Mother, Catherine de Medici, and that of her Valois sons, as they struggled to contain the ambitious Guise family.

The outbreak of the Dutch Revolt in 1572 complicated affairs and drew England and France closer together. Elizabeth and Catherine signed the Treaty of Blois, which offered them mutual protection, and established a trading base in France as an alternative to the Netherlands. The St Bartholomew's Day massacre of thousands of Huguenots in August 1572, however, caused Elizabeth to suspend this agreement, but only temporarily since she knew she would need France as an ally if relations with Spain began to worsen.

7.3 The wooing of Anjou and Alençon

In 1572 the privy council was divided over what to do. Walsingham and Leicester wanted Elizabeth to intervene in the Netherlands against Spain; Burghley and Sussex saw France as a greater threat to England's trade and security. Elizabeth decided to befriend Henry of Anjou, heir to the French throne, in the hope that she might discover and then influence French policy towards the Netherlands. When Anjou became King of France (1574), Elizabeth transferred her attention to his younger brother, Francis of Alençon.

From 1579 he was given money and encouraged to lead troops against the Spanish Army of Flanders. In return he hoped to marry Elizabeth, although this was probably not part of the queen's strategy. In 1584 Alençon died, having achieved very little.

7.4 Henry of Navarre

Henry of Navarre became heir presumptive to the French throne in 1584. As leader of the Huguenots, he asked Elizabeth for help but, although she sympathised with his cause, she could not afford to lose the support of Henry III as war with Spain drew closer. Her moderation brought its reward in 1588 when the Spanish Armada was denied entry to a French port until the last moment, thereby frustrating Philip's forward planning.

Henry III's death in 1589 enabled Elizabeth to assist Navarre openly in his attempt to take the French throne. He was no longer a rebel but king-designate. Between 1589 and 1593, four English expeditions sailed for France and Elizabeth sent £300,000 to help Henry of Navarre. He was crowned king in 1594, having first converted to the Catholic faith. Elizabeth's contributions to Henry's successful campaign had been marginal but she remained on good terms with him during her war with Spain.

EXAMINER'S TIP

This subject appears at AS in the OCR specification and at A2 in the OCR, Edexcel and AQA (Alternative N) specifications. The connection between events in France, the Netherlands and Scotland, and England's changing relations with Spain, need to be understood if you are to appreciate fully why Elizabeth kept out of French affairs after 1564. Decide whether her strategy, particularly her wooing of Anjou and Alençon, was a sensible or a foolish piece of diplomacy. Elizabeth's Anglo–French relations proved successful in the end, but was this due more to luck or to skilful management?

(1) What were the main causes and effects of rising prices?
(2) How serious a problem were enclosures?
(3) How were towns affected by social and economic developments?
(4) How effectively did Tudor governments tackle the problem of poverty?
(5) How far did agriculture, industry and trade change between 1509 and 1603?

1 What were the main causes and effects of rising prices?

1.1 Background

In 1348–49 much of England had been ravaged by the Black Death. The population fell by one third, land became abundant and, as demand for food was small, prices and rents remained low. By the end of the fifteenth century, population levels were growing again, fertile land was at a premium and prices were rising. The sixteenth century witnessed a fourfold increase in grain prices, with the steepest rises occurring in the middle and at the end of the century.

1.2 Causes

Population growth

This was the most important cause of price inflation. Between 1500 and 1600, population levels probably doubled from 2 to 4 million. The absence of domestic and foreign wars for much of the sixteenth century ensured the survival of more males, younger couples married and families increased in size. At the same time, agricultural improvements provided more food, and better living conditions reduced the incidence of disease. As a result, the rise in population created a demand for grain and work, while surplus labour ensured wages generally lagged behind prices.

Land shortage

To meet the growing demand for food, waste land was cultivated and some landowners increased their rents. As rents went up, land prices increased, which in turn made food products more expensive.

Bad harvests

On average, one in every four harvests failed. For much of the sixteenth century harvests were fair or good, but periodically they were poor. If bad harvests coincided with war, rebellion or an outbreak of plague, then grain prices rose steeply. This happened in 1548–49, 1557–58 and 1594–97.

Enclosures

Before 1500 farmers frequently enclosed their fields with fences and hedges in order to farm more efficiently. Sheep farmers in particular employed fewer labourers, which increased profits and made wool prices very competitive, but if fields were converted from arable to pasture then the cost of grain went up. Contemporaries believed that enclosures were the main cause of inflation but this was not so. Less than 3% of the country was enclosed between 1509 and 1603; much more damaging was the decline of tillage, which did not always accompany enclosures.

Debasement

The coinage was first debased in 1526 and 1543–51. Although the Crown profited by extracting gold and silver from coins, the actual value of newly minted currencies was much less than their face value, and so demand for coins increased and with it inflation. This explanation was forcefully expressed by Sir Thomas Smith in *A Discourse of the Common Weal* in 1549.

Influx of silver

In the seventeenth century commentators were convinced that the importation of American silver into Spain and western Europe had caused inflation in England in the sixteenth century. In fact, the impact on England appears to have been negligible. Some native merchants imported coins containing silver but the Dutch Revolt and subsequent Anglo–Spanish wars kept the volume of trade between England and the continent to a minimum.

Impact of war

The Tudors engaged in few wars before 1585 and the impact upon inflation was limited. In 1512–14, 1522–24, 1542–50 and 1557–58 prices did rise when the Crown exercised its rights of purveyance and there was a rise in government expenditure, but the main effects of war occurred in the 1590s.

1.3 Effects

Landowners

The Crown was the principal landowner and suffered most from price inflation. As land prices rose it was expected to honour the terms of leases and was only able to raise its rents and entry fines when a lease expired. This could be any period of time from 21 to 99 years. The Crown also paid for its goods and services in cash and now had to pay more for both.

Few landowners farmed their land directly. Nobles leased their estates to tenant farmers and raised their rents when their lease expired. Inflation forced many nobles to sell their property and find alternative sources of income to meet rising costs of living. The gentry, yeomen and merchants were in a position to benefit and bought property from the Crown and nobility. But Richard Tawney's view that this period saw 'the rise of the gentry' is no longer accepted by historians. No single class rose or fell as a result of rising prices.

Tenant farmers

Wealthy tenant farmers were able to adjust to inflation more easily by raising the price of their goods at markets. Poorer tenants, however, such as **copyholders** and **tenants at will**, were less well placed. Many were evicted or forced to pay high rents and live in poverty. 'Rack-renting' was one of the rebels' complaints in the 1536 Pilgrimage of Grace, and high entry fines were among the grievances voiced in Kett's Rebellion in 1549.

Labourers

Wage-earners were at a great disadvantage. Agricultural wages began to rise in London in the 1520s and elsewhere in the 1540s and 1550s; craftsmen's wages started to rise in the 1530s, but all wages consistently lagged behind prices. Urban workers suffered most of all because, unlike farm-hands, who received higher wages for seasonal work and were often paid in kind, labourers were paid daily rates and the rising population kept wages down. The labouring classes probably numbered between half and two thirds of the population and very few wage-earners had landholdings to fall back on.

copyholders: tenants who held a copy of the manor court roll, which detailed the terms and conditions of their tenure.

entry fines: sums of money payable by tenants when they renewed their leases.

tenants at will: tenants who held land at the will of their lords; they had no security of tenure.

This topic appears at AS in the OCR specification and at A2 in the AQA (Alternative N) specification. At AS you might be asked: 'Assess the main causes and effects of the sixteenth-century price inflation.' You should present a balanced assessment of both causes and effects. The highest marks will be awarded for answers that explain why some factors were more important than others and why different social groups had varying experiences.

2 How serious a problem were enclosures?

2.1 Background

Between 1450 and 1509 there was a steady rise in the number of landowners enclosing their fields. Some enclosed arable lands to gain a better crop yield. Most did so when the demand for wool increased and farmers converted fields from arable to pasture. Enclosures were less frequent in the period 1509–50 and they declined further when the Antwerp cloth market collapsed in 1551. They did not become a target for criticism again until the 1590s, when grain prices rose sharply in the wake of poor harvests.

2.2 Why were enclosures a problem?

A number of reasons account for the widespread condemnation of enclosures in the sixteenth century. The main ones are as follows:

- Landowners enclosed fields without the consent of and to the detriment of their community. They were accused of profiteering and causing grain prices to rise.
- Farmers converted arable land to pasture, which created grain shortages.
- Unemployment went up because less labour was needed for pasture land.
- The commons became overstocked with sheep and cattle, some of which were owned by the enclosers.
- Tenants at will, who had no rights of tenure, were evicted and became vagrants. Villages declined in population and some settlements became deserted.
- Wealthy farmers bought up neighbouring fields from less prosperous freeholders and engrossed the properties. Unwanted farm buildings then fell into decay.

2.3 Who complained?

The main complainants were small farmers and tenants, who were driven off the commons and open fields. As prices and rents rose they could not compete with larger sheep farmers and they naturally resented enclosures, since they gained nothing from them. As good, fertile land was scarce and wasteland and commons were already heavily used, enclosures hurt the landless peasants. Disgruntled copyholders could take their grievances to court, but litigation could take years and unscrupulous landlords might use their influence to obstruct the law. Some peasants protested in anti-enclosure riots by killing sheep and pulling down fences and hedges.

Among the publications criticising enclosures were *Utopia*, written by Thomas More (1516), and *A Discourse of the Common Weal* by Sir Thomas Smith (1549). Preachers like Hugh Latimer, Robert Crowley and Thomas Lever complained about greedy landlords engrossing farms which, in their view, was worse than creating enclosures.

2.4 Were the complaints justified?

Modern economic historians have concluded that in a few areas of the country complaints were justified. Northamptonshire, Leicestershire, Warwickshire, Buckingham-shire and Bedfordshire, in particular, saw more new enclosures than elsewhere: by 1600 some 30% of Leicestershire had been enclosed. If arable land was converted to pasture or if enclosures occurred without the consent of villagers, then their complaints were probably justified. Enclosure could also cause depopulation. When this took place in coastal areas, such as Hampshire and Dorset, the land was vulnerable to invasion and piracy.

It is also clear that very little land was enclosed between 1500 and 1600. Prejudices against rich landlords exploiting poor commoners survived from the fifteenth century but such allegations were rarely sustained in the sixteenth century. This did occasion-ally happen in the sixteenth century, however. In 1549, when Lord Herbert encroached on common land in Wiltshire, local peasants destroyed his hedges. Enclosure riots were exceptional though, and mainly confined to 1536, 1549, 1569 and 1596. The problem of overstocking the commons was in fact more a result of engrossment than enclosures.

2.5 Government action

Tudor governments held two major enclosure commissions, in 1517 and 1548, and several proclamations and some 10 acts were passed between 1509 and 1603. The most important pieces of legislation were as follows:

1518 A proclamation prohibited enclosures without the consent of commoners.

1533 An act was passed against engrossing; farmers could only rear 2,400 sheep and own two farms.

1536 An act was passed against the conversion of arable land to pasture.

1549 A tax was put on sheep and wool to discourage enclosures and pasture farming (repealed in 1550).

1551 Enclosures were allowed again, following the collapse of the Antwerp wool market.

1555 Farmers who owned over 120 sheep had to keep at least two cows.

1593 Limits on enclosure were lifted due to a grain surplus, but a series of bad harvests saw anti-enclosure legislation restored (1597).

2.6 Conclusion

Governments were increasingly alarmed at the grain shortages. Famine resulted in considerable suffering and sometimes disturbances; enclosures were regarded by many as a major source of the trouble. Wolsey, Cromwell and Somerset tried to prevent illegal enclosures but their proclamations and acts of Parliament were largely ineffective. This was because JPs were often landowners, who sympathised with the enclosers rather than the complainants. Although enclosures tended to occur at the beginning and end of the sixteenth century, most administrations did little to curb them and instead let market forces determine their growth and decline.

UNIT 6

3 How were towns affected by social and economic developments?

3.1 Background

At the start of the sixteenth century most of the 600 or so English towns had less than 1,500 people. A few towns, like Norwich, Coventry, Bristol and York, had a population of between 8,000 and 10,000. All were outstripped in size, wealth and importance by London, which probably had a population of 50,000. It has already been noted that the country's population doubled in the course of the sixteenth century, but London's population tripled, making it one of the largest cities in Europe.

3.2 London

As the country's capital and the centre of administration and law courts, London had long been established as a centre of trade. In 1500, 80% of England's trade went through London. As its wealth grew, thousands of people moved to the city seeking their fortune. Some were merchants, traders and craftsmen; some were professionals such as lawyers, clerics and doctors; some were gentry and yeomen; and many — perhaps the majority — were domestic servants, casual labourers and beggars.

By 1603 the population was probably in excess of 150,000 and the city was teeming with tens of thousands of poverty-stricken people living in tenements and poor housing. About one quarter of the poorest people lived outside the city walls in suburbs like Southwark and Islington. Vagrants and beggars were a constant problem. They carried disease, committed crimes and were a burden upon society wherever they went. The city corporation began to address the issue from the beginning of the century: cheap corn was stored, parishes made collections, beggars were licensed, and in the 1540s and 1550s hospitals were given extra funding to tackle different types of poor people. As London became more overcrowded, plague and fire remained serious hazards. Attempts were made in the 1580s to stop further building inside the city, and within 3 miles of the city walls, but the laws were probably not enforced.

3.3 Provincial towns

All towns owed their livelihood to trade; as patterns of trade changed, so did their fortunes. Some towns that had been thriving in the fifteenth century began to decline. York lost many of its weavers to the new towns of Leeds and Halifax; and Coventry saw its population halve due to its limited communications and reluctance to develop new trades and industries. Lincoln, Winchester and Salisbury, which were also cathedral towns, similarly saw a slowing down in their growth. Nearly all English ports lost most of their continental trade to London. In contrast, provincial towns that depended on woollen cloth prospered. In East Anglia, Yorkshire and the West Country, for instance, there was plenty of work between 1509 and 1603. The second half of the sixteenth century also saw several towns expand rapidly as they developed new industries, e.g. Manchester (linen cloth), Newcastle (coal-mining) and Birmingham (metal trades).

3.4 Was there urban decay?

Most social historians believe that there was a general recession in the late fifteenth century, which intensified between 1520 and 1570 before finally stabilising. As a result, almost every provincial city and market town — with the notable exception of Exeter — was affected. Rising urban taxes and competition from rural trades and industries brought significant changes in the traditional patterns of employment. In the 1530s Cromwell tried to protect boroughs from rural competition but government intervention appears to have had little success. By 1603 towns that had adapted to changing conditions were prospering and those towns that lacked enterprise were showing signs of decay.

Norwich, for example, developed **new draperies** rather than relying on its traditional production of worsted cloth and, in spite of a devastating outbreak of plague in 1579–80, it turned its ailing industry around by 1603. Though London surged ahead of other towns, and often at their expense, about 100 towns held large markets and fairs and had populations of between 1,500 and 7,000. Many had impressive public buildings, stone and brick houses and well-maintained roads and bridges; and some corporations made provision to keep their streets clean and supply piped water and public lighting.

GLOSSARY

new draperies: lighter but less durable material produced by weaving long-staple wool.

EXAMINER'S TIP

This topic appears at AS in the OCR specification and at A2 in the AQA (Alternative N) specification. Questions on urban development are likely to be quite general but will still require specific examples to illustrate the various changes. London is the most obvious illustration but you should refer to a range of towns to highlight and explain why some were more flourishing than others. A typical AS question is: 'How far did towns become more prosperous between 1509 and 1603?'

4 How effectively did Tudor governments tackle the problem of poverty?

4.1 Background

Poverty has always existed but the sixteenth century seems to have witnessed a dramatic increase in the number of poor people and vagabonds. The end of civil war and limited foreign wars reduced the need for retainers, the decline in feudalism made tenants more vulnerable to social and agrarian change and, as already noted, a rising population, enclosures and intermittent poor harvests and plague all aggravated a worsening problem and forced governments and local authorities to take action (see section 1.2 of this unit).

4.2 Contemporary opinions

Sixteenth-century writers offered a variety of explanations for the growth in poverty and vagabondage. Henry Brinklow, in *The Complaynt of Roderyk Mors* (1543), and Henry Wriothesley, in *A Chronicle of England* (1549), attributed the large numbers of 'sturdy beggars' to the loss of hospitality and monastic charity following the dissolution of the monasteries. In fact, historians now believe that the closure of the monasteries made little difference to the numbers of poor. Another writer, Sir Thomas Smith, in *A Discourse of the Common Weal* (1549), held the engrossing of farms and greedy landlords to be the main culprits. Most contemporaries seem to have exaggerated the size and extent of the problem. Nevertheless, the presence of 'stout rogues'—beggars and vagrants—as well as the vast numbers of genuine poor, was a matter of real concern for authorities at the time.

4.3 Government legislation

In the course of the sixteenth century the government passed a number of acts designed to combat the problem of the poor. Few remedies were entirely successful but important lessons were learned in the process, and by 1603 laws were in place that were to survive well into the nineteenth century.

1531 Act

Poor people who were old and impotent were given licences to beg; the able and idle unemployed were to be whipped, publicly disgraced and made to work. In practice this act proved to be unsuccessful because there was insufficient work for everyone and the genuine poor were still dependent on local charity.

1536 Act

Money was to be raised voluntarily by the parish to look after the poor. This was unsuccessful in towns because the poor constituted a migrant population.

1547 Act

Beggars were to be branded and enslaved for 2 years and their children seized and apprenticed to anyone willing to teach them a trade. This was unsuccessful because parish constables were reluctant to condemn a person to slavery. The act was repealed in 1550.

1552 Act

Two parishioners were appointed to collect alms each week; registers of the poor were compiled and unwilling taxpayers were 'persuaded' to contribute. This did not work because donations remained voluntary.

1563 Act

Parishioners had to donate money and goods to the poor or face punishments. This was more successful, although minimum contributions enabled many to evade the spirit of the reform.

1563 Act

Craftsmen had to serve 7-year apprenticeships and anyone not training in a craft was to be given work in the fields. This was not very successful since JPs, who were expected to enforce the law, lacked the resources to check up on workers and their employers.

1572 Act

Every parish, village and town had to levy a weekly poor rate, supervised by overseers; if parishes could afford it they were to start 'houses of correction'; and vagrants were to be whipped and a hole pierced through their ear. These reforms were more successful

as the distinction between the genuine poor (who were to be helped) and the idle (who were to be punished) was enforceable in practice.

1576 Act

The poor and unemployed in every town were to be found work in houses of correction; wool, hemp, flax and iron materials were provided and workers were paid for the goods they produced. Beggars unable to work due to old age, injury or lack of opportunity were to be licensed. This was another effective measure as it tackled the problem of insufficient work for the unemployed.

1598 and 1601 Acts

The most successful pieces of legislation were drawn together in 1598 and repeated with minor changes in the Poor Law Act of 1601. These declared that:

* unemployed able-bodied workers would be made to work in houses of correction
* genuine poor were to be accommodated in 'houses of dwelling'
* children of the poor were to be apprenticed: girls until 21 and boys until 24
* a compulsory poor rate was to be collected by four overseers in the parish
* neighbouring parishes had to assist less prosperous ones
* vagabonds were to be whipped and returned to their place of origin

4.4 Local initiatives

Almost all government legislation followed initiatives by county towns. Gloucester, Lincoln, Cambridge and York, for instance, licensed beggars well before the 1531 Act. Compulsory poor rates were first levied in London (1547), Norwich, Cambridge and York, in advance of the 1572 Act. Ipswich, York and Norwich also followed London's example in establishing hospitals, some incorporating houses of correction. Norwich led the way in many initiatives:

* Its citizens were the first to organise a collection to reduce the number of beggars in the town.
* It made begging illegal.
* It conducted a survey to find the extent of poverty.
* It set up its own hospital and **Bridewell**.
* It pioneered a scheme to compel wealthier parishes to subsidise the poorer ones.

4.5 Public and private charity

Until the 1530s very little cash, goods or land were given to charity. The monasteries, for example, contributed less than 3% of their entire income and most private endowments went to the Church. After the Reformation the Church received few donations, whereas poor relief, schools and hospitals saw a dramatic increase from public and private donors. Many of the donations came from merchants who (individually or as a group) founded permanently endowed institutions in or near their home towns. London merchants gave money and property to found grammar schools and colleges in the city and around the country. Corporations, such as Norwich and Bristol, also acquired ex-monastic almshouses and schools but not all towns were so fortunate. York lost more than half of its hospitals at the dissolution.

Bridewell: a house of correction where the poor and 'idle' were made to work.

This subject appears at AS in the OCR specification and at A2 in the AQA (Alternative N) specification. A typical AS question is: 'Assess the main causes of poverty during this period.' If you are asked at A2, 'How effectively did Tudor governments tackle the problem of poverty?', you should assess the principal pieces of legislation, examine contemporary reactions to the problem and the complementary role of private and public contributions. Local initiatives invariably presaged government legislation. Does this mean that governments were usually slow to tackle the problem?

5 How far did agriculture, industry and trade change between 1509 and 1603?

5.1 Agriculture

Types of farming

In 1500 most people worked on the land. Their work depended on where they lived. Sheep farming was most common on the uplands of Wales, Northumberland and on the open fields of Salisbury Plain and the North York Moors. Cattle were farmed mainly on the lowlands. Arable farming — growing wheat, barley, oats, rye, peas and beans — took place principally in the middle, eastern and southern counties. Mixed farming (pasture and arable) was also practised in the wetland and woodland regions. In the southwestern counties, for example, farmers combined corn growing with fattening of livestock; and in forested areas such as the Weald (in Kent) and Sherwood Forest (Nottinghamshire), dairy farming and stock-keeping could be found alongside arable farming. Most villages were divided into three large fields that were communally dedicated to meadow, arable and pasture use.

Land tenure

In theory all land belonged to the lord of the manor, who held it from the Crown. In practice, by 1500 country-dwellers were either freeholders, leaseholders or landless peasants. Freeholders had no restrictions on their property but leaseholders could be subject to a range of customary practices. For instance, copyholders were generally protected by the terms of their agreement and had tenure for the lives of three named persons (i.e. usually for the tenant, his wife and his heir). Tenants at will, on the other hand, had no security and could be ejected at the will of the landlord. All tenants who could not pay entry fines when leases expired, or who fell behind with their rents, were liable to eviction, and unscrupulous landlords increased these payments whenever they could.

Between a quarter and a third of the rural population consisted of cottagers and labourers. Cottagers held a handful of acres comprising a cottage, garden and small-holding and frequently owned a few animals. Labourers held no land and survived by working seasonally on the farms and supplementing their wages with local crafts and trades. It was a meagre existence and led many into begging and vagrancy.

Agrarian changes

In the early twentieth century Richard Tawney claimed that between 1500 and 1600 a 'peasant' economy, which was largely **subsistent**, was replaced by a 'capitalist' agrarian economy. Rising prices, enclosures, the conversion of arable land to pasture and owners engrossing farms had forced the smaller tenant farmers to sell their farms and businesses to greedy capitalists.

In the 1960s this **Marxist** view of an 'agrarian revolution' was rejected by Eric Kerridge. He argued that although important agricultural changes had occurred in the second half of the sixteenth century, these were due to innovations in land use and more efficient practices like drainage fens and **marling** soils. Moreover, market forces, not capitalist-minded landlords, had brought about a decline in the number of tenant farmers.

Revisionism
Revisionist historians have suggested that neither of these interpretations is entirely correct. Instead it is argued that:
- Land was used more efficiently, areas under cultivation were increased, subsistence farming and smallholdings declined, and commercialised farming and large estates became more common.
- The mainspring of change was the need to solve the basic problem of how to feed a growing population. In some areas (e.g. the Midland counties) common fields were enclosed, depopulation and overstocking of commons resulted and there were many complaints.
- Elsewhere, enclosures generally occurred with the consent of all interested parties and there were few or no complaints.
- On the other hand, market forces — rising population, price inflation, land shortages — did produce changes in land tenure. Successful landowners increased the size of farms and some customary tenants bought their own holdings; unsuccessful ones were forced to sell their farms, and manorial tenants, who were unable to renew their leases, became landless.

Conclusion
- There is some evidence to suggest that grain production increased in the course of the century: more grain was exported than imported and most towns had sufficient stocks of corn to overcome bad harvests.
- More areas of woodland, upland, fens and marshes were brought under cultivation.
- There were no major inventions in farm machinery.
- The main changes were marling arable land, draining marshes, planting rape, watering meadows, and the introduction to England of Friesian cattle, Hungarian horses, and Dutch carrots and turnips.

5.2 Industry

The cloth industry
Most people who lived in towns were employed in a craft or trade connected with the cloth or leather industries. Some towns specialised in particular trades (e.g. leather in Nottingham, cloth in Worcester). By 1600 nearly all wool was spun or woven into a wide variety of fabrics. Heavy broadcloths were produced mainly in the West Country, Yorkshire and Suffolk. Lighter bays, says and serges, known as new draperies, were produced in East Anglia and the West Riding. Though the majority of spinners and weavers worked at home, some clothiers had begun to develop industrial practices such as buying wool and taking it to carders and combers, spinners and weavers, before selling the unfinished cloth for dyeing. A small number of entrepreneurs, like John Pawson of Leeds and William Stumpe of Malmesbury, combined these processes under one roof.

The mining industry

The sixteenth century saw a considerable growth in the mining industries. The coal industry expanded more rapidly than any other due to the shortage of wood and demand from the iron industry and shipbuilding, and coal was also used in brewing, glass-making and the manufacture of gunpowder. Coalfields were operating in Northumberland, Durham, the Midlands and Wales. The use of blast furnaces in the 1540s led to an expansion in copper, lead and iron-mining. By 1603 iron production, for instance, had increased by 200%. A few landowners, like the Earl of Rutland, who discovered iron ore on his estates, began to mine, refine and work the iron on site in the 1570s.

Other industries

Traditional industries dependent upon raw materials continued, such as pottery, brewing, domestic and farm materials, glass-making and shipbuilding. Several new industries began, for example nail-making in Staffordshire, stocking-knitting in Wakefield, crystal glass-making in Essex and salt panning in Tyne and Wear. The use of charcoal blast furnaces led to important changes in the iron, copper and bronze industries. In the 1560s Italian and French glaziers introduced refined techniques for making windows and crystal glass. Finally, in the 1590s William Lee developed a knitting-frame that speeded up and standardised the production of stockings. It was the only significant invention in this period.

Was there an industrial revolution?

J. U. Nef once argued that the century following 1540 saw the start of England's 'Industrial Revolution'. It was characterised by a rapid expansion in coal production, new industries and inventions, which paved the way for further progress. It is now acknowledged that this view exaggerated the extent to which coal was used commercially in the sixteenth century, that new industries only contributed a fraction of the country's output and that a handful of technological developments hardly constituted an 'industrial revolution'.

5.3 Domestic trade

Most trade was domestic, serving local and regional markets by land, river and sea. Distances were short and goods were carried by wagon, ship and pack-horse. Transport was difficult by road and only a few rivers, such as the Thames, Trent and Severn, were navigable for long stretches. By far the largest market was London, dominated by its 12 great livery companies, though it drew most of its raw materials from areas around the Thames Valley, Kent and Essex.

Other provincial towns, such as Exeter, York and Norwich, exercised a similar pull on their hinterland. Ports on the east, south and southwest coasts traded with each other and with continental ports but they fell increasingly behind London. Newcastle (coal) and King's Lynn (grain) prospered due to London's demand for these wares but ports like Southampton and Bridgwater declined. The second half of the sixteenth century, however, saw the beginning of overseas trade, which subsequently transformed England's position in the world.

5.4 Overseas trade

Wool and cloth

In 1509 most English trade was with the Netherlands, France and Germany. Raw wool was exported by the Merchants of the Staple to Calais and unfinished cloth by the

Merchant Adventurers to Antwerp. Raw wool exports were already declining. Government customs duties and competition from Spanish and Flemish merchants reduced their profits and the staplers struggled to survive as the century progressed. The loss of Calais (1558) was a further blow to the wool trade.

In contrast, cloth exports expanded steadily at first, and then rapidly in the 1540s, until the market collapsed in 1551. Since one third of all Antwerp's trade was in English cloth, the depression had a serious effect on both the Dutch and the English clothiers. Nevertheless, trade soon recovered, such that by 1603 over 80% of all English exports were in woollen cloth. Two important changes had taken place, however:

- Very little raw wool was exported by 1603.
- Many merchants began to consider investing in alternative markets outside the traditional trade routes.

By the end of the century English trade was neither exclusively focused on wool nor on Europe. There remained, however, a heavy dependence on foreign imports of manufactured goods and on the export of West Country woollen cloth.

Africa

Trade with Morocco began in 1551 when English merchants John Lok and William Towerson sailed to Guinea selling new draperies in exchange for sugar, gold and saltpetre. The Barbary and Africa trading companies were set up in the 1580s.

America

In the 1560s John Hawkins began to transport African slaves to Spanish colonies in America in return for silver, gold and hides. In 1567 his third expedition was attacked and his goods seized by Spanish officials. Francis Drake, who was with him, retaliated in the 1570s and 1580s by capturing silver bullion shipments bound for Spain from Mexico and Peru. Trade links with Newfoundland, pioneered by John and Sebastian Cabot, brought profits to Bristol fishermen. Other transatlantic voyages were undertaken by explorers like Walter Raleigh, who landed in Virginia in the 1580s, and by Martin Frobisher and John Davis, who went in search of the northwest passage to China and the Far East.

The Far East

After Drake's circumnavigation of the globe (1577–80), English merchants were confident that they could establish trade routes with the Far East via the Cape of Good Hope. The Levant Company, established in 1581, traded in the eastern Mediterranean with Turkey, selling cloth for raw silk. Some of these merchants formed the East India Company in 1600 to develop the spice trade in the Indian Ocean and the South China Seas.

France, Spain and Italy

As more English ships were built in Henry VIII's reign, merchants from Bristol, Southampton and London increased their trade with France and Spain. The Andalusia Company, established in 1531, exported cloth for Spanish wine, oil and soap. Venice, which had monopolised the carrying trade in the fifteenth century, reasserted its influence in the 1550s but a war with Turkey in the early 1570s again enabled English merchants to venture into the Mediterranean, exporting cloth, lead, tin and coal to Sicily, Malta and Venice itself. By 1603 the Levant Company had extended its trade routes throughout the Mediterranean. Although from the 1580s England's war with Spain disrupted the trade of the newly formed Spanish Company, its merchants seem to have continued to trade by disguising their wares as Flemish goods.

The Baltic

In 1509 Scandinavian and Baltic trade was controlled by the Hanse, and English merchants were excluded. In the course of the sixteenth century the Hanse's monopoly declined and more English traders were trading with north Germany, Denmark and Poland. In 1579 the **joint-stock** Eastland Company was formed. In return for English cloth, Polish naval supplies — hemp, tar and sailcloth — were imported, all vital for the shipbuilding industry.

Equally significant was the demise of the Hanse's privileges in London. In 1552 these were temporarily suspended and although Mary restored them, the German merchants never really recovered their position in London. In 1598 their main base — the Steelyard — was closed down.

Russia

In 1553 Willoughby and Chancellor set out to find the northeast passage through the Arctic to the Far Fast. Their expedition proved unsuccessful but Chancellor went on to establish trade links with Archangel, and the Russia Company was founded in 1555.

GLOSSARY

joint-stock: a company whose members were jointly responsible for funding voyages and shared any profits according to the size of the capital they had invested.

marling: the process of adding lime to clay to make it more fertile.

Marxist: one who follows the ideas of Karl Marx, a nineteenth-century philosopher. He believed that the working classes were exploited by their employers, who were only interested in profiting from their labours.

subsistent: producing food for one's own consumption.

EXAMINER'S TIP

This topic appears at AS in the OCR specification and at A2 in the AQA (Alternative N) specification. Questions that are concerned with agriculture, industry and trade usually require an assessment of the main developments in the course of the period. For example, at AS: 'Explain any two ways in which industry in England changed between 1509 and 1603.' Avoid narratives and descriptions, which score low marks; instead focus on two industries (e.g. cloth and coal) and explain two key changes (e.g. decline in raw wool and wood resources, and increasing demand from the continent).

UNIT 7 Spain, 1469–1556

KEY QUESTIONS

(1) How effectively did Isabella and Ferdinand restore royal authority in Spain, 1469–1516?

(2) What was the importance of religion between 1469 and 1516?

(3) How far was Spain a united country by 1516?

(4) How successful was Charles I in his domestic policies, 1516–56?

(5) What were the strengths and weaknesses of Spain's economy, 1469–1556?

(6) What were the main achievements in foreign policy between 1469 and 1556?

1 How effectively did Isabella and Ferdinand restore royal authority in Spain, 1469–1516?

1.1 The condition of Spain in 1469

Spain did not exist in 1469. The Iberian peninsula comprised six kingdoms and an emirate:

- Castile — ruled by Henry IV (1454–74).
- Aragon, Catalonia and Valencia — ruled by John II (1458–79).
- Navarre — independent but ruled by Aragon until 1462.
- Portugal — ruled by Alfonso V.
- Granada — a Moorish emirate ruled by the Nasrids.

1.2 The main developments in Castile, 1469–79

Henry IV and civil war

Civil war plagued Castile between 1469 and 1479. Initially it was caused by disgruntled nobles and bishops who were no longer prepared to put up with Henry's high-handed style of rule. The king chose to ignore many of the leading families and attempted to disinherit his half-sister, Isabella, by claiming that he had fathered a daughter, Joanna. Support for Henry began to dissolve as nobles like Mendoza, Medina Sidonia and Cabrera changed sides. Many reached a deal with Isabella. At Henry's death, only the Villena family seemed unwilling to accept Isabella when she was crowned queen in December 1474.

Isabella's marriage

In 1469 Isabella married Ferdinand, heir to the Aragonese throne. It was a defining moment in Spanish history. Popular with most Castilian nobles, the union soon produced a daughter. Meanwhile, Ferdinand directed military operations against rebellious towns.

War of Succession, 1475–79

There were three main sources of resistance to Isabella's accession:

- grandees and bishops, like the Marquis of Villena and Archbishop Carrillo of Toledo
- towns, mainly in the centre and south of Castile, like Toledo, Seville and Burgos
- Alfonso of Portugal, who announced his intention to marry Joanna and assert her claim

Isabella overcame this opposition by a mixture of bribes, threats, executions and military victories. Alfonso was halted at the battle of Toro (1476) and Carrillo at Olmedo (1476).

Ferdinand's troops also forced recalcitrant towns to surrender, while the **Santa Hermandad** pacified much of the countryside. Peace between warring factions was reached at Alcaçovas (1479).

1.3 The political condition of Aragon, 1469–79

The kingdom of Aragon was a federation of states. Each of the three kingdoms of Aragon, Catalonia and Valencia had its own assemblies and resisted attempts by the king of Aragon to interfere in its affairs. Rivalry between nobles and towns deepened the political disunity, which was further exploited by foreign powers. France held the Catalonian counties of Roussillon and Cerdagne, and lay claim to Navarre. Civil wars in Catalonia ended in 1472, when Barcelona fell to John, but his subjects remained discontented. The peasantry wanted more freedom, there were disputes between nobles and knights, and arguments broke out in Barcelona's city council. Everyone looked to Ferdinand to solve their problems when he became king in 1479.

1.4 The restoration of royal authority, 1479–1516

Two of the greatest obstacles facing Isabella and Ferdinand were the Castilian nobility and the weak condition of the royal finances.

Castilian nobility

The clergy and nobility owned 90% of Castile and controlled massive private armies. To weaken this power, Isabella and Ferdinand:

- recovered royal lands at the Toledo **cortes** (1480), destroyed unlicensed castles and imposed heavy fines upon lawbreakers (e.g. the Marquis of Cadiz)
- took control of the three military crusading orders (Santiago, Calatrava and Alcantara) and their 1 million retainers
- encouraged the *Santa Hermandad* to subdue disorder in the countryside, and local *hermandades* imposed speedy justice. The contemporary chroniclers Pulgar and Palencia claimed these troops were vital to the Crown's restoring its authority over the nobility

The following concessions to the nobility were also made:

- they were exempt from taxation and from imprisonment for debt
- they were allowed to assess and collect their own **alcabala**
- they received patents of nobility and land grants
- their right of inheritance was confirmed in 1505
- they were appointed to the highest political and administrative offices

In effect, the nobility remained in control of regional politics and many still kept their castles and retainers in defiance of royal commands.

Royal finances

In 1474 only one sixth of expected revenue actually reached the Crown. Many tax collectors made fraudulent claims and pocketed rents. Enquiries into **mercedes** and tax auditing saw a massive improvement in the first few years, and revenue trebled by 1504. Most of the money came from the *alcabala*, the *Hermandad*, *cortes* and the Church. But serious problems remained:

- corruption among tax officials was not stamped out
- many claimed to be nobles to avoid paying direct taxes
- government expenditure increased fourfold due to the cost of war
- loans (known as *asientos*) and state bonds (*juros*) mortgaged future income

Justice

The queen attended public hearings every Friday in the **alcazar**. Permanent courts of appeal (*audiencias*) were set up at Valladolid and Granada, and provincial courts at Santiago and Seville. Magistrates (*alcaldes*) imposed justice in towns and, if required, were assisted by **corregidores**. The *Santa Hermandad* operated between 1476 and 1498, and rural *hermandades* continued thereafter. In the Aragonese kingdoms local militia were directed by towns and nobles.

For the first 15 years of their reigns, justice was effectively enforced but in the 1490s the Crown increasingly sided with the nobility in disputes with towns. Burgos, Toledo and Segovia all complained in vain and by 1516 disturbances were widespread in Navarre, Léon and Andalucía.

Administration

Isabella ruled Castile and Ferdinand ruled Aragon; when they left their kingdoms, viceroys assumed control. Most of their working lives was spent in Castile travelling from town to town, for there was no fixed capital and effective government depended on their regular consultation with town officials. Advising the monarchs were leading nobles and clergy who, together with **letrados**, were put in charge of departments of state (e.g. finance, justice, inquisition).

The *cortes* met in each of the kingdoms to pass laws and more usually to vote money (*subsidio*) to the Crown. The Castilian *cortes* only represented 17 towns and was more compliant than the other *cortes*. It met 16 times, mainly between 1498 and 1516. The *cortes* in Aragon, Catalonia and Valencia were less cooperative, more self-interested and, as a result, were called less frequently.

Towns

For most of her reign Isabella had a good relationship with her town councils. They were usually protected from aristocratic interference — *regidores* (town councillors) were often appointed by the Crown and *corregidores* could be sent to deal with particular problems. By 1516 the number of *corregidores* had increased from 19 to 64. Ferdinand exercised less control over towns in Aragon. His attempt to introduce election by lot to town councils was generally resisted and the idea of appointing *corregidores* was totally rejected.

Conditions in 1516

In the years following Isabella's death (1504) many grandees exploited the succession dispute, first between Ferdinand and Philip of Burgundy and then, after Philip's death (1506), between Ferdinand and Joanna (Isabella's eldest surviving, but mentally unstable, daughter). As rival factions took sides, civil war was only prevented when Ferdinand raised an army and subdued nobles like Medina Sidonia, Villena and Priego.

Between 1506 and 1516 Ferdinand ruled Castile in the name of Joanna but the administration was handled by Cardinal Cisneros and royal secretaries, supported by noble families (e.g. Mendozas, Enriquez, Velascos), who again built up their power at the expense of the Crown and town authorities. By 1516 royal administration was showing signs of breaking down.

1.5 Conclusion

Historians now recognise that although Isabella and Ferdinand restored the prestige and authority of the Crown and ended civil wars in Castile and Aragon, tension between

towns and nobles was as strong in 1516 as it had been in 1469. As Charles I found to his cost within a few years of his accession, this could easily spill into disorder and threaten royal authority.

alcabala: a 10% sales tax.

alcazar: a town castle or fortress.

corregidores: royal governors appointed to Castilian towns.

cortes: representative assembly in each kingdom.

letrados: law graduates.

mercedes: a royal grant or gift.

Santa Hermandad: the Holy Brotherhood, which became a permanent national militia in 1476.

This topic appears at AS in the OCR specification. Questions tend to be of two main types: they can focus on an assessment of the achievements and limitations of Isabella and Ferdinand or on a comparison of the Castilian and Aragonese administrations. For example: 'How successful was Isabella's administration of Castile, 1474–1504?' She was not entirely successful, so make sure you present a balanced argument.

2 What was the importance of religion between 1469 and 1516?

2.1 Background

Castile and Aragon were multiracial kingdoms with a long tradition of **convivencia**. About 150,000 Jews and 20,000 **conversos** lived in Spain, mainly in towns; over 300,000 **mudéjars** lived in Aragon and a much smaller number of **moriscos** lived in Castile. Most Spaniards were Christians but many had little understanding of their faith. The Church seemed more interested in its material well-being than in instructing the people or improving its own condition.

2.2 The Spanish Church

The aims of the Catholic Monarchs were to:
- improve the spiritual condition of their clerical and lay subjects
- reform the standard of the monastic orders
- wrest more authority from the Pope

Improvements in the secular clergy and laity

Most Spaniards experienced few, if any, religious changes in their lives. They remained strongly attached to local rituals, worshipped saints and attended processions. Attempts were made to improve the clergy: colleges to train priests were founded at Valladolid and Alcalá, and some bishops (e.g. Mendoza, Cisneros, Talavera) led ascetic lives. In general, however, the Church attracted low-calibre priests: cases of absenteeism, clergy living with mistresses, and monks who had not taken holy orders continued to be reported throughout this period.

Monastic reform

Each of the major orders saw reforms. The main changes were:
- re-housing Benedictine nuns in Galicia

- reforming Dominican friars in Burgos and Seville
- forcing Franciscan friars to become more 'observant'

Papal relations

Relations with the Pope were generally good. Although there were clashes over three main issues, the monarchs emerged with more revenue and authority:

- Isabella won the right to appoint her bishops (1482); the Pope merely confirmed her nominations. Control of clerical patronage in Granada and the Canaries (1486) and the Americas (1508) was also gained.
- All appeals from 1488 were to be held in Spain.
- From 1482 a papal tax (*cruzada*) and one third of all Castilian tithes (*tercia real*) were used to fund crusades against the Muslims and finance Ferdinand's foreign policy (after 1508).

2.3 Jews and *conversos*

Judaism was a minority faith in Spain and wealthy Jews, although tolerated, were resented; *conversos* were frequently suspected of being false converts. In 1478 Isabella gained papal permission to set up the Castilian Inquisition to investigate secret judaisers. The Aragonese Inquisition was also begun by Ferdinand in 1481.

Inquisition

In the 1480s some nine towns established tribunals in Castile. Not everyone welcomed them: Seville, Toledo, Teruel and Barcelona argued strongly against the Inquisition — but the Crown was insistent. Those suspected of reverting to Judaism were arrested, tried and sentenced. Most received lenient sentences but many who refused to be 'reconciled', or who were found guilty a second time, were imprisoned or burned at the stake. Exact numbers will never be known but several thousand may have died between 1480 and 1492.

Expulsion of the Jews, 1492

The Inquisition had no jurisdiction over Jews. From 1480, however, several towns began to discriminate against them. Cordoba, Seville and Cadiz, for instance, forced Jews to wear yellow badges and segregated them into *aljamas* (ghettos). In the opinion of Torquemada, the inquisitor-general, the strategy of preventing Jews from having contact with *conversos* was not a success and stronger measures were required. On 31 July 1492 Jews were told they had to emigrate or convert to Christianity.

Effects of the expulsion

Historians disagree over how many Jews emigrated. It was perhaps 50 % — but many returned as *conversos* in the 1490s. In fact, far from eliminating the problem of suspected heresy, the Crown had made it worse. Inquisitors were kept very busy for the rest of this period and most of their victims were *conversos*. At Toledo 250 were burnt at the stake between 1485 and 1501. The expulsion not only ended *convivencia*, it also put at risk the future of *moriscos* and *mudéjars*.

2.4 Islam, reconquest and *moriscos*

The *moriscos* in Castile and the *mudéjars* in Aragon presented no serious threat to the Catholic Monarchs. They had been assimilated into society and played a significant part in the eastern kingdoms' economy since the thirteenth-century reconquest. To the south of Castile, however, lay the Muslim state of Granada, which Isabella and Ferdinand were determined to conquer.

War in Granada, 1482–92

Viewed as a holy war, Ferdinand's army drew crusaders from all over the peninsula. Isabella raised money from the *Hermandad*, *cortes* and Church and (allegedly) sold some of her jewels. Both monarchs accompanied the troops in what turned out to be a long war of sieges — notably at Ronda (1485), Malaga (1487), Almeria (1489) and Granada (1492). A hundred thousand Muslims died or were imprisoned; 200,000 emigrated to north Africa and 200,000 became *mudéjars*.

Convivencia and expulsion, 1492–1502

For much of the 1490s *convivencia* continued in Granada. Christians and *mudéjars* coexisted, prayers were said in Castilian and Arabic, and a policy of persuading *mudéjars* to accept conversion seemed to be working. The queen and Cisneros disagreed, however, claiming that the close proximity of the Granadan *mudéjars* and north African Muslims presented a security risk. Between 1500 and 1502 *mudéjars* were ordered to convert or leave Granada. In 1502 a decree applied to the whole of Castile. The majority chose to stay and became *moriscos*.

Mudéjars in the eastern kingdoms

Ferdinand took no steps to convert or expel the *mudéjars* from his lands. They were too numerous and, as craftsmen and farmers, were much valued by the nobility. As long as socioeconomic conditions remained stable, all groups in Aragon were content with the status quo.

2.5 Conclusion

Isabella and Ferdinand had a mixture of success and failure in their religious policies. They achieved:

- greater Christian uniformity in Castile
- the completion of reconquest by victory over Granada
- total control of clerical patronage and increasing papal revenue
- an inquisition, which protected Spain from heresy and helped to unify the kingdoms

Among their failures were:

- a largely unreformed clergy
- widespread ignorance of Christianity among the laity
- the ending of *convivencia*
- a sense of distrust and suspicion, which accompanied the Inquisition

GLOSSARY

conversos: former Jews who had been converted to Christianity.
convivencia: the coexistence of different religious faiths (e.g. Christianity, Islam and Judaism).
moriscos: former Muslims who had been converted to Christianity.
mudéjars: Muslims living under Christian rule.

EXAMINER'S TIP

This subject appears at AS in the OCR specification and at A2 in the AQA (Alternative B) specification. It is a popular topic with examiners, so make sure you understand the more important terms, such as '*convivencia*', '*conversos*' and '*moriscos*'. A typical A2 question is: 'Assess the motives and consequences of Isabella's and Ferdinand's religious policies.' Keep the link between motives and consequences in mind. Note that a 'motive' is not the same as an 'aim' and consequences could usefully be assessed in terms of short- and long-term results.

3 How far was Spain a united country by 1516?

3.1 Arguments in favour of unity

Historians R. Menendez Pidal and John Lynch believe that the reigns of Isabella and Ferdinand saw the beginnings of a national identity:

- The marriage united the medieval kingdoms and the incorporation of Granada, the annexation of Navarre and the recovery of Roussillon and Cerdagne (see section 6.2 of this unit) completed the unification of Spain.
- Only one king (Charles I) ruled Spain in 1516.
- Only one faith existed in Castile.
- Inquisitions operated in each of the Hispanic kingdoms.
- Royal administration was centred upon Castile.
- The army was drawn from the whole country.
- All kingdoms used a gold ducat, a common exchange rate and the same unit of account.

3.2 Arguments against unity

Historians Glyn Redworth and M. A. Ladero Quesada have stressed the diverse features of the country. They argue that each kingdom had:

- Its own constitution, *fueros* and separate *cortes*.
- Different royal officials (e.g. there were no *corregidores* in Aragon).
- Trade barriers within and between kingdoms, and Aragon was excluded from trading with America.
- Its own currency as well as a gold ducat common to each kingdom.
- A variety of languages — Castilian, Catalan, Basque, Romance.
- Different foreign policies. For example, Naples was annexed to Aragon and Navarre to Castile.

3.3 Conclusion

Considerable advances towards a unitary state occurred between 1474 and 1516, but Spain was still a disunited country.

GLOSSARY

fueros: Aragonese laws and privileges.

EXAMINER'S TIP

This topic appears at AS in the OCR specification. Consider the question: 'Isabella and Ferdinand established a dynastic union but not a united country. Discuss.' First, you need to think carefully about the meaning of 'dynastic union' and 'united country'. It may help if you ask a number of sub-questions. For instance, were the kingdoms unified administratively as well as politically? Did Castile and Aragon develop separate or similar economies (see section 5)? Did the monarchs' religious policies help to unite Spain? Was a common foreign policy pursued (see section 6)? Questions like this will help you to clarify your ideas and explanations.

4

How successful was Charles I in his domestic policies, 1516–56?

4.1 Charles' inheritance

Sixteen-year-old Charles was King of Spain, Naples, Sicily, Sardinia, the Balearics, the Canaries and the Indies, and Archduke of Austria and Duke of Burgundy. Three years into his reign he would also become the Holy Roman Emperor.

4.2 The revolt of the *comuneros*, 1520–22

The death of Ferdinand unleashed many complaints from **comuneros** across the peninsula at the Crown's failure to keep control of the nobility. Cisneros, regent between 1516 and 1517, proved ineffectual, and measures taken by Charles on his arrival in Spain from Burgundy worsened the situation. In 1520 many Castilian towns were in revolt.

Causes of the revolt

- Charles had appointed Burgundians, like Adrian and Jean Le Sauvage, to prominent government and Church offices, and then naturalised them to honour his promise not to favour foreigners.
- Charles mishandled the *cortes*. Having received over 1 million ducats between 1518 and 1519, he convened another *cortes* at Santiago in 1519. Taxes were still being collected, no *cortes* had ever met there and a Burgundian was appointed as its president.
- Towns and lesser nobles, led by Juan de Padilla, held deep-seated grievances against lawless nobles who infringed their rights and seized urban lands.
- Charles left Castile in 1519 to contest the imperial election. He was likely to be absent for several years and, while some complained at his absence, others feared that Castile would be used to fund his other commitments.

The rebels' demands

In November 1520 the rebels called for four main reforms:
- Charles must return from Germany and get married
- the Castilian *cortes* must meet regularly and play a major part in government
- only Castilians should hold Church and state offices
- all taxes should be reduced

Events during the revolt

In 1520–21 serious riots occurred in Toledo, Salamanca, Valladolid, Segovia and Medina del Campo, and Tordesillas was captured but Joanna, Charles' mother, who lived there, refused to support the rebels. The tide turned against them when leading grandees were appointed to the council of state, the regent (Adrian) promised not to favour any more foreigners, the latest **servicio** was cancelled, and grandees found that their own lands were under attack. At Villalar (1521) royalist troops backed by the grandees defeated the main rebel army.

Results

The revolt settled political and social unrest and strengthened Charles' authority in Spain:
- Nobles and grandees retained their social privileges and kept control of the provinces in return for supplying royal troops and exclusion from central government.

- Towns retained their rights and privileges but *corregidores* were given extra powers of intervention.
- *Cortes* would only meet when called and taxation had to be approved before representatives could discuss their grievances.

4.3 Revolt of the Germania, 1520–24

The Germania, a military brotherhood composed mainly of urban workers, protested at the nobility infringing their rights and the growth in numbers of *mudéjars* who, in many cases, were tenants of the nobles. The failure of Charles to call a *cortes* where the towns' representatives could voice their grievances sparked off the revolt. It began in Valencia where rebels, led by Vicent Peris, seized the city, and soon spread to Aragon and Majorca. The nobles finally suppressed the revolts and hundreds of rebels were executed. The Crown was powerless to intervene.

4.4 Government reforms

Charles returned to Spain in 1522, stayed for 7 years and introduced several administrative reforms. Most changes built upon the councils established by Isabella and Ferdinand, but there were some innovations too.

Central administration

- The Council of Castile was reformed and took control of internal affairs.
- The Council of State, from 1526, contained leading advisers.
- Councils of Finance (1522), War (1522), the Indies (1524) and Italy (1555) were created.
- Unpopular and incompetent officials were removed.
- Most councils were now staffed by *letrados*.
- Royal secretaries grew in power, especially Gattinara (died 1530), Los Cobos (who administered Spanish and Mediterranean affairs) and Perrenot (who administered the Netherlands, Indies and Americas).

Local administration

Nobility and grandees remained as governors and viceroys in the provinces and lands overseas.

Cortes

The principle of voting taxation before discussing grievances remained in spite of an attempt in 1523 to reverse the order, but towns were allowed to collect their own *servicios*, which opened the door to malpractice.

The eastern kingdoms

Aragon, Catalonia and Valencia were left alone. The Council of Aragon dealt mainly with judicial matters and did not interfere with the internal administration of the other kingdoms.

4.5 Finance

There were serious problems due to the inequitable tax system and the rising costs of government and war. Charles relied heavily on Castilian taxation.

- Fifteen Castilian *cortes* were held (only ten occurred in the three eastern kingdoms, which voted small sums).
- Attempts to tax the clergy and nobility (1527) or to get them to pay a ***sisa*** (1538) failed.

- The amount of American silver and gold bullion steadily increased: average annual receipts rose from 324,000 ducats in the 1530s to 871,000 ducats in the early 1550s.
- Most revenue came from the *alcabala*, which was fixed in 1534.
- The Church contributed 25% of all revenue in taxes (*tercias reales* and *cruzada*) and donations.
- *Juros* were sold but repayments cost 500,000 ducats a year.
- *Asientos* were negotiated with bankers, resulting in debts of 14 million ducats.
- Public offices and certificates of nobility were sold by the Crown.
- Italian and Dutch subjects contributed but after a revolt in Ghent (1539), Charles was unwilling to press them too hard.

In 1556 the government had a debt of 36 million ducats. All revenue for the next 4 years was earmarked for military costs and repayments on debts and loans.

4.6 The Church

- Little was done to reform the Spanish clergy. Most bishops did not reside in their dioceses and were engaged in state administration.
- The Inquisition investigated suspected *conversos* and *moriscos*.
- Aragonese *mudéjars* were forced to convert or emigrate in 1526; most remained and became *moriscos*.
- **Illuminists**, **Erasmians** and Lutherans were persecuted in the 1520s.
- A list of censored works was drawn up by Salamanca University theologians in 1547.

4.7 Conclusion

After a difficult start, Charles became a successful ruler of Spain. No further revolts occurred after 1524 in spite of heavy taxation and his frequent absences in the 1530s and 1540s. Charles viewed Spain as the centre of his monarchy; and he chose to die there in 1558. In concert with the nobles — who governed the provinces, the Church and the Inquisition, which prevented the spread of Protestant heresy — and the towns, whose *fueros* were respected, the king came to be admired and loved. Finance was his only serious failure.

5 What were the strengths and weaknesses of Spain's economy, 1469–1556?

5.1 Background

Throughout this period the economies of the Spanish kingdoms developed at different rates. No attempt was made to establish a single economic policy: each kingdom was left to its own devices and resisted state intervention. As a result, some towns and regions (e.g. Seville and Andalucía) flourished, and others (e.g. Barcelona and Catalonia) declined.

5.2 Population

Strengths

The population of Spain rose steadily between 1480 and 1580, particularly during Charles' reign, from about 5 to 6.5 million by 1556.

Weaknesses

Over 70% of the population lived in Castile. The high demand for food led to shortages and famine; the rural areas of the eastern kingdoms were underpopulated.

5.3 Agriculture

Strengths

Sheep farming provided the main employment. In 1489 the *Mesta* (corporation of sheep-owners) was allowed to extend sheep walks (*cañadas*); in 1501 its right to graze sheep on any pastureland and on migratory routes was confirmed. This secured the woollen trade and provided a regular source of revenue from wool and cloth exports.

Weaknesses

Most fertile land was sacrificed to sheep. Limited areas along narrow coastal strips and river valleys were cultivated but arable farming was neglected. Grain shortages occurred regularly after 1502 and food imports began in 1506. There were no new farming practices and soil erosion and deforestation increased.

5.4 Trade

Strengths

- Well-established and new trade routes flourished during this period.
- Bilbao, Santander and Seville thrived. The main imports were gold, sugar, grain and slaves from north Africa; cloth from Bruges and Antwerp; wine and metals from northern Europe; silk and spices from the Far East; and hides, tobacco, cocoa, sugar, dyes, gold and silver from the Indies.
- Exports of leather, wool, wine, fruit and olive oil went mainly to northern Europe; oil, wine and biscuits went to America.
- Navigation acts were passed by Ferdinand to increase shipbuilding.
- *Consulados* were established in Burgos (1494), Seville (1503) and Bilbao (1511).
- A 1497 decree established a common exchange rate between Castile, Valencia and Catalonia, which was a step towards economic integration.
- Bullion imports provided money for Charles' wars and enriched many Castilian nobles and merchants. The amount of bullion received trebled between 1503 and 1516, and produced 10% of Charles' income in 1556.
- The volume of trade with America rose from 300 tons a year in 1503 to more than 3,000 tons in 1516, and steadily increased thereafter.

Weaknesses

- There was widespread smuggling and illicit trade, as well as avoidance of customs duties, on the transatlantic routes.
- Seville and Castile monopolised the American trade to the detriment of other regions but they were unable to meet the demand of colonists, which was instead met by Flemish and Italian merchants.
- No free trade existed between the kingdoms; tolls were levied at the borders.
- Transportation was very difficult due to many unnavigable rivers and poor roads.
- The economy depended heavily on exporting good-quality wool. Several northern towns declined in the early sixteenth century as more expensive cloth was imported. Antwerp's collapse in 1551 also had an adverse effect on the wool towns of Old Castile.

5.5 Industry

Strengths

- There was a wide range of small industries (e.g. silk in Granada, pottery and soap in Seville, ceramics and leather in Cordoba, shipbuilding in Barcelona, iron works in Vizcaya).
- The main source of employment was the woollen industry, especially in the northern towns of Segovia, Toledo and Cuenca.
- Guilds in Valencia and Catalonia regulated manufacture and protected workers' rights.

Weaknesses

- The Crown failed to promote native industries.
- Charles increased taxation, which discouraged investment.
- Guilds, which were introduced to Castile by Ferdinand, were generally resented and opposed innovations.
- The expulsion of the Jews reduced levels of investment and production of luxury crafts.
- The expulsion of *mudéjars* adversely affected leather, pottery and silk production.
- American silver was not invested in industry; instead it contributed to inflation (2 % p.a.), which made Spanish goods more expensive to produce, buy and sell.

5.6 Conclusion

Isabella, Ferdinand and Charles had no coherent economic policies. Each kingdom was treated as a separate economic unit, and opportunities to develop trade with America and to invest in native industries were not taken due to short-term expedients.

GLOSSARY

consulados: boards of directors responsible for controlling a town's trade and commerce.

EXAMINER'S TIP

This topic appears at AS in the OCR specification. You are likely to have to assess the strengths and limitations of the economic policies of either the Catholic Monarchs or Charles I. This type of question is best answered by examining the strengths and weaknesses of the state of Spain's finances (see sections 1.4 and 4.5), agriculture, trade and industry, before reaching a conclusion. Remember to evaluate rather than describe the policies and developments.

6 What were the main achievements in foreign policy between 1469 and 1556?

6.1 Isabella and Ferdinand's aims

Ferdinand assumed the leading role in directing the affairs of both Castile and Aragon. He was mindful, however, of their diverging interests: Castile was mainly concerned with Portugal, north Africa, Granada and the Atlantic; Aragon was concerned with France, the Pyrenees, Italy and the Mediterranean. Isabella and Ferdinand's main aims were to:
- remove French threats from the Pyrenees
- prevent French ambitions in Italy from being realised
- wage war against Islam
- develop Atlantic colonisation

6.2 Achievements, 1469–1516

Portugal

In the War of Succession (1475–79), Ferdinand successfully prevented Portugal from deposing Isabella, and the Treaty of Alcaçovas laid the foundations of a long period of peace. A series of marriages between the Portuguese and Castilian royal families further strengthened ties:
- Isabella, daughter of the Catholic Monarchs, married Prince Alfonso (1490).
- After Alfonso's death (1497) Isabella married King Manoel.
- When Isabella died (1500) Manoel married Maria, daughter of the Catholic Monarchs.

The Canaries

At Alcaçovas Portugal ceded to Castile all claims to the Canaries. As a result, between 1482 and 1493 the main islands were conquered and colonised.

The Americas

In 1492 Isabella gave her support to Columbus to sail across the Atlantic. He landed in the Bahamas, and three further voyages led to Castile's laying claim to Cuba, Hispaniola, Puerto Rico and Trinidad. By 1516 settlers, soldiers and missionaries were regularly crossing the Atlantic.

North Africa

The conquest of Granada (1492) opened up the opportunity to conquer and settle parts of north Africa. Success would increase trade, reduce pirate attacks on the Spanish mainland, establish Christian settlements and enhance Castile's international standing. The capture of Mers-el-Kebir (1505), Cazaza (1506), Peñón de Vélez (1508), Orán (1509), Bougie, Tripoli and Algiers (1510) gave protection to the west Mediterranean sea routes. Colonies were not established, however, and instead permanent garrisons were needed to protect these trading bases.

The Pyrenees

Ferdinand recovered Roussillon and Cerdagne in Catalonia (1493) in return for acknowledging the French rule of Brittany. Navarre was occupied (1512) and partitioned between France and Castile (1515).

Italy

In 1495 Ferdinand joined the Holy League to oust France from Italy and to protect the papacy. He denied any interest in claiming lands for himself, but after victories at Cerignola and Garigliano (1503) he was able to control Naples and Sicily.

The Duchy of Milan was the gateway to Italy and, when Louis XII of France lay claim to it, Ferdinand was keen to stop him. In 1511 he persuaded Pope Julius II to construct a Holy League comprising English, German, Italian, Swiss and Spanish troops. For 3 years, following an allied victory at Novara (1512), Ferdinand appeared to have succeeded but a new French king, Francis I, unexpectedly won the battle of Marignano (1515) and, with it, control of Milan.

6.3 Charles I's aims

Charles' aims were to:
- protect his inheritance and drive France out of Italy
- secure settlements in north Africa and trade in the west Mediterranean
- fight Islam

6.4 Achievements, 1516–56

War against France

1521–29   Charles defeated Francis I of France at Pampeluna in Navarre (1521), at Bicocca (1522), when Spain seized Milan, and again at Pavia (1525), when Francis was taken prisoner. Charles, however, failed to follow up his victories until Landriano (1529), when Francis finally yielded claims to Milan, Naples and Genoa (which became a Spanish protectorate).

1529–44   Francis I was a poor loser and at the first opportunity renewed his quest to recover Milan. In 1535 the Duke of Milan, Francesco Sforza, a Spanish ally, died. French troops threatened to overrun Milan and captured the neighbouring Duchy of Savoy, which Charles acknowledged in the Treaty of Nice (1538). When fighting recurred in 1542, however, France lost the Duchy of Savoy at the Treaty of Crépy (1544).

1544–56   The death of Francis (1547) brought Henry II to the French throne. He was able to construct an unlikely alliance of German Protestants, Turkish Muslims and French Catholics against Charles in the 1550s. As a result, French troops won a handful of victories in northern Italy and threatened Milan. In 1555 the Pope urged Henry to use his troops to expel Spain from Naples. In the depths of depression, Charles abdicated control of Spain to his son, Philip, who was left to deal with the problem (see Unit 8, section 4.3).

War against Islam

Berber pirates raided the southeast of Spain, Muslim tribes attacked African settlements and Turkish fleets threatened trade routes between Naples, Sicily and Tunisia. In defending his territories in the Mediterranean and north Africa, Charles was also fighting a holy war against Islam.

In 1516 Barbarossa, a Muslim pirate, established himself in Algiers. The Turkish sultan, Suleiman, appointed him grand admiral of the Ottoman fleet and his seizure of Tunis (1534) endangered Spain's north African and Mediterranean shipping lanes. Charles recaptured Tunis (1535) but failed to recover Algiers (1541). In the 1550s Tripoli, Peñón de Vélez and Bougie also fell to the Turks. In the course of his reign Charles lost four African settlements and only retained Melilla, Orán, Mers-el-Kebir and Tunis, protected by the fortress of La Goletta.

6.5 Conclusion

Between 1469 and 1556 Spain emerged as the leading power in Europe. It had captured Granada, Milan and Naples, and settlements in north Africa; it had prevented France from claiming lands in Italy and the Pyrenees; it had established itself in the Canaries and gained control of the Americas; and it had achieved peaceful coexistence with Portugal. By a series of marriage alliances, the Spanish Habsburgs had a claim to most of the royal houses in Europe. Less successful were Spain's wars against the Turks, who still threatened Spain's garrisons in north Africa and its west Mediterranean trade routes. Equally worrying was the rising cost of defending this world-wide empire.

EXAMINER'S TIP

This topic appears at AS in the OCR specification. You may well be asked: 'How far did either the Catholic Monarchs or Charles I achieve the aims of their foreign policy?' You could start by establishing their aims and then develop your answer, possibly country by country. In this way you can comment upon both successes and failures and largely avoid a narrative approach. Remember that an argued explanation will always score higher marks than a narrative account.

(1) How effectively did Philip II govern Spain and his *monarquía*?
(2) How far was Philip the 'Most Catholic King' of Spain?
(3) What were the causes, events and outcome of the Dutch Revolt?
(4) How far did Philip's foreign policy change between 1556 and 1598?

1 How effectively did Philip II govern Spain and his monarquía?

1.1 Style of government

Philip II assumed total responsibility for government decisions. He took all decisions slowly, and had difficulty discriminating between important and trivial matters. He preferred to govern by paper but the number of **consultas** requiring his attention overwhelmed him, even though he annotated an average of 40 papers a day. Endless discussions took place, and months often passed before decisions were taken.

Conciliar administration

Philip governed Spain through 14 councils based, from 1561, in Madrid. Six councils dealt with different territories; eight were departments of state. All councils were dominated by *letrados* (law graduates) and by Castilians. Resentment built up among those excluded and, although a few advisers were non-Castilian (e.g. Moura was Portuguese), contemporaries were convinced that the old Castilian aristocratic families (e.g. the Mendozas and Guzmans) were favoured.

The king increasingly relied on his secretaries — Eraso (1556–66), Espinosa (1566–72) and Vazquez (1573–91). They presented memoranda and *consultas* for the king to read and drafted his replies. It was probably Vazquez who suggested that he should consult *juntas* in the 1580s.

1.2 Factions

The council of state was Philip's most important advisory council. It soon came to be divided by factions as rival nobles competed for government offices, power and patronage.

Eboli vs Alva, 1559–73

Ruy Gomez de Silva, the Prince of Eboli, consistently clashed with Fernando Alvarez de Toledo, the Duke of Alva. Traditionally, historians have regarded their attitude towards the Netherlands as the main source of disagreement — Eboli supported peace and diplomacy whereas Alva favoured war and aggression. More recently, historians have questioned this interpretation. Henry Kamen has argued that the councillors did not consistently adopt either diplomatic or confrontational stances. Albert Lovett, on the other hand, has suggested that the council was divided over whether Spain should develop a centralist (favoured by Alva) or a federal administration (Eboli's preference).

Pérez vs Alva, 1573–79

Eboli's death in 1573 saw his protégé, Antonio Pérez, become Alva's rival until both Pérez and Alva fell from office in 1579. Pérez was arrested, accused of plotting against the king; it is likely that Philip felt he could no longer trust him to keep state secrets.

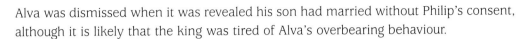

Spain, 1556–98

Alva was dismissed when it was revealed his son had married without Philip's consent, although it is likely that the king was tired of Alva's overbearing behaviour.

Juntas, 1585–98

In 1579, 62-year-old Cardinal Granvelle became president of the council while Philip prepared to go to Portugal. Upon the king's return (1583) control passed to Zuñiga, Moura, Idiáquez and Chinchón; and from 1585 these men dominated the newly created *juntas*:

- *Junta de Noche*: three councillors and a secretary met at night to advise the king.
- *Junta Grande*: eight to ten councillors reviewed the *consultas*.
- *Junta de Gobierno*: a governing committee displaced the *Junta Grande* in 1593 and comprised three councillors, Archduke Albert and Prince Philip.

1.3 Provincialism

Castilian administration

The provinces were controlled by grandees and nobles. They had the wealth to raise, pay and command an army and were vital to the maintenance of law and order. Provincial viceroys, governors and captain-generals possessed immense power and were only held in check by courts of appeal (*audiencias*).

The *corregidor* (Castilian royal governor) was the Crown's main servant in local government. Sixty-six were appointed by Philip to manage town councils and secure royalist elections to the *cortes*. Attempts to influence local decisions were fiercely resisted. *Corregidores* also ensured that royal decrees were enforced and justice was upheld. Although laws were generally obeyed and Philip acquired a reputation as a 'just' king, there was much corruption among local Crown servants.

The Castilian *cortes*

The *cortes* of Castile met frequently and sessions became longer as Philip's reign progressed. Historians disagree over whether it became more subservient (the view of Griffiths and Pierson) or more awkward (the view of Woodward and Jago).

- In 1566 it would not approve a *servicio* (parliamentary tax) until Philip had responded to its grievances over rising taxes, a practice repeated in 1571 and 1573.
- In 1575–77 Philip agreed to reduce the **encabezamiento** and to listen to any grievances if the *cortes* first approved his request for a *servicio*.
- In 1590 the *cortes* attached over 100 conditions before approving the *millones* tax.
- In 1596 nearly half the delegates refused to extend a *sisa* tax to wine and food.

The Aragonese *cortes*

The Aragonese *cortes* insisted that financial grants should be spent mainly in their own provinces, and resisted any infringement of their customary rights (*fueros*). The king could only appoint the viceroy; the **justiciar** held office for life and was a native-born noble. The limits of Philip's authority were revealed in 1591 when he tried to extradite Pérez to Castile. Riots broke out, the viceroy was murdered and the Inquisition's headquarters was burned down. Order was only restored when Philip sent 14,000 troops and executed over 20 rebels. In 1592 the Crown extended its authority by modifying Aragon's charter. Henceforth:

- the *justiciar* could be removed at will
- non-Aragonese officers could be appointed
- prisoners could be extradited to Castile
- the *cortes* could no longer control how financial grants were to be spent

Italy

Spanish viceroys governed the Italian states of Milan, Sardinia, Naples and Sicily but relied totally on local nobles. Claiming poverty, the states paid nominal taxes to Madrid and were generally obedient: only once, in 1585, did serious food riots break out in Naples.

Burgundy

The 17 provinces of Burgundy and Franche-Comté were recent acquisitions. Their States-General (national assembly) was riven with class factions and provincial rivalry but members were united by a common desire to preserve as much of their independence as possible. The king was equally determined to govern them more effectively by appointing Spanish-born councillors. The result was the most serious rebellion ever to confront the Spanish Habsburgs (see section 3 of this unit).

1.4 Royal finances

Philip was regarded by contemporaries as a 'prudent king' yet his financial administration was little short of disastrous. His problem was not that he received inadequate revenue: between 1556 and 1598 it increased four times to nearly 13 million ducats.

- Most revenue came from Castilian taxes, especially the *alcabala* and *servicios*.
- All sectors of society (except the nobility) saw a steep rise in taxation. The clergy, for instance, contributed 20% of Spain's revenue.
- More silver also arrived from America: the annual average rose from 300,000 ducats in the 1550s to 3 million ducats in the 1590s.

Philip's real problem was expenditure, especially the cost of defending his empire:
- Between 1550s and 1590s the cost of the armed forces rose from 2 million to 10 million ducats.
- Money was borrowed and government bonds, crown lands, titles and offices sold.
- In 1557, 1575 and 1596 decrees of bankruptcy were issued and interest payments suspended.
- Between 1556 and 1598 crown debts rose from 36 million to 84 million ducats.

1.5 Was the government absolute?

Arguments supporting this view

- In theory all monarchs were subject to God alone and therefore 'absolute'.
- Some contemporary jurists (e.g. Suarez) claimed Philip could act 'above the law'.
- Philip condoned the trial and execution of Egmont and Hornes, though they should have been tried by the Order of the Golden Fleece (see section 3.2), and he insisted on the execution without trial of the Aragonese *justiciar* (in 1592).
- Philip may have connived at the state murders of Montigny (1570) and Escobedo (1578).
- There were centralist and autocratic developments: Madrid became the capital; the army expanded to 80,000 troops; Philip controlled the Church and the Inquisition.
- Biased contemporary writers (e.g. William of Orange, Santa Cruz and Antonio Pérez) and some modern historians (e.g. Motley, Dominguez Ortiz, Kiernan, Lynch) have claimed that Philip exercised as much absolute authority as was possible in the sixteenth century.

Arguments against this view

- Philip lacked the means to impose his will on most subjects: there was no police force outside Madrid; there was only a small army in Iberia; he had financial problems; there were only 66 *corregidores* in Castile.

- Outside Castile, autonomous states resisted centralisation; there was no Inquisition in Naples and Milan; there were no *corregidores*; viceroys (e.g. Peru and Mexico) were largely independent.
- Philip ruled according to the law (e.g. the Inquisition did not abuse its power).
- Real power rested with the nobility and town authorities.
- Many contemporaries were biased against Philip (e.g. the **Black Legend** developed as a result of Italian, English and Dutch propaganda) and their allegations were repeated by later historians.
- Revisionist historians (e.g. Thompson, Woodward, Parker, Kamen) claim Philip had no aspirations to become an absolute ruler. Moreover, in Thompson's view: 'Absolute monarchy is to be judged not by what it looked like but by how it worked.'

Black Legend: a myth that Spaniards were an arrogant and imperialist nation.
consultas: summaries of council meetings.
encabezamiento: the assessment and collection of the *alcabala* tax by a town or region.
juntas: small committees of royal advisers.
justiciar: an Aragonese law officer in charge of justice.

EXAMINER'S TIP

This topic appears at AS and at A2 in the OCR specification. At AS, ensure that you know the meaning of terms such as '*corregidores*', '*juntas*', '*consultas*' and '*letrados*', and that you understand the strengths and limitations of Philip's administration. A typical AS question is: 'How successful was Philip II in dealing with the problems of court faction and the provinces?' At A2 you may have to explain why some but not all historians have regarded Philip as an absolute king.

2 How far was Philip the 'Most Catholic King' of Spain?

2.1 Background

Philip was devoted to the Catholic faith. He attended Mass daily, received communion regularly, endowed monasteries and shrines, and kept religious books at his bedside. From his room in the Escorial palace he overlooked the monks of San Lorenzo at prayer. There was, moreover, a strong belief among Spaniards that the king had a prime duty to defend the Church.

2.2 Philip's aims

Philip II's aims were to:
- support the Inquisition in eliminating Protestant heresy and investigating *conversos* and *moriscos*
- improve the spiritual condition of the clergy by better training and removing clerical abuses (e.g. absenteeism and pluralism)
- educate the laity in Christian beliefs and discourage local religious practices
- maintain good relations with the papacy

2.3 Reforms in the Spanish Church

Philip waited until the conclusion of the Council of Trent in 1563 before introducing reforms based on its recommendations. Among the most important changes were:

- Twenty seminaries were established to educate the clergy.
- Seven new dioceses and a new archdiocese of Burgos were created.
- Regular meetings of bishops were held to discuss reforms.
- New monasteries were built (e.g. 80 **discalced** Carmelite convents were founded by Teresa of Avila).
- Decayed monasteries were closed or amalgamated; links with foreign houses were abandoned.
- Priests had to preach a weekly sermon, give religious instruction and start Sunday schools.
- Priests had to wear vestments in public and not socialise during religious festivals.
- Congregations were required to attend weekly services, take communion at Easter and learn the Ten Commandments and Creed.
- Jesuits were encouraged to spread Christianity to all areas of Spain.

Impact of the reforms

The quality of the clergy appears to have improved and some bishops (e.g. Quiroga of Toledo and Ribera of Valencia) raised the level of spirituality in their dioceses. Towns in Old Castile saw a marked improvement. Rural and more isolated areas, however, made less progress:

- In Galicia there were insufficient priests.
- In Granada and Navarre people still worshipped pagan images.
- In the west and south missionaries and inquisitors reported apathy and ignorance.

2.4 The role of the Inquisition

Philip presided over the Suprema, which controlled the 15 mainland and 6 overseas tribunals. The Spanish Inquisition was much cherished by the king; without it, he believed, he could not have ruled so effectively. It was mainly concerned with:

- wiping out heresy: mystics were silenced (e.g. Luis de Léon, an Augustinian friar, was imprisoned for 5 years) and Protestants were arrested and purged (e.g. 278 were tried at Seville and Valladolid in 1559–62 and 77 were burned at the stake in *auto-de-fés*)
- investigating *conversos* and *moriscos*: Inquisitor-General Valdez was particularly interested in verifying people's purity of blood to prove that they were not of Jewish or Muslim descent. Cases concerning *conversos* increased in the 1580s and 1590s after the annexation of Portugal and the arrival of immigrants into Castile. *Moriscos* were investigated in Granada in the 1560s and in Valencia and Andalucía thereafter
- censoring books and teaching: a decree of 1558 ordered a list (the 'Index') of prohibited books to be drawn up. Six hundred and seventy titles were banned, extended to over 2,300 (mainly foreign) titles in 1583. Castilian students abroad were ordered home in 1559. Inquisitors collaborated with Salamanca University to purge unorthodox teaching
- maintaining standards of behaviour: the Inquisition saw itself as the guardian of public morality. It devoted much of its time to investigating cases of blasphemy, bigamy and sexual misconduct

Historical controversy

In recent years historians have revised traditional views of the Inquisition. The old view is that:

- the Inquisition was an instrument of political power
- it used torture indiscriminately

- its concern for purity of blood led to the persecution of thousands of innocent people
- its censorship stifled free speech and isolated Spain from European culture

Revisionists (e.g. Henry Kamen and Jaime Contreras) have challenged these beliefs, claiming that:

- the Inquisition had a very limited political impact, was not a secular arm of the state and had its powers restricted by various *cortes* (e.g. Valencia in 1568)
- torture was not widely used, was always lawfully applied and instruments of torture were a myth created by Dutch propagandists
- censorship had little effect on Spanish literature, science or freedom of speech. Books were easily smuggled into Castile from Aragon (where censorship did not apply) and scholars and politicians enjoyed more freedom of expression than most Europeans
- educating Castilians and upholding moral standards were positive social contributions that enabled the Inquisition to champion the Catholic Counter-Reformation and combat heresy. Most of the *conversos* and *moriscos* who were interrogated were found to have been non-practising Christians

2.5 Papal relations

Philip acknowledged that the Pope was God's representative on earth but the king effectively controlled the Church in Spain. Between 1556 and 1598 the papacy clashed with him on three main issues: his **regalian rights**, the Jesuits and foreign affairs.

Regalian rights

Philip had the right to:

- register or reject papal bulls
- deny appeals to Rome
- appoint all ecclesiastical offices
- retain 50% of clerical revenue

Philip yielded none of these rights in spite of pressure from Pius IV and Pius V. His lawyers also scrutinised all papal bulls (e.g. the 1564 **Tridentine Decrees**) before authorising their publication. If he disagreed with a papal policy (e.g. a decree to ban bullfighting), then he ignored it.

Jesuits

Philip believed that the Jesuits had an important role to play in furthering the Catholic Reformation and at first he welcomed their presence in Spain. All Jesuits took an oath to serve the Pope, however, and the appointment of Aquaviva (1581) — an Italian — as general of the Jesuits convinced the king that they needed to be closely watched. In 1586 the Inquisition arrested Marceu, the Jesuit principal of Toledo, but Pope Sixtus V demanded his release. Philip reluctantly complied and, in spite of royal protests, failed to get the papacy to allow him greater control over Jesuit activities in Spain.

Foreign affairs

Most of the popes openly criticised Philip's foreign policy. They believed that, as the Most Catholic King, he should be actively at war with heretics but that in fact he was more interested in expanding Spanish power. Paul IV went to war with Spain (1556–59), Gregory XIII condemned his truce with Turkey (1578) and Sixtus V threatened to excommunicate him (1590). For his part, Philip resented the papacy's persistent anti-Spanish sniping.

GLOSSARY

auto-de-fés: ceremonies at which penitents were encouraged to abdure their heresy before receiving sentence from the Inquisition.

discalced: bare-footed.

regalian rights: rights belonging to the Crown.

Tridentine Decrees: decrees issued by the Council of Trent.

EXAMINER'S TIP

This subject appears at AS in the OCR specification and at A2 in the OCR and AQA (Alternative B) specifications. Philip's religious affairs are a regular exam topic and you need to have a clear understanding of his main aims, successes and limitations. For instance, at AS you might be asked: 'How far was Philip II motivated by religious beliefs in ruling Spain?' At A2 you should focus on historical interpretations of the work of the Inquisition and the extent to which the Spanish Church had been reformed by 1598. You might be asked: 'Why has the role of the Spanish Inquisition under Philip II been the cause of controversy among historians?'

3 What were the causes, events and outcome of the Dutch Revolt?

3.1 Background

The 17 provinces constituting the Netherlands had been transferred from the Holy Roman Empire to Spain in 1555. Philip stayed there for 4 years. When he left in 1559 there were already signs of trouble. Disturbances occurred in 1566–67 (often referred to as 'the first revolt') and an even more serious uprising began in 1572 and lasted until 1609.

3.2 Causes

Spanish taxation

Philip believed the Dutch should contribute substantial grants to his administration but the provincial estates, led by Brabant, resisted. In 1559, 3.6 million ducats were voted to him but the Dutch insisted on collecting the grant and stated that it would have to last for 9 years. In 1569 the States-General (national assembly) rejected a proposed 5% tax on land sales and a 10% tax on other sales. When Spanish officials tried to collect both taxes in 1571 without Dutch consent, widespread protests and a tax strike ensued.

Ecclesiastical reforms

To prevent the spread of Calvinism and increase his control over the Dutch, Philip introduced several changes in 1561:

- Three archbishops and 14 bishops were created.
- Cardinal Granvelle became the new Archbishop of Malines.
- All bishops were to be graduates, assisted by two inquisitors and funded by local abbeys.

These reforms were resented by nobles, who had no university qualifications, by abbots, whose income was reduced, and by all who feared the Inquisition. In 1564 Philip

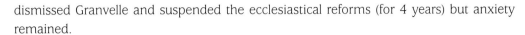

dismissed Granvelle and suspended the ecclesiastical reforms (for 4 years) but anxiety remained.

Calvinism

Between 1559 and 1565 many Dutch nobles had become Calvinist (e.g. Egmont, Hornes, Marnix and Brederode). Egmont visited Philip in 1565 and believed the king was willing to relax the heresy laws but Philip's 'Letters from the Segovia Woods' in October stated he was not. The lesser nobles armed themselves and forced the regent, Margaret, to support their demand for the heresy laws to be lifted and the Inquisition removed. Calvinist preachers provoked disturbances in 1566–67 in the 'iconoclastic fury': Catholic churches were sacked and priests attacked. Only when the grandees intervened was order restored. The execution in 1568 of several Calvinist nobles (e.g. Egmont, Hornes, Brederode) did little to quell Dutch opposition to Spanish Catholicism and the Inquisition. Calvinism was always a minority faith but the willingness of its followers to die for its beliefs was an obstacle Philip never overcame.

Alva's army

Philip kept 3,000 troops in the Netherlands at the end of his war with France in 1559. They were never liked and, although he withdrew them in 1561, the outbreak of riots in 1566–67 prompted him to send 10,000 troops under General Alva. Alva's strong-arm methods soon alienated Dutch Catholic and aristocratic subjects — the very people who had earlier stood by the king. Alva's Council of Troubles subsequently arrested over 12,000 rebels, seized the lands of 9,000 and executed more than 1,100.

Dutch liberties

The Dutch always suspected that Philip wanted to suppress their liberties and centralise the provinces into a single country. The deputies in the States-General, therefore, consistently defended their rights to consult their provincial estates before agreeing to Spanish taxation. The grandees also expected to be given more authority in the absence of the king; William of Orange, in particular, resented the power exercised by Granvelle, and then by Alva. Orange was horrified by the trial and execution of his colleagues Egmont and Hornes. As Knights of the Golden Fleece, they were entitled to a trial by their own order but Alva had treated them as common rebels. Between 1568 and 1572 Orange, from his exile in Germany, encouraged the Dutch to defend their 'lives, property and wealth', not as rebels but as 'liberators'.

Philip's mistakes

The king made a number of serious mistakes, which contributed to the outbreak of the revolt:

- When he left the Netherlands in 1559 he promised to return, but he never did.
- He appointed his sister as regent but refused to let her make any decisions.
- He showed poor political judgement in appointing Granvelle, an arrogant, ambitious man.
- Philip's refusal to withdraw the army and Inquisition, or to allow religious tolerance, left the Netherlands in a permanent state of unrest.
- He acted like a despot by endorsing Alva's execution of rebels.

Sea beggars

In April 1572 Dutch 'sea beggars' (pirates), led by William de la Marck, sailed into the ports of Brill and Flushing. An inadequate Spanish garrison failed to defend them and their capture sparked off a wave of uprisings in the eastern and western provinces, while Orange invaded the Netherlands from the east.

3.3 Main events, 1572–98

1572	Alva's troops took 6 months to capture Mons and 7 months to take Haarlem, and then unwisely massacred the garrison.
1573	Requesens replaced Alva as governor-general. Orange became a Calvinist. Spanish troops failed to capture Alkmaar.
1575	Peace talks failed. Orange demanded religious toleration and the restoration of 'ancient privileges and liberty'. Philip refused.
1576	Requesens died. Unpaid Spanish troops sacked Antwerp and killed 8,000. The States-General pledged to unite against Spain in the 'Pacification of Ghent'. All but Holland and Zealand signed.
1577	Don John, the new governor-general, agreed to withdraw the troops, allow toleration and restore political privileges in the Perpetual Edict. Three months later the troops returned.
1578	Don John died. The Duke of Parma assumed command. Divisions began to appear between Calvinists and Catholics in the States-General. French and German mercenaries assisted the rebels.
1579	Three Catholic-controlled provinces in the south formed the Union of Arras and stopped fighting. Six more northerly provinces signed the Union of Utrecht: Calvinism was established and they vowed to continue the revolt.
1580	Philip declared Orange an outlaw. Orange, in his 'Apology', condemned Philip as a tyrant and murderer.
1581	The States-General issued an Act of Abduration, which denied Philip his right to rule them. Ten provinces signed it. Francis, the Duke of Anjou, agreed to become their new sovereign.
1584	Orange was assassinated. Anjou died of fever.
1585	Only Holland and Zealand remained unconquered. England signed the Treaty of Nonsuch and sent 7,000 troops to help the Dutch.
1587–88	Parma was told to focus on the war against England; on his return from Dunkirk his troops failed to capture Bergen-op-Zoom.
1589–90	Parma was told to assist the French Catholic League. In his absence the Dutch won further victories.
1591–92	Parma returned to the Netherlands. Philip again insisted he should return to France, where he died of wounds received at Rouen.
1596	Archduke Albert of Austria became the governor-general.
1598	Albert married Isabella, Philip's daughter. Together they governed the ten southern 'obedient' provinces; the seven northern provinces were still in revolt and in all but name had won their independence.

3.4 Reasons for Spain's failure

Historians agree that no single factor accounts for Spain's failure. Dutch writers, however, have tended to attach importance to qualities inherent in their people, faith and physical conditions, whereas Spanish historians have stressed the logistical problems, imperial commitments and intervention of other states. The main reasons for Spain's defeat are seen as:

• the strength and organisation of Calvinism as a faith at war: the sea beggars were fanatical Calvinists and unwilling to submit
• the leadership of William of Orange. He overcame Dutch particularism, united their opposition and turned the revolt into an international conflict

- Dutch military and naval strength. Maurice (William's son) led the troops in the 1590s, and the navy ensured that trade with the Baltic and Mediterranean sustained the economy
- the fact that Spanish administration could not solve the problem of long distances, and insufficient money and troops
- the low-lying land, wide rivers and isolated communities, which made any permanent conquest impossible to sustain
- Philip's serious misjudgement in declaring war on England and France and expecting Parma's army to fight on three fronts simultaneously
- the fact that assistance from France, Germany and England in the 1580s was decisive
- the fact that Spain's commitment to defeating the Turks between 1565 and 1578 diverted money, men and resources at a crucial time

EXAMINER'S TIP

This subject appears at AS in the OCR specification and at A2 in the OCR and AQA (Alternative B) specifications. You will need to understand the causes of the revolt and the nature of the fighting before you can explain why Spain was unable to suppress it. A typical AS question is: 'How far does religion explain the outbreak and continuation of the Dutch Revolt?' At A2 different historical interpretations must be understood. You might be asked, for example: 'Did the Dutch rebels challenge Philip II's rule primarily in defence of their liberties?'

4 How far did Philip's foreign policy change between 1556 and 1598?

4.1 Aims

Historians have long argued over Philip's foreign policy aims. Part of their problem is that he did not write down any objectives or principles that may have constituted a policy. Although it is generally agreed that he did not pursue a single objective and would not have separated political from religious motives, four possible aims have been suggested:
- to expand the Spanish empire
- to defend the Catholic faith
- to defend his and his country's reputation
- to react to opportunities as they occurred

Contemporaries were similarly perplexed. The papacy was convinced that Philip wanted to 'safeguard and increase his dominions'. The Venetian ambassador, on the other hand, believed the king did not want to wage war but to make peace 'so that he can keep the lands he has'.

4.2 Strategy

For the first 20 years of his reign Philip focused on the Mediterranean, stemming the advance of Turkish fleets and defending Spanish trade routes and possessions in north Africa and Italy. Financial, military and naval resources were limited for much of this period. He was unable to pursue the aggressive policy that his councillor Alva recommended; instead, peaceful diplomacy prevailed to the satisfaction of Eboli (see section 1.2). England's friendship was also most useful at a time when there was a civil war in France and a revolt in the Netherlands.

The years 1578–80 proved a critical turning-point:

- Relations with England deteriorated.
- A truce was reached with the Turks.
- Philip took possession of Portugal.
- Revenue from the New World increased. As a result, Philip was able to turn his attention to northern Europe to concentrate on the Dutch Revolt, to declare war on England and to intervene in the French wars of religion.

4.3 Relations with France

War, 1556–59

Between 1556 and 1559 French and papal troops unsuccessfully attacked Spain's Italian lands; in France, Philip won the battle of St Quentin (1557) and Henry II captured the English town of Calais (1558). As a result of the Treaty of Cateau-Cambrésis (1559):

- France kept Calais
- Spain kept its Italian lands
- Philip married Elizabeth, daughter of Henry II of France

Henry of Navarre

Philip stayed out of French affairs until 1584, when he pledged money and troops at the Treaty of Joinville to stop Henry of Navarre from becoming the next king of France. Henry was leader of the French Protestants, King of French Navarre and heir to the French throne. The subsequent murder of Catholic nobles and the assassination of Henry III, King of France (1589), convinced Philip that he should send a much larger army into France and offer Isabella, his daughter, as an alternative claimant to the French throne. France rejected her and accepted Navarre once he had renounced his faith and become a Catholic (1593).

War, 1595–98

Henry IV declared war on Spain. Both sides had victories and defeats before bankruptcy and Philip's declining health ended the conflict at Vervins (1598). Neither France nor Spain gained any land, but Henry IV won a moral victory; Spain was no longer invincible.

4.4 Turkey

In the 1550s the Turks were securing more bases in north Africa and threatening Spain's Italian territories and trade routes in the west Mediterranean. The loss of 10,000 men and eight galleys at Djerba (1560) focused Philip's mind upon revenge, and the recapture of Peñón de Vélez (1564) and the relief of Malta (1565) went some way towards restoring Spain's ailing reputation.

Lepanto, 1571

Although not over-keen, Philip agreed to join Venice and the papacy in a crusade against the main Turkish fleet; and the king more than enjoyed the subsequent victory at Lepanto. The Turks showed that they were not a spent force, however, when 300 galleys recaptured Tunis and threatened Sicily.

Peace

The death of Selim (1575) brought a new sultan, Murad, to power. He was more interested in fighting Persia than waging war against Spain. Philip took the opportunity to negotiate a truce (1578), which became a peace (1581) that held for the rest of his reign. Criticised by the Pope, Venetians and Spanish clergy, Philip believed that he was acting in Spain's best interests.

4.5 Portugal

Philip's claim to the Portuguese throne

In 1580 Henry, King of Portugal, died, leaving three claimants:
- Philip, whose mother was Portuguese.
- Catalina, the Duchess of Braganza, who was the queen mother.
- Don António, Henry's illegitimate nephew.

Philip had the best claim but left nothing to chance. He took the following steps:
- He persuaded Catalina to withdraw her claim.
- He bribed leading members of the *cortes* to back him.
- He offered merchants the prospect of trading with Castile and America.
- He sent troops to defeat António's supporters.

Results

- In 1581 Philip was crowned king and was well received.
- Portugal kept its constitution, *cortes*, administration, laws and language.
- The Spanish empire became the largest in the world, though more vulnerable to attack.
- The unification of Iberia brought security and prestige.
- Portuguese *galleasses* (warships) gave the Spanish Navy greater flexibility.
- António was still at large and supported by France and England until his death (1595).

According to the historian Peter Pierson, the annexation of Portugal was Philip's 'greatest triumph'.

4.6 England

Tudor friendship with Spain had begun in 1489 and, in spite of occasional difficulties, was still sound in 1556. It was based on family ties, trade and a mutual hostility towards France. Philip's marriage to Mary (1554) thus followed a well-established dynastic tradition.

Years of friendship, 1556–67

Philip spent 17 months in England in 1554–55 and 1557. He was not well liked and, by enticing Mary to join him in war against France, he lowered his reputation even further. Calais was lost and Spain was blamed. Queen Elizabeth and Philip enjoyed a pragmatic relationship: she needed his support to secure her position with Catholics; he wanted her support to limit the growing power of the Guises in Scotland and France. As a result, he dissuaded the papacy from excommunicating the queen.

Worsening relations, 1568–85

Relations with England steadily deteriorated for a number of reasons until open warfare occurred in 1585 (see Unit 5, section 5.3 for more details):
- Spain denied English merchants the right to trade in America. Hawkins' ships were seized at San Juan d'Ulloa (1567) and in return Drake attacked Nombre de Dios (1573); other merchants/pirates targeted Spanish silver convoys. By the 1580s Drake was regularly attacking Spanish and Portuguese ships as well as mainland ports.
- The arrival of Mary, Queen of Scots in England (1568) threatened Elizabeth's life and her religious settlement. Spain gave encouragement to the northern rebellion, the Ridolfi plot, Irish revolts and Throckmorton's plan to put Mary on the throne.
- The arrival of 10,000 Spanish troops in the Netherlands (1568) threatened English trade, the liberty of the Dutch and the future of Protestantism. By the 1580s the army was in excess of 60,000, English trade had stopped and security was endangered.

War and defeat, 1585–98

Between 1585 and 1588 Philip planned an armada. Its aims were:

- to force Elizabeth to withdraw troops from the Netherlands and ships from the Channel
- to be compensated for the cost of the Armada
- to convert England to Catholicism or establish toleration for English Catholics

Admiral Medina Sidonia successfully sent 122 ships to Calais, where he waited to escort Parma's army across the Channel — but Parma was 30 miles away at Dunkirk. Instead, English fireships attacked and scattered the fleet. The plan of invasion failed, and one third of the crew and ships were lost.

Two more armadas were sent, in 1596 and 1597, only to be dispersed by gales. English privateers also counterattacked with varying degrees of success but neither England nor Spain was capable of delivering a decisive blow. By 1598 Spain's invincible reputation was in shreds.

UNIT 9 Luther and the German Reformation, 1517–55

KEY QUESTIONS

(1) What were the causes of the German Reformation in 1517?
(2) What were Luther's main ideas?
(3) What progress had Lutheranism made by 1555?

1 What were the causes of the German Reformation in 1517?

1.1 Background

The Reformation began in Germany when Martin Luther asked questions about the sale of indulgences in 1517. Several preconditions brought this about: Desiderius Erasmus and **humanism**; the printing press; and the condition of the Roman Catholic Church.

1.2 Erasmus and humanism

Erasmus was principally a Christian humanist. He believed that Christianity was essentially a simple faith that had become materialistic in the hands of theologians. In a series of publications, notably *The Handbook of a Christian Soldier* (1503), *In Praise of Folly* (1509), *Julius Exclusus* (1513) and a new translation of the original Greek New Testament (1516), he expressed the following ideas:

- The Scriptures should be the basis of all Christian beliefs.
- The original Hebrew and Greek manuscripts should be studied because the Catholic Latin Bible (known as the Vulgate) contained errors.
- Inner spirituality was more important than outward devotional practices such as going on pilgrimages, collecting relics and worshipping saints.
- The Roman Catholic Church was full of clerical abuses: popes behaved like princes, many clergy were greedy and corrupt and the laity had been led astray.

German Protestant reformers, like Luther and Bucer, later found inspiration from reading Erasmus' books, even though few shared his love of humanism. Erasmus, however, was a Catholic scholar who wanted to see the Church reform its ways, not publicly and discordantly, but peacefully and by the Pope, so as to ensure Church unity. Schism was never his intention and he condemned Luther and other reformers who challenged the primacy of the papacy and the fundamental beliefs of the Catholic faith.

1.3 The development of printing

By 1500 most western European countries had a printing press. Germany had 64, mainly in Frankfurt, Cologne, Nuremberg, Augsburg, Strassburg and Wittenberg — Luther's university town. Both Protestant and Catholic printers published mainly devotional and religious material but by the mid-sixteenth century Protestant printers outnumbered Catholic ones by 20 to 1. Historians, such as Elizabeth Eisenstein, have argued that printing played a major role in bringing about the German Reformation. This was because:

- the number of books in circulation increased, and ideas spread much more rapidly and extensively. Erasmus' *Adagia*, for instance, sold 72,000 copies in the years between 1500 and 1525

- the Scriptures were published in the vernacular (native language) for all to read. Between 1522 and 1534 Luther's German translation of the Greek New Testament sold over 200,000 copies
- woodcuts (pictures) often accompanied the text to help the illiterate and semi-literate
- differences between the Vulgate and original manuscripts were revealed, which cast doubts about the integrity and significance of the priesthood
- the volume of publications was too great for the Church and state to censor

1.4 The condition of the Catholic Church

The papacy

The Pope, as bishop of Rome, claimed to be the representative of St Peter. Although he did not claim infallibility, he did not expect to be challenged on spiritual matters. Some popes abused their authority: Sixtus IV appointed friends and relatives as cardinals, Alexander VI fathered illegitimate children, Julius II led an army into battle in order to extend his lands, and Leo X sold papal offices. Not everyone, however, accepted the basis of papal power. General councils of the Church claimed to be Christ's representatives on earth and a council of 1415 had declared that it was superior to the Pope. Some secular rulers (e.g. French, English and Spanish kings) largely controlled Church patronage in their country and pocketed considerable sums of clerical money through taxation and rents.

The German Church

In Germany secular authorities were less influential and papal power remained strong. Taxes, fees and the appointment of Italian cardinals to German churches caused much resentment. Princes and cities regularly complained to the emperor, but to little effect. There were also numerous complaints about the quality of the priesthood. Most priests were poorly educated, many held several offices or were absent from their parishes; some seemed more interested in managing their estates and collecting rents and tithes.

Holy relics, indulgences and chantries were particularly popular in the early sixteenth century as people pursued 'good works' to reduce the time their soul would inevitably have to spend in purgatory. Religious works and catechisms, which taught basic Christian beliefs, were also popular. Kolde's *Mirror of a Christian Man*, for example, was printed in 1470 and ran to 19 editions by 1517. And preachers who stressed the importance of the Bible, like Staupitz in Nuremberg and von Kaisersberg in Strassburg, drew very large crowds.

GLOSSARY

humanism: a movement of people who became more civilised and better trained to play an active role in the life of the state by studying art, architecture, language, rhetoric, grammar and literature.

EXAMINER'S TIP

This topic appears at AS in the Edexcel and AQA (Alternative B) specifications. Questions might require you to assess the contribution of the printing press to the German Reformation or the relationship between Erasmus and Luther. For instance: 'How did Luther's criticisms of the Church differ from those of Erasmus?' Be aware of the different factors in 1517 that account for the origins of the Reformation in Germany.

---

2 *What were Luther's main ideas?*

2.1 Background

It took Luther more than 15 years to develop his theological ideas fully. In his search for salvation he had turned his back on a life of monasticism and instead immersed himself in study. At Erfurt and Wittenberg universities he read and rejected the traditional authorities of Aristotle and Aquinas, found the writings of St Augustine too oppressive and those of Occam and Scotus inadequate. The ideas of mystics like Tauler and humanists like Erasmus were enlightening but not totally satisfying. Finally, in 1515, he discovered the key to his salvation while reading St Paul's Epistle to the Romans. As he subsequently defended his ideas in writing and debate, Luther rejected much of the penitential system and papal authority that endorsed it. Gradually he developed his own theology, which was finally summarised in the Augsburg Confession (1530).

2.2 Luther's ideas

Indulgences

These pieces of parchment were incapable of releasing a soul from **purgatory** and, in selling them, the papacy was exploiting the people. On 31 October 1517 Luther pinned his 95 Theses to his church door in Wittenberg to explain why people should not buy indulgences.

Good works

In 1518–19 Luther questioned the **Treasury of Merits**, the worshipping of saints and the existence of purgatory — all of which he later rejected. Good works, such as acquiring holy relics or going on a pilgrimage, did not make a person 'good', although a 'good person' might do these things.

Sola fide (by faith alone)

God had revealed the true path to salvation through the death of Christ. According to St Paul's Epistle to the Romans, 'the just shall live by faith'. Luther fully developed this 'theology of the cross' in his pamphlet *On Christian Freedom* (1520).

Predestination

Man had no freedom to decide how he should lead his life; God alone determined his fate. All that Luther could do was to follow the precepts of Christ. This idea was expressed in Luther's *The Bondage of the Will* (1525) in response to Erasmus' *A Discourse on Free Will* (1524).

Sola scriptura (by the Scriptures alone)

Since only the Scriptures were free from error, they must be the basis of Christian teaching. In a debate at Leipzig (1519) Luther denied the authority of popes, claiming that only church councils could rule on matters of faith and that both popes and councils were capable of making mistakes.

The papacy

In his *Address to the Christian Nobility of the German Nation* (1520) Luther called on all Germans to:

- stop paying fees and taxes to the Pope
- end appeals to Rome
- insist that the emperor appointed bishops to German dioceses

In his pamphlet *Babylonish Captivity of the Church* (1520) Luther claimed that:
- the Church had been forced into a state of paganism by a Babylon-styled papacy
- the Pope was really the Antichrist, intent upon destroying the German people

Sacraments

In 1519–20 Luther developed his ideas on the **seven sacraments**. He believed that only three were to be found in the Scriptures: baptism, the **Eucharist** and penance (later he rejected penance as well). By denying the other four sacraments he implied that priests were in no way special, declaring in the *Babylonish Captivity of the Church*, 'we are all equally priests'. As a result, Luther claimed that both bread and wine should be offered to the laity at communion and that Christ was really present (consubstantiation) but did not enter the communicant (Catholics believed that the substances of bread and wine did change into the body and blood of Christ — a belief known as transubstantiation).

Eucharist: also known as the Mass, the Eucharist was a ceremony in which the priest blessed the bread and wine at the altar in celebration of Christ's suffering on the cross.
purgatory: where souls are purged of sins before entering Heaven.
seven sacraments: baptism, confirmation, marriage, extreme unction (last rites), penance, the Eucharist and ordination were the basic beliefs of the Christian faith taught by the Roman Catholic Church.
Treasury of Merits: in 1343 the papacy declared that, as a result of Christ's suffering on the cross and the good works of saints, it had unlimited merits at its disposal to enable penitents to go to Heaven.

This topic appears at AS in the OCR, Edexcel and AQA (Alternative B) specifications. You might be asked: 'How did the views and theology of Luther differ from those of the Catholic Church?' Ensure that you understand the main terms associated with Luther's ideas, such as indulgences, *sola fide*, *sola scriptura*, consubstantiation and purgatory, before discussing his motives in challenging the papacy and orthodox Catholic beliefs.

3   *What progress had Lutheranism made by 1555?*

3.1 Reaction to Luther by secular authorities, 1517–21

Frederick the Wise

As patron of Wittenberg University, Frederick the Wise, the Elector of Saxony, took a keen interest in the welfare of his professor of biblical studies. Frederick was also anxious to safeguard his lands from his cousin, George, Duke of Saxony, whom he suspected would seize the chance to use the heretical Luther as a pretext for war. As a German prince, Frederick was in theory subject to the emperor but in practice he was more than capable of protecting Luther. Indeed, he refused to hand Luther to the papal authorities until he had had a fair hearing. When this occurred at Worms in 1521, Frederick absented himself but arranged for Luther to be 'kidnapped' and spirited away to a secluded castle at Wartburg (Saxony) for his own protection.

Charles V

Elected Holy Roman Emperor in 1519, Charles met Luther for the only time at the Diet of Worms. Having listened to Luther expound his views and then refuse to compromise or recant, Charles banned him from the empire and called upon the princes to enforce the ban. In fact, he could do little more: he had no army, little money and many other problems to consider both in Germany and in the rest of his monarchy. Moreover, he had to rely on Frederick and princes like him if he were to establish his authority in the empire.

3.2 Reaction to Luther by religious authorities, 1517–21

Dominicans

The Dominicans opposed Luther for a number of reasons and in a number of ways:
- Luther was a member of the rival Augustinian order of monks.
- John Tetzel, who had hoped to sell indulgences in Wittenberg, was a Dominican and in 1518 he accused Luther of being a heretic.
- Cardinal Cajetan, the official Dominican representative in Rome, was sent to Germany in 1518 to make Luther take back his views on indulgences.
- Dr Eck, a theology professor from Ingolstadt, debated with Luther at Leipzig University (1519), a Dominican stronghold in ducal Saxony. Eck taunted Luther by calling him a **Hussite**. Luther retorted by declaring that Hus was not a heretic.

The papacy

Pope Leo X (1513–21) had a personal interest in German indulgences. Most of the money collected went to him and anyone who condemned this practice had to be silenced. In 1518 Prierias, a papal spokesman, wrote to Luther reminding him that popes were infallible and Cardinal Cajetan, the papal legate in Germany, tried to get him to admit at Augsburg that he was in the wrong. Luther refused. Prierias condemned Luther and confirmed papal infallibility in the Refutation (1519), which goaded Luther into writing three pamphlets in 1520: *Address to the Christian Nobility of the German Nation*, *Babylonish Captivity of the Church* and *On Christian Freedom*.

In the 1520 bull '*Exsurge Domine*' the papacy listed 41 errors in Luther's teachings. When Luther burned the bull in a public ceremony in Wittenberg (December 1520), the papacy officially excommunicated him (1521) and left his fate in the hands of the emperor.

3.3 The progress of Lutheranism, 1521–30

Imperial knights

A small group of knights took up Lutheranism for a number of reasons:
- Franz von Sickingen, a nationalist, saw a chance to seize Church lands and extend his power.
- Ulrich von Hutten, a humanist, was proud of German culture and wanted to end papal and clerical influence in Germany.
- All knights were anxious to halt their political decline at the hands of princes and cities. In 1522 they used their armies to besiege Church lands belonging to the Archbishop of Trier. The knights were finally beaten at Landstuhl (1523) by the princes and their troops. Von Sickingen was killed and von Hutten fled to Switzerland.

Peasants

Many peasants supported Luther in the early 1520s. They saw him as a prophet sent by God to lead them against their oppressive landlords. Some interpreted Luther's

references to 'Godly law' and 'we are all one body' as messages of equality and freedom, and as justification to seize Church property. Rising levels of taxation, poor harvests in 1523–24 and landlords' attempts to reintroduce feudal practices brought as many as 100,000 peasants to revolt, mainly in the west and south of Germany. A list of grievances, the Twelve Articles of Memmingen, was drawn up in 1525. Luther was appalled and condemned their acts of violence in *Against the Robbing and Murdering Hordes of Peasants*. The revolt was brutally put down by the princes at Frankenhausen (1525). Rural support for Luther, although strong, was never again so widespread.

Princes

Between 1524 and 1529 six princes, led by Philip of Hesse, Albrecht of Hohenzollern and John of Saxony, committed themselves to Lutheranism. Their main motives were to:

- eliminate clerical corruption
- spread Lutheranism in Germany
- get control of Church assets
- prevent further peasant revolts
- increase their political power at the expense of the emperor

The majority of princes stayed loyal to the emperor and Pope in the 1520s, although none attempted to enforce the ban against Luther. Those in the south of Germany had to take into account the Catholic orthodoxy and military power of the Wittelsbach and Habsburg families. In the centre, Duke George of Saxony and in the west the prince-bishops of Mainz, Trier and Cologne deterred many from open conversion. Charles was absent from Germany, however, and his brother Ferdinand was preoccupied with the Turks for much of the 1520s. As a result, in 1526 at the Diet of Speyer, princes were allowed to practise Lutheranism if they wished. Only in 1529, when Ferdinand was in a stronger position, was this decree reversed. Six princes 'protested'.

Towns and cities

Recent studies have revealed that towns and cities reacted to Lutheranism in different ways. In some:

- the council introduced vernacular services, a mixture of traditional and new prayers, and ensured that reforms were introduced slowly (e.g. at Wittenberg)
- a debate was followed by a referendum on whether to reform the Church (e.g. at Ulm)
- preachers persuaded the council to introduce changes, but all decisions were taken constitutionally (e.g. at Nuremberg)
- local guilds played a decisive role in influencing the council's decision (e.g. at Memmingen)
- to maintain order and minimise changes, Lutheran, Catholic and radical sects were tolerated (e.g. at Strassburg)
- strong anti-clerical attitudes proved decisive (e.g. at Lübeck)

By 1529 some 14 out of 65 imperial or 'free' cities had joined six princes in signing the Protestation against the imperial decree banning Lutheran practices.

Luther's view of radicals

Luther was always concerned about the unity of the Christian Church and in the 1520s he became alarmed at the growing number of radical sects, each of which claimed to profess the true faith:

- Ulrich Zwingli, a Swiss reformer, had much in common with Luther. They met at Marburg (1529) and agreed on all but one article of faith — the Eucharist. Luther believed in consubstantiation (Christ was present in the sacraments); Zwingli believed in sacramentarianism (the sacraments symbolised the body and blood of Christ). By 1529 Zwinglianism was practised in at least six south German cities (e.g. Ulm and Augsburg).
- Andreas Carlstadt, a lecturer at Wittenberg, demanded the immediate reform of Catholic images, monasteries and **celibacy**. In 1521–22 he was joined by the **prophets of Zwickau**, who smashed churches, attacked the clergy and rejected the Mass in favour of a vernacular service. Luther condemned this iconoclasm in a series of sermons — the '*Invocavit*' (1522) — and the radicals were expelled from the town by the council.
- Anabaptists denied child baptism and were condemned by Luther as revolutionaries. Some, like Thomas Müntzer, rejected the Bible in favour of the 'inner word' and reform by the sword; some believed in the fellowship of all men, women and children and in the common possession of goods. All believed that the world was about to end and Christ would return to earth to save the chosen few.

The importance of printing

The press gave Luther the means to attack the Church, to reveal the true faith and to become a national celebrity. In the 1520s he published:

- a German New Testament based on Erasmus' Greek edition
- a German Mass
- a textbook of sermons
- a book of hymns
- a small and a great catechism (for children and adults respectively)

3.4 The progress of Lutheranism, 1530–55

The Schmalkaldic League, 1531

Philip Melanchthon, Luther's principal spokesman, drew up the Augsburg Confession (1530), which outlined their main beliefs. At the Diet of Augsburg, held later that year, Charles rejected it, fearing any agreement might lead to a permanent schism in the Church. Several German princes and cities reacted by forming an army and at Schmalkalden they pledged to defend their right to worship freely.

In the course of the 1530s, support for Lutheranism grew as preachers travelled to the north and west of the empire. Charles was preoccupied for much of this period, having to contend with persistent challenges from the Turks and France. He hoped in vain that the Pope would call a general council to resolve the issue. In 1541 Charles agreed to a meeting at Regensburg where Melanchthon met Contarini, a leading Catholic theologian. Their failure to secure a settlement did not spell the end of reconciliation — further talks were held at Speyer and Regensburg, and offers of toleration were dangled in front of the Lutherans — but Charles was playing for time. By 1546 he was ready to take military action. He had an army, the support of several princes, and was confident that neither France nor the Turks would interfere.

Mühlberg, 1547

Charles' army, composed of Spanish, Italian and German troops, defeated the Lutheran princes at Mühlberg in 1547. Their leaders — John Frederick of Saxony and Philip of Hesse — were taken prisoner. On the strength of this success, Charles proposed the

Interim (1548) as a compromise solution to the religious problem, but it was rejected by both Catholics and Lutherans. Furthermore, in 1550 several northern princes revived the League of Torgau to defend Lutheranism, and in 1551 Maurice of Saxony, disappointed at not being well rewarded for supporting the emperor, defected to them.

The Peace of Augsburg, 1555

The emperor was represented by Ferdinand at the Diet of Augsburg, where it was declared that:

- princes were allowed to establish either Lutheranism or Catholicism — a principle known as 'cuius regio, eius religio'
- territories ruled by a Catholic in 1552 had to stay Catholic
- no Catholic state was allowed to convert to Lutheranism but a Lutheran state could return to Catholicism — a clause known as the 'ecclesiastical reservation'

Conclusion

In 1555 the majority of German princes and at least 50 of the 65 free cities had become Lutheran. Although only states ruled by princes were acknowledged at Augsburg, Lutheranism continued to be practised in the majority of imperial cities and towns in the empire. Other Protestant faiths, however, such as Zwinglianism, Calvinism and Anabaptism, were still not legally recognised.

GLOSSARY

celibacy: the belief that priests should be unmarried.

Hussite: a follower of Jan Hus, a Bohemian heretic who rejected the authority of the Pope and was burned at the stake in 1415.

prophets of Zwickau: a handful of Bohemian preachers who travelled to Zwickau and were expelled on account of their radical views.

EXAMINER'S TIP

This subject appears at AS in the OCR, Edexcel and AQA (Alternative B) specifications. You might be asked: 'Why did Luther appeal to so many people in Germany?' You should consider the motives of Luther's supporters, which aspects of his theology they found attractive and why the Reformation began in Germany. Analyse 'people' according to princes, knights, humanists, peasants and urban dwellers.

(1) How did Charles V's political relations with his German subjects change, 1519–56?

(2) How was the Holy Roman Empire affected by Charles V's wars, 1519–59?

1 How did Charles V's political relations with his German subjects change, 1519–56?

1.1 Charles' inheritance

In 1519 Charles was elected Holy Roman Emperor. He was already Duke of Burgundy (1515), King of Spain (1516) and Archduke of Austria (1519). His *monarquía* comprised:

- Franche-Comté, Luxemburg and the Netherlands
- Spain, Naples, Sicily, Sardinia and the New World (see Unit 7)
- Austria, including Styria, Carinthia, Carniola, Tyrol, Alsace, East Swabia, the Vorlande and Upper Rhineland
- the Holy Roman Empire, comprising over 300 German states

1.2 Problems in the empire

There were several problems connected with the Holy Roman Empire, including:

- powerful German knights and princes
- ineffective government: Charles had no army, no regular taxation and no central administration
- the Lutheran threat to Church unity
- French claims to Burgundy
- the Turkish threat to east German and Austrian Habsburg lands

Charles' greatest problem was keeping effective control over such a massive monarchy. His enemies were likely to exploit his absences and force him to divide his financial and military resources.

1.3 Charles' aims

Charles' aims were:

- to protect his inheritance
- to rule his lands effectively with the minimum of change
- to defend the Catholic faith from Muslims and Protestants

1.4 Burgundy

The eight provinces of the Netherlands, Franche-Comté and Luxemburg were governed by a succession of Habsburg regents: Charles (1515–17), his aunt Margaret (1518–30) and his sister Mary (1531–55). Rudimentary machinery for a more centralised government existed — a council of state, privy council, States-General (national assembly), law courts and provincial assemblies — but Charles and his regents were unwilling to risk losing the support of the most politically important groups. The grandees were thus admitted to the prestigious Order of the Golden Fleece and enjoyed the benefits of ducal

patronage, the nobility were left in charge of provincial administration, and wealthy merchants continued to dominate town politics.

Policies

- To bring the states under more central control.
- To extend Charles' rule over adjoining provinces.
- To increase taxation to fund his monarchy.
- To eliminate heresy.

Main developments

The eight provinces had little in common with Charles or each other but between 1515 and 1543 Charles acquired nine more states by military and political pressure: Tournai (1521), Friesland (1523), Utrecht (1527), Overjssel (1528), Groningen and Drenthe (1536), Cambrai, Zutphen and Gelderland (1543). In 1548 they were organised into a single unit independent of the empire. A new court of appeal and a council of finance (1531) gave the administration a veneer of centralisation but in practice the 17 provinces known as the Netherlands had little political unity.

When changes did occur there was opposition in three areas of the administration:

- The establishment of the Inquisition (1522). It was set up to prevent the spread of Protestantism but was viewed as a means of extending state authority.
- A plan to introduce a standing army (1534) was vigorously opposed by the States-General.
- Increases in taxation provoked riots and disturbances at Tournai, Bois-le-Duc, Brussels and Ghent. Charles was particularly severe on his birthplace: as a result of its rebellion in 1539 Ghent lost its charter, was heavily fined and had a new fortress built in the town.

Conclusion

Charles received substantial taxes from the Netherlands, which enabled him to wage war against French, German and Turkish enemies. In return his regents recognised the need to work with the grandees, nobles and merchants, and to preserve the states' privileges and federalism. The towns bore the brunt of taxation, which led to poverty, revolts and resentment.

1.5 Austrian lands

In 1522 Charles transferred the administration of his family estates in Austria to his brother Ferdinand. Ferdinand's main policies were:

- to enlist Hungarian and Austrian nobles to collect taxes and enforce the law
- to defend his lands from the Turks (see section 2.2 below)
- to leave untouched the regional diets and chancelleries
- to reform Catholic churches to counter the growth of Protestantism

1.6 Germany

The Holy Roman Empire was divided into ten administrative circles. Each one supervised justice, finance and defence in the name of the emperor, although in practice real authority rested with the sovereign princes, imperial knights and free cities. For instance, the princes controlled the Swabian League, which upheld order in southwest Germany. In advance of his election in 1519, Charles had to promise constitutional reforms which in theory would give the princes even more power (e.g. he promised not to employ foreigners in his government).

At the Diet of Worms (1521) the princes also requested:

- the restoration of the supreme court
- the right to appoint 18 of the 22 members of a new regency council

In practice, neither reform had a lasting effect. The supreme court never commanded the support of princes and cities, and had no jurisdiction over religious matters; and the council only met in the emperor's absence and ceased to function after 1530.

Following his victory at Mühlberg over the Lutheran princes, Charles for the first time felt strong enough to insist on major constitutional changes. At the Diet of Augsburg (1547–48) Charles declared that:

- a new supreme court would be established, which would hear ecclesiastical cases
- a new regency council would be set up but without any princes
- a military league would be formed under his control and funded by princes and cities

In effect, these proposals were short-lived. Once Charles' authority declined in the early 1550s in the face of opposition from both Catholic and Lutheran princes, none of these reforms was implemented. German princes and cities were not willing to see the creation of a strong imperial monarchy.

1.7 The political impact of Luther

Charles first confronted Luther at Worms in 1521. Having decided to ban him from the empire, the emperor needed his princes to carry out the edict. None was willing to do so and some, such as Frederick of Saxony and Ludwig of the Palatinate, never signed the ban. Divisions between Catholic and Lutheran princes deepened at the Diets of Nuremberg (1522–24) and resulted in the formation of two armed groups, namely:

- the League of Dessau (1525), formed by Catholic princes (e.g. the Duke of Bavaria)
- the League of Torgau (1526), formed by reformist princes (e.g. Philip of Hesse)

Between 1524 and 1526 both Catholic and Lutheran princes took action to suppress the peasant revolts. Once order had been restored, the Lutherans pressed for religious freedom. In 1526 Ferdinand, acting on behalf of the emperor, conceded this demand at the first Diet of Speyer (known as the 'recess') but 3 years later he revoked his decision at the second Diet of Speyer. He declared that:

- no freedom would be granted to Lutherans in Catholic lands
- Catholics must be tolerated in Lutheran states
- there must be no more evangelical reforms

The resulting protest, from six princes and 14 cities, saw the birth of Protestantism (1529) and the formation of the Schmalkaldic League (1531) to defend them. The likelihood of war breaking out between rival confessional groups in Germany existed but did not occur in the 1530s because the emperor was preoccupied with defending his Mediterranean possessions (see section 2 below).

In 1547 Charles was ready to attack but his victory at Mühlberg was too decisive. The Catholic princes, who had supported him, rejected his plan to establish an imperial army and the Lutheran princes resurrected the League of Torgau. When French and Turkish troops joined the league in 1552, Charles' humiliation was complete. Ferdinand negotiated a truce with the Lutherans but was unable to stop France from seizing the German bishopric of Metz. Charles was a broken man.

Ferdinand attended the Diet of Augsburg (1555), which conceded to the princes the right to decide the religion of their lands. Charles never returned to Germany. In a series of

carefully staged ceremonies in 1555–56 he abdicated first as Duke of Burgundy, then as King of Spain and Duke of Milan, and finally as Holy Roman Emperor (though he retained this title until 1558). Throughout the later Middle Ages the German princes had consolidated their power, but it was Lutheranism that had finally enabled them to assert themselves at the emperor's expense.

This topic appears at AS in the OCR and Edexcel specifications and at A2 in the AQA (Alternative B) specification. You might be asked to explain why Charles' authority in Germany was so ineffective. The relationship between princes, knights, peasants, towns and emperor needs to be examined, as well as the impact of Lutheranism and Charles' commitments elsewhere. In the limited time you have at your disposal, ensure you give a balanced response.

2 How was the Holy Roman Empire affected by Charles V's wars, 1519–59?

2.1 The Habsburg–Valois conflict, 1521–59

Between 1494 and 1516 France and Spain had been contesting the right to rule Naples and Milan. Their dynastic conflict was fought out mainly in Italy but it had occasionally spilled over into Burgundy and Navarre, and involved England, Venice, Florence, the papacy and the emperor. At Charles' accession to the imperial throne, he held Naples and was keen to oust French troops from Milan, which was a vital link in the Austrian–Spanish Habsburg line of communications. On the other hand, Francis I, King of France (1515–47), was desperate to break this potential Habsburg encirclement of his country.

Events, 1521–29
- French troops invaded Spanish Navarre but were beaten at Pampeluna (1521).
- The Spanish Army defeated France at Bicocca and seized Milan (1522).
- The French Army was beaten at Pavia (1525); Francis I was taken prisoner to Madrid.
- On his release, Francis formed the League of Cognac (1526) and allied with the Turks against Charles.
- Imperial troops occupied the Papal States and sacked Rome (1527).
- The French campaign against Naples ended when the Genoese naval commander, Andreas Doria, deserted to Spain (1528).
- Imperial troops defeated a French army at Landriano (1529).

At the Treaties of Barcelona (between Charles and the Pope) and Cambrai (between Charles and Francis), signed in 1529:
- France gave up its claim to Milan, Naples, Genoa, Artois and Flanders
- the Medicis were restored to Florence as papal clients
- the Sforzas were restored to Milan as Spanish clients

The Pope recognised Charles as Holy Roman Emperor (1530) and Ferdinand as his successor, King of the Romans (1531). The Habsburgs effectively ruled Italy and were close to encircling France.

Events, 1536–59
- In 1536 the Duke of Milan died. French troops occupied Savoy and invaded Milan.

- Charles allowed Francis to keep Savoy at the Truce of Nice (1538).
- Following the murder of two French envoys Francis invaded Nice (1542) and lay claim to Artois, Brabant, Luxemburg, Milan and Roussillon.
- Charles recovered Savoy (1543), captured Cambrai and kept both of them at the Treaty of Crépy (1544).
- Henry II, King of France (1547–59), signed the Treaty of Chambord (1552) with Lutheran princes in return for holding the German bishoprics of Metz, Toul and Verdun.
- Charles' failure to recapture Metz sapped his morale (1553).
- French troops invaded Milan and Naples (1555).
- Charles abdicated, handing over Burgundy (1555) and Spain (1556) to Philip.
- Ferdinand became emperor (1558).

At the Treaty of Cateau-Cambrésis (1559), negotiated by Philip II and Henry II:
- Spain was confirmed as the ruler of Milan and Naples
- France kept the imperial towns of Metz, Toul and Verdun, as well as Calais from England

Conclusion

After more than 60 years of fighting, Spain emerged as the dominant power in Italy but France had reduced the Habsburg threat of encirclement. Both countries were financially exhausted. The Holy Roman Empire no longer included Milan and the Netherlands, and three bishoprics had been lost to France; but more importantly, the emperor had seen German Lutherans, French Catholics and Turkish Muslims combine to weaken his power in the empire.

2.2 The Ottoman conflict

In 1519 the Ottoman Turks were advancing westwards through the Balkans towards Hungary and the eastern Adriatic, southeastwards into Syria and Egypt, and threatening central and eastern Mediterranean trade routes (see Unit 7). The Muslims were intent on a holy war against Christianity and the western empire looked to Charles to counter them.

Events, 1521–58

- Suleiman the Magnificent, the Turkish sultan (1520–66), seized Belgrade (1521) and Rhodes (1522) and expelled the Knights of St John, who went to Malta.
- Charles, preoccupied in Spain and Italy for most of the 1520s, delegated the defence of his Austrian lands to Ferdinand (1522).
- Suleiman killed the King of Hungary at Mohacs (1526).
- Turkish troops besieged Vienna for 3 weeks (1529) before retreating 80 miles away.
- Charles repelled Turkish armies at Güns (1532).
- Ferdinand retreated from Buda (1541) and lost most of Hungary.
- Ferdinand agreed at Adrianople (1547) to pay the sultan an annual tribute of 30,000 ducats.
- Imperial troops failed to remove the Turks from Transylvania (1550).
- Spanish garrisons were expelled from Tunis (1534), Algiers (1541), Tripoli, Bougie and Peñón de Vélez (1550s) in north Africa.

Conclusion

The western expansion of the Ottoman Empire contributed to and benefited from the disunity in the Holy Roman Empire. German princes exploited the Ottoman threat by

forcing the emperor to make political and religious concessions at Speyer (1526) and Nuremberg (1532), when his fortunes were low. Charles later admitted that he had been forced to compromise his faith to attend to the Turks. Indeed, his only significant triumph against the Lutherans, at Mühlberg (1547), was achieved safe in the knowledge that Suleiman was engaged in wars against Persia.

EXAMINER'S TIP

This topic appears at AS in the OCR specification and at A2 in the AQA (Alternative B) specification. If you are asked to explain how Charles' wars influenced affairs in the Holy Roman Empire, you should discuss the nature of his religious, political and financial problems in Germany and how his French, Lutheran and Turkish enemies exploited them. Studying a map of Charles' monarchy will help you to understand why its size and lack of unity proved so troublesome. A typical AS question is: 'How serious for the Holy Roman Empire were the results of Charles V's prolonged wars with the kings of France?'

(1) What was significant about Calvin's ideas and influence in Geneva?
(2) Why was Calvinism popular in France and the Netherlands?
(3) How effective was opposition to Calvinism in France and the Netherlands?

1 What was significant about Calvin's ideas and influence in Geneva?

1.1 Background

Born in France in 1509, Calvin studied theology and law at university. In 1531–32 he underwent a religious experience, convinced that he was 'chosen by God to proclaim the truth'. His Protestant views were unpopular in Paris and in 1534–36 he travelled to Switzerland, Germany and Italy before arriving in Geneva. Having just published his *Institutes of the Christian Religion* (1536), he was persuaded to help reform the city.

1.2 Calvin's ideas

The *Institutes* outlined Calvin's main theological ideas. Written as a six-chapter introduction to the Christian faith, they were subsequently revised three times until the final edition of 1559 comprised four books and 80 chapters. Calvin's main ideas concerned:

- justification by faith alone: God was all-knowing and all-powerful. The only way to understand God's word was to study the Scriptures and lead a morally pure life
- predestination: those with faith were sure of salvation — a doctrine known as 'single predestination'; those without faith were certain to be damned — known as 'double predestination'. God, not man, had chosen the elect and the reprobates (damned)
- good works: like the first generation of Protestant reformers, Calvin denounced indulgences, pilgrimages, fasting, the collecting of relics and similar 'good works'
- sacraments: only baptism and the Eucharist had any scriptural basis. He rejected the Catholic belief in transubstantiation, arguing that Christ was spiritually present at communion (Luther believed in the real presence and Zwingli in the symbolic presence of Christ)

The *Ecclesiastical Ordinances* (1541) explained how Calvin intended to organise the Church and to reform Geneva as a model city:

- The Church would be ruled by four officers: pastors (who belonged to the Venerable Company and were required to preach, teach and administer the sacraments); doctors (teachers who were assisted by a catechism written by Calvin in 1542); deacons (who cared for the sick and poor); and elders (who maintained standards of behaviour).
- Religious, social and moral discipline was imposed by a consistory (made up of all of the pastors and 12 elders). Punishments ranged from gentle rebukes to public confession, from exclusion from communion to excommunication, and occasionally exile or death.

Calvin's ideas were not original. Most could be found in the writing of St Paul and St Augustine and had been voiced by Luther, Zwingli and Bucer. Calvin brought two distinctive qualities to the Reformation, however:

- He explained complex ideas clearly and logically to a lay audience.
- He created a Church organisation that embraced social and moral issues as well as religion.

1.3 Calvinism in Geneva
Genevan politics, 1536–41

In 1536 the city of Geneva was in political and religious turmoil. Its 10,000 citizens were governed by four syndics drawn from the Small Council of 24 members and elected by a General Council of 200. The Small Council was divided by rival factions — some politicians were pro-Bernese, some pro-French and some pro-Savoy. Most were anxious to retain the city's recently won independence and were keen to reform the Church but unsure how best to proceed.

Between 1536 and 1540 the prevailing Articulant faction sought an alliance with neighbouring Berne and expelled Calvin (in 1538). The council wished to keep control over Church affairs and resented his uncompromising views. They soon lost much of their Church revenue and political independence to Berne, however. In 1541 a new faction, the Guillarmins, won control and invited Calvin to return.

Politics, 1541–54

Between 1541 and 1554 Calvin's position was far from secure. He was consistently criticised by opponents who despised his influence, his radical ideas and the fact that he was a foreigner. On several occasions he was brought before the consistory to explain his conduct:

- In 1547 he was cautioned for remarks made in his sermons.
- In 1548 he was reprimanded for calling the magistrates 'gargoyle monkeys'.
- In 1552 he refused to baptise a child with the name of Claude because he considered it to be unchristian.

Dealing with opposition

Calvin liked to appear as the defender of Christian values and a man of moderation. In practice he was intolerant of any critic or dissenter, and backed the secular authorities in imposing harsh punishments upon his opponents:

- In 1544 Sebastian Castellio, a teacher, was expelled for claiming that the biblical 'Song of Songs' was an erotic poem.
- In 1546 Pierre Ameaux, a councillor, was ordered to beg forgiveness from the city magistrates for accusing Calvin of teaching 'false doctrine'.
- In 1547 Jacques Gruet was executed for ridiculing the Bible.
- In 1551 Jerome Bolsec was exiled for criticising the doctrine of predestination.
- In 1553 Michael Servetus, a Spanish theologian, was burned at the stake for rejecting the **Trinity**, justification by faith and infant baptism in a book, *The Restoration of Christianity*.
- In 1555 Ami Perrin, captain-general of the city's militia and councillor, claimed that Calvin and his French pastors were trying to take over Geneva. When Perrin was voted off the council his supporters (known as Libertins) resorted to public demonstrations and were condemned to death or exile. Perrin fled the city.

Reforms, 1555–64

More than 7,000 French refugees entered Geneva in the early 1550s. Many gained citizen status and voted a majority of Calvinists onto the council. After 1555 they in turn controlled the selection of elders. As a result, the consistory acquired magisterial authority and exercised its right to excommunication. Henceforth Calvin's position was secure.

Calvin's *Ecclesiastical Ordinances* created a civil and religious structure whereby he could shape the city spiritually, morally and politically. Magistrates and clergy worked together in the consistory to enforce the city's laws and implement reforms in the following areas:

- Morality: Calvin set out his moral code in a *Book of Discipline*. Gambling, swearing, drunkenness, dancing in public, wearing ostentatious clothes and Sabbath-breaking were all condemned.
- Religious education: to ensure all citizens knew the basic Christian theology, the consistory conducted tests every year. Communion was withheld until they had proved their competence or undertaken extra lessons each Sunday.
- The Academy: established in 1559 for the training of future missionaries and political leaders, the Academy was run by Theodore Beza (Calvin's successor). By 1564, at Calvin's death, it had over 1,500 students.
- Quarrels: every effort was made to resolve private arguments, especially between a husband and wife. The consistory stressed the importance of living together harmoniously; divorce was countenanced, but only as a last resort.

Conclusion

At his death Calvin left Geneva with:

- a Church and state that worked together and had clearly defined functions
- a learned company of pastors
- an internationally renowned academy
- a consistory that effectively enforced moral and religious discipline

In the opinion of John Knox, a leading Scottish Calvinist, it was 'the perfect city of Christ'.

GLOSSARY

Trinity: the belief that there is one God and that the Father, the Son and the Holy Spirit are each God and that they are also each a distinct person.

EXAMINER'S TIP

This topic appears at AS in the AQA (Alternative B) specification and at A2 in the Edexcel specification. A typical AS question is: 'Calvin's success in Geneva was due to the organisation and discipline of the movement rather than to his theology. How far do you agree with this statement?' You should assess both the structure and the ideas of Calvinism, compare their relative merits and link them to the movement's success before reaching a verdict. Try to identify one factor as being more important than any of the others.

2 Why was Calvinism popular in France and the Netherlands?

2.1 France, 1541–62

In the course of the 1550s Calvinism became a popular minority faith in France. Though Catholicism was the only lawful religion and the death penalty awaited any heretic, the numbers of people converting to the reformed Church dramatically increased.

- In 1555 the first Calvinist church was established in Paris.
- In 1557 a synod at Poitiers approved a set of articles binding on all Calvinist churches.
- In 1559 a group of aristocrats met in Paris to agree on a French confession of faith.
- In 1562 one contemporary estimated there were 2,150 Calvinist churches. They were mainly located in a wide arc, stretching from the west coast south of the Loire to Périgord and the Dordogne, and east to Provence and Dauphine.

Reasons for the growth of Calvinism in France

- Calvin was French. In 1541 he published a French edition of his *Institutes* and *Ordinances*, and he kept in close contact with his homeland. In 1544 he wrote an open letter to the **Nicodemites**, calling upon all French people to reject the Mass and be ready to accept persecution.
- Geneva was situated close to France. When the French government persecuted Protestants, more than 5,000 refugees arrived in the 1550s. Many exiles trained at the Academy to be pastors and missionaries — 88 pastors returned to France between 1555 and 1562.
- French nobles saw the chance to gain control of their Church and to introduce reforms. Over one third of ministers who left Geneva for France were nobles. Many converted their friends and relatives until, by 1562, 50% of all nobles had become Calvinist.
- Many literate urban groups, lesser clergy and mendicant friars were drawn to Calvin's theology.
- In the growing climate of persecution Calvinism fostered a sense of self-assurance and the inevitability of its eventual triumph over Catholicism.
- Its hierarchical structure of district consistories, regional colloquies (conferences) and national synods (assemblies) gave Calvinism a cohesion and unity, making it capable of expansion.
- The monarchy was weak after 1559. The deaths of Henry II (1559) and Francis II (1560) and the fact that Charles IX was a minor brought Catherine de Medici to power as regent. She proclaimed her tolerance of Calvinists in the Edict of January (1562): Calvinists were allowed to worship and preach outside towns, and the nobles held services on their own lands.

2.2 The Netherlands, 1555–72

Charles V had established an inquisition in the Netherlands in 1522 and was keen to enforce the heresy laws. A spirit of free criticism prevailed, however — Erasmus was popular and Lutheranism was practised in the more literate circles. The absence of a centralised administration saw Protestantism flourish in the 1540s, and in the 1550s Calvinism became a popular faith in the southern towns. In 1554 a reformed Church was established in Antwerp and, in the course of the next decade, 10% of the population took up the faith.

Reasons for the popularity of Calvinism in the Netherlands

- Bibles, catechisms and the *Institutes* were published in Dutch; in 1560 Calvin appealed to people to declare their faith openly.
- Refugees went to stranger churches in London and Emden (in Germany) in the 1540s and returned in the 1550s. Further persecutions in the 1560s saw 7,000 refugees flee to England and Germany. Their determination to survive increased the appeal of their faith.
- Theories of resistance were developed. In 1561 Calvin had suggested that, although

subjects had a duty to obey their magistrate (governor), if that magistrate was a royal prince who in turn rebelled against a sovereign ruler for reasons of conscience, then subjects could also resist their ruler.

- Lesser nobles (e.g. Philip of Marnix and Louis of Nassau) adopted Calvinism in protest against the policies of Philip II, especially his attempts to hispanicise the Dutch and use the Inquisition to stamp out heresy. Dutch liberties were at stake. By 1565 some 400 nobles had signed the Compromise, opposing the nature of Spanish rule.
- French Calvinism (known as Huguenotism) spread in the 1560s. Some Dutch grandees were related to French converts (e.g. the Hornes and Egmonts were related to the Montmorencies, and Baron Montigny's cousin was the Constable of France).
- The Spanish governor, Margaret, weakened in the face of growing Dutch demands for religious toleration. **Hedge-priests** exploited the absence of an effective central administration and drew massive crowds outside the towns. In 1566 preachers led 5 days of iconoclasm and rioting in Antwerp and nearby towns in Flanders and Holland.

GLOSSARY

hedge-priests: preachers who delivered a sermon in open fields and disappeared over hedges when the authorities tried to arrest them.

Nicodemites: they (like Nicodemus) hid their true feelings to avoid detection.

EXAMINER'S TIP

This subject appears at AS in the AQA (Alternative B) specification and at A2 in the Edexcel specification. You might be asked: 'How do you explain Calvin's appeal in France and the Netherlands in the period up to 1572?' This kind of question requires you to offer an explanation and, where possible, to find reasons that were common to both countries (e.g. the oppressive nature of Catholicism, the weakness of central governments after 1559, and predestination).

---

3 How effective was opposition to Calvinism in France and the Netherlands?

3.1 France (to 1562)

The majority of French people were Catholic and expected their king to uphold his coronation oath to defend the Church. Therefore:

- Francis I banned Calvin's works in 1542
- Henry II set up the Chambre Ardente (1547) to try heresy cases: by 1550, 500 heretics had been sentenced
- the Edict of Chateaubriand (1551) imposed heavy fines and imprisonment on anyone who was in contact with Calvinists
- the Edict of Compiègne (1557) imposed the death penalty on all heretics

The *parlement* of Paris and the Sorbonne also took a firm stance against heresy. The main source of opposition to Calvinism, however, came from the Guise family, especially in 1559–62, when the Crown was weak. Sectarian murders increased as Catholics took the law into their own hands (e.g. the Duke of Guise and his troops murdered 70 Calvinists in a barn at Vassy in April 1562 and massacres occurred at Sens, Tours, Anjou,

Carcassonne and Bar-sur-Seine in August of that year).

3.2 The Netherlands (to 1572)

Philip II's presence in the Netherlands between 1554 and 1559 alerted him to the growing number of students who were taking up Calvinism. As a result, in 1557 he ordered the Delft Inquisition to be more active. Reforms to the dioceses (1561–64) were intended to increase the number of bishops and inquisitors in order to prevent the growth of Calvinism, and 600 prosecutions followed in 1562. The reforms were suspended between 1564 and 1567, however, and Calvinism spread. The arrival of Alva and 10,000 troops in 1568 led to the establishment of the Council of Troubles (nicknamed the 'Council of Blood') and the arrest of 12,000 suspected heretics, of whom 1,100 were executed.

3.3 Conclusion

The authorities in France and the Netherlands had mixed success in their attempts to suppress Calvinism. On the one hand, Calvinism never expanded beyond 10% of the population in both countries — although some of the most influential families adopted the reformed faith. On the other hand, Calvinists, confident that they were the elect, refused to yield to the reprobate Catholics. Politically and socially, France was to be divided by religious intolerance for more than 100 years, while Spain suffered an 80-year war in the Netherlands, which it finally lost.

GLOSSARY

parlement: a body of lawyers who registered royal edicts, heard appeals and presented local grievances to the king.

EXAMINER'S TIP

This topic appears at AS in the AQA (Alternative B) specification and at A2 in the Edexcel specification. You might be asked: 'How effective was opposition to Calvinism in France and the Netherlands in the period to 1572?' Events in both countries need to be evaluated using a balanced approach. One measure of effectiveness is the extent to which Calvinism spread during these years. Explain why no more than 10% of the population was converted.

KEY QUESTIONS

(1) What political and financial problems faced French monarchs, 1515–59?
(2) How absolute was Francis I's government and administration?
(3) What religious issues and problems faced the French Church, 1498–1547?
(4) How successful was France during the Italian and Habsburg–Valois wars, 1499–1559?

1 What political and financial problems faced French monarchs, 1515–59?

1.1 The kings' personalities

Francis I, 1515–47

- Six feet tall, athletic, enjoyed hunting, military campaigns, very courageous.
- Married Claude of France (died 1524) and Eleanor of Portugal (died 1558) and had several mistresses.
- Patron of painters (e.g. Leonardo da Vinci), established Fontainebleau school of art, literate and a bibliophile.

Henry II, 1547–59

- Married Catherine de Medici (died 1589). Was an unfaithful husband — fathered several illegitimate children.
- Stubborn, determined, vindictive.
- Enjoyed sport, especially tennis, jousting, riding.

1.2 Relations with the nobles

Francis I and Henry II relied upon the nobility to provide troops for military campaigns, to keep order in the provinces and to enforce their laws effectively. If the monarch was weak the nobles could present a serious threat to the Crown; if the monarch was strong his aristocratic governors complemented his power. Francis kept his nobles in check in a variety of ways.

Charles of Bourbon

As Constable of France and owner of vast estates in Burgundy, Charles of Bourbon was the most powerful noble in France. When Francis claimed part of Charles' family lands in 1523, Charles plotted against the king and then fled the country. *Parlement*'s report on the case was suppressed by the king because it found against him, but the Crown still took possession of the lands.

Baron de Semblançay

In 1527 the treasurer, Baron de Semblançay, was found guilty by a biased court of defrauding the Crown of 1 million livres and was sentenced to death. In fact, the king owed him money.

Montmorency

Montmorency, the governor of Languedoc, was dismissed in 1542 along with all other governors. All except Montmorency were subsequently reappointed, however.

1.3 Judicial problems

The Crown faced a number of judicial problems in the early sixteenth century. These included:

- lack of uniform administration: procedural confusion existed between central provincial and local courts of law, and in judgements given by itinerant magistrates and appeal court judges. Attempts to reform the system in 1539 failed
- absence of a single law code: Roman law prevailed in the south and **customary law** was practised mainly in the north and centre of France
- limited jurisdiction: the Crown had no legal jurisdiction over the counties of Foix and Périgord, the viscounties of Bigorre, Nebouzau and Soule, or over the principalities of Dauphiné, Béarn and Navarre
- conflict with the *parlements*: Paris and the six regional *parlements* were determined to defend their rights in the face of royal interference. Francis was equally set upon making them submit. In 1518 he threatened the Paris *parlement* with closure if it did not register the terms of the Concordat of Bologna (see section 3.1 below). In 1540 the king suspended the Rouen *parlement* and dismissed its councillors

1.4 Financial problems

Finance was the most serious problem facing Francis I and Henry II. Inherited debts, an inequitable tax system, corrupt officials, inefficient methods of collecting revenue, a decentralised administration and unrealistically high war expenditure caused financial crises in the sixteenth century.

- Francis inherited a debt of 3 million livres, which rose to 6 million in 1547 and 12 million in 1559. Interest repayments were reduced (in 1557), suspended (1558) and finally stopped (1559) when the Crown was effectively bankrupt.
- Corruption existed at every level of the administration (e.g. tax farmers in the 1530s, who collected indirect revenue, only forwarded 25 % to the Treasury).
- The nobility, clergy, royal servants, professional groups, universities and certain towns (e.g. Paris, Lyons) were exempt from paying the main tax on property — the *taille*.
- The *gabelle* tax on salt was only effectively levied on the northern, central and south-eastern provinces.
- Different methods of tax assessment and collection existed in the **pays d'états** and **pays d'élections**. When, in 1519, Francis attempted to extend the appointment of **élus** to Languedoc and Guyenne, the politically important groups objected and he backed down. In Burgundy no new taxes were introduced, nor old ones increased, for fear of rebellion.
- There was no central administration. Instead, two departments operated side by side: one handled ordinary revenue (crown rents and feudal dues); the other dealt with extraordinary revenue (land and indirect duties).
- Wars cost an excessive amount: Francis' first Italian campaign (1515–17) cost 1.8 million livres; his campaigns in the 1530s cost 5 million; and those in the 1540s cost over 20 million livres.

Solutions

Attempts were made to remedy the situation. The most important were:

- a variety of expedients to increase revenue (e.g. the sale of government bonds, crown lands, and offices; the imposition of forced loans); public loans were negotiated (e.g. the Grand Parti de Lyon in 1555); direct and indirect taxes were extended

- a central treasury, the Trésor d'Epargne, which was set up to supervise administration in 1523
- the division of France into 16 districts (généralités) in 1542 to centralise the collection of all royal income and end the dual revenue system

Conclusion

The Crown's financial administration became more centralised, uniform and simplified during the period 1515–59. Royal revenue doubled due to the increase in taxation but the methods of assessment and collection remained anomalous; corruption went unchecked and expenditure outstripped income.

customary law: laws drawn from feudal and local traditions.
élus: the Crown's chief financial inspectors in local administration.
pays d'élections: provinces where taxes were levied by Crown officials.
pays d'états: provinces where taxes were levied by local estates.

This topic appears at AS in the OCR specification. If you are asked to examine the Crown's financial problems in the period 1515–59, you will need to assess the financial administration, the sources of revenue and expenditure, and explain why attempted solutions fell short of their expectations. Try to avoid overcrowding your essay with facts and figures but do include enough to highlight the main points of your argument.

2 How absolute was Francis I's government and administration?

2.1 The nature of the government and administration

The king took all decisions but was advised by the *Conseil des Affaires*, an inner ring of councillors drawn from the *Conseil d'Etat* (state council). Royal councillors, comprising the *noblesse d'épée* (aristocracy), princes of the blood, household officers, clerics and lawyers, attended by invitation only and accompanied the king when he travelled around the country. Once decisions were taken they were turned into laws by some 50 *maîtres* (lawyers who worked in the chancery), and then passed to provincial governors to enforce.

The 11 provincial governors (16 by 1547) exercised considerable authority as army commanders, political leaders and patrons. Francis favoured his relatives and upper nobility, and encouraged hereditary appointments. Below the governors were *baillis* (local officials) but low wages produced a culture of bribery and corruption.

In his early years Francis consulted several representative groups. An Assembly of Towns met in 1517 and Notables in 1527 but he never called the Estates-General (national assembly). He was also wary of the *parlements*. In 1515 there were seven: Paris (by far the most important), Toulouse, Bordeaux, Aix, Rouen, Dijon and Grenoble. In their opinion, the king held his power from the people and *parlements* were the guardians of the people's rights.

The administration was still decentralised. The absence of a professional bureaucracy, the profusion of local rights, favouritism and corrupt practices made it hard for the king to enforce his will over all his subjects; nevertheless, the French administration was the largest and most specialised in western Europe.

2.2 Budé and Seyssel's views on the monarchy

Budé

Guillaume Budé was secretary to Francis I and wrote *L'Institution du Prince* in 1518. He claimed that the king could exercise independent power if he wished, make his own laws without consulting his subjects and impose taxes without their consent. The aristocracy might assist in government but he was under no obligation to involve them.

Seyssel

Claude de Seyssel published *La Monarchie de France* early in Francis I's reign. He believed that while the king held his power from God and was therefore in theory absolute, in practice he was restricted by certain obligations — he had a duty to provide justice for his subjects, to defend his kingdom, its laws and its Catholic faith. *Parlements* and the aristocracy therefore acted as a brake against a possible royal tyranny.

2.3 The extent and limits of Francis' authority

Historians have long argued over the extent of Francis I's authority. In the opinion of Robert Knecht, for instance, while 'absolutism in practice has always fallen short of its theoretical completeness…Francis would appear to have been about as absolute as any European monarch of his day could hope to be'. Russell Major, on the other hand, has argued that Francis was a constitutional monarch, since there were 'significant institutional, theoretical and/or practical limitations upon the authority of the king'.

Arguments supporting absolutism

- All sixteenth-century monarchs claimed to hold divine power and so they exercised absolute authority.
- The royal prerogative (what the king could and could not do) was undefined.
- Francis never called an Estates-General.
- He levied taxes without his subjects' consent.
- He would not be limited by *parlement* (e.g. in 1527 the Paris *parlement* was forbidden from interfering in affairs of state or modifying future royal legislation).
- He victimised opponents (e.g. the Duke of Bourbon (1523), Admiral Chabot (1541), Chancellor Poyet (1543)).
- He acted arbitrarily (e.g. following a rebellion at Lagny-sur-Marne (1544) the town was sacked, its inhabitants denied the right of appeal, and *parlement* was told not to investigate the case).

Arguments supporting a limited monarchy

- The king took a coronation oath to uphold the laws of the land; *parlements* were guardians of the law and could hold the king accountable.
- The absence of a centralised administration, judicial system and legal code presented obstacles to royal authority.
- There was no standing army or police force.
- Political power effectively rested with the nobility and provincial governors.
- Francis' authority did not extend throughout the whole country.
- Taxes were not imposed on certain provinces (e.g. Provence, Vendée and Brittany) for fear of rebellion.

Conclusion

In many respects 'absolutism' is an inappropriate term to describe a sixteenth-century monarchy. In theory Francis could act beyond the law and — occasionally — he did, but he was also well aware that his power was really limited. 'Autocratic' seems a more suitable description of his behaviour. Until he had enough revenue to rule independently, a standing army to enforce his will and a judicial and government administration that was subservient, his authority would be limited.

EXAMINER'S TIP

This topic appears at AS in the OCR specification. A typical AS question is: 'To what extent do you agree with the view that Francis I was an absolute monarch?' The best answers will present arguments for and against absolutism, and evaluate 'extent', before coming to a judgement. You will not be expected to include a detailed analysis of each issue but you should explain and illustrate your points with relevant examples.

3 What religious issues and problems faced the French Church, 1498–1547?

3.1 Relations with the papacy

Since 1438 the king had elected all clerical officers and collected papal taxation. He effectively controlled episcopal and monastic patronage, ecclesiastical property and revenue, and decided how much money should be forwarded to the Pope.

The Concordat of Bologna, 1516

Francis negotiated an agreement (concordat) with Pope Leo X. It stated that the king was allowed to nominate priors, abbots and bishops, who had to be at least 27 years old, university graduates and be appointed within 6 months of a vacancy. The Pope would confirm these royal nominations.

The Paris *parlement* reacted angrily and refused to register the edict (until 1518). It alleged that Francis had allowed the papacy to interfere in French affairs and the concordat infringed the liberties of the Gallican Church. This does not appear to have been the case, however; the Paris *parlement* simply overreacted in its desire to protect the French Church.

3.2 Christian humanism

Lefèvre d'Etaples

The late fifteenth century saw a small number of French intellectuals take up Christian humanism. Foremost among them was Lefèvre d'Etaples. He was dissatisfied with the traditional methods of teaching at the Sorbonne (the theological faculty at the University of Paris). Instead of relying on Latin translations of the Scriptures by medieval scholars, he favoured a study of the texts in their original language, as had Erasmus in the Netherlands. In 1509 Lefèvre published a Psalter and in 1512 a French edition of St Paul's Epistles. Six years later he became a client of the Bishop of Meaux.

The Bishop of Meaux

When Guillaume Briçonnet became Bishop of Meaux in 1518 he realised how much his diocese needed reforming. He recruited several humanists (e.g. Lefèvre, Farel and Roussel) and encouraged them to preach their evangelical ideas to the clergy and laity.

Though criticised by Franciscan friars, who saw their livelihood as travelling preachers under threat, and by the Sorbonne, who claimed humanism would open the door to Lutheranism, Meaux and his circle of humanists were defended by Francis and his sister, Margaret, Queen of Navarre.

In 1524 the king rejected the Sorbonne's attempt to ban all Greek, Hebrew and French editions of the Scriptures. In 1527 he ordered the Paris *parlement* to stop its investigations into Meaux and his associates.

3.3 The impact of Lutheranism to 1547

The dilemma facing Francis was how to distinguish between humanists, who were scholars, and Lutherans, who were heretics. The Sorbonne had no difficulty: both were guilty of heresy. Luther's works first appeared in Paris in 1519 and, after careful deliberation, were condemned as heretical in 1521. Some of Luther's ideas were well received by French humanists (e.g. his denunciation of indulgences) but Lefèvre and others could not accept his reduction of the sacraments from seven to two. Nevertheless, orthodox Catholics were convinced that humanism fuelled heretical thinking and both the Sorbonne and the Paris *parlement* demanded severe sentences for all dissidents. In 1528 Louis de Berquin, a Lutheran scholar, was burned. In 1533 the university complained about a sermon delivered by its rector, Nicolas Cop, and forced him to flee France to avoid persecution. Fifty alleged heretics were subsequently arrested in Paris but most were released without punishment when the king discovered that the Sorbonne and *parlement* had falsified the charges.

The Day of the Placards, 1534

A turning-point in Francis' relations with French Protestants came on 18 October 1534. Posters ridiculing bishops and the Catholic Mass appeared in Paris and several other towns. One was allegedly found outside the king's bedroom at Amboise. These placards were viewed as a violent attack on the most sacred of sacraments and convinced Francis that a stand now had to be taken to prevent radicalism from spreading. He ordered that:
- all heresy cases were to be tried by lay courts so that death sentences could be passed
- there was to be no right of appeal
- prosecution could be based on hearsay, oral or written evidence, defined as 'all words contrary to the Holy Catholic Faith and the Christian Religion'

As a result, Francis now worked with his *parlements* to stop the growth of Protestantism. Six Lutherans were burned in Paris in 1534. In January 1535 a state procession attended by the king, which glorified the Catholic faith, ended with the burning of another six Lutherans. Between 1540 and 1547 the persecution of Lutherans intensified:
- The Edict of Fontainebleau (1540) granted control of heresy cases to secular courts.
- In 1543 secular as well as Church authorities were given the right to search and arrest heretics.
- The Sorbonne defined the 25 articles of the Catholic faith and published an index of 65 prohibited books (1543).
- Heretics in Provence were massacred (1544) with the consent of the *parlement* at Aix.
- In 1545 the Aix *parlement* sentenced to death over 6,000 Waldensian heretics.

Conclusion

By 1547 the Crown stood firmly behind the Sorbonne, Paris and provincial *parlements* in their persecution of heresy. Humanism and Protestantism were treated alike. In some provinces, however, such as Guyenne, Normandy and Dauphin, French Protestantism went largely unpunished. There the ideas of Calvin had become popular among the nobility, lesser clergy and urban groups, and as a result there were fewer prosecutions.

This topic appears at AS in the OCR specification. You might be asked: 'How far did heretical groups seriously challenge the Catholic Church in France during the period 1515–47?' You should be aware of the limited support for humanism, Lutheranism and Calvinism, how Church and state institutions reacted to unorthodoxy, and the conflicting signals coming from Francis I before 1534.

4 How successful was France during the Italian and Habsburg–Valois wars, 1499–1559?

4.1 The legacy of Louis XII, 1498–1515

In 1494 Charles VIII of France invaded Italy, marched south with a vast army and laid claim to the kingdom of Naples. His success was short-lived. By 1498 he had been driven out by a military alliance centred upon Ferdinand of Aragon (his rival claimant), the papacy and several Italian states.

Louis XII

Louis XII not only renewed the French claim to Naples but he also intended to take control of the duchy of Milan, the gateway to southern Italy. Opposition from Ferdinand of Aragon intensified and superior Spanish armies won decisive battles at Cerignola and Garigliano (1503). As a result, Louis yielded his right to Naples and returned to France. In 1508 Louis was again tempted to invade Milan. He joined the League of Cambrai against Venice, won the Battle of Agnadello (1509) and shared the republic of Venice with Ferdinand of Spain. In 1511 Louis became the target of ambitious Italian princes who were egged on by Pope Julius II. A heavy French defeat at Novara (1512) saw Louis' hold on Milan and Venice slip away. Worse, Swiss mercenaries invaded eastern France and Spanish troops occupied French Navarre. Louis died in 1515, having lost all Italian territories and leaving the country in danger of losing lands in France itself.

4.2 Francis I, 1515–47

Aims

Francis I's aims were to:

- avenge the defeat of Louis XII at Novara
- acquire Milan and if possible Naples
- prevent the encirclement of France by the Spanish and Austrian Habsburgs
- demonstrate his superiority over Charles V

Problems

- Charles V's military power and resources were greater than those of Francis.
- Francis' allies were unreliable (e.g. Andreas Doria of Genoa defected in 1528).
- Henry VIII supported Charles at critical moments (e.g. 1522–24, 1542–46).
- Francis showed great courage but had limited diplomatic and military expertise.

Achievements and failures

- Francis won a famous victory at Marignano (1515) against the best mercenaries in Europe and held Milan for 6 years, but subsequent defeats at Bicocca (1521), Pavia

(1525) and Landriano (1529) saw the permanent loss of Milan at the Peace of Cambrai (1529). Francis kept Burgundy and recovered his two sons, who had been held hostage in Spain, but he gave up his claims to Italy and lost his rights to Flanders, Artois and Tournaisis.

- Francis spent 400,000 crowns in bribes but failed as a candidate to the imperial throne (1519).

He spent 200,000 livres entertaining Henry VIII at the Field of the Cloth of Gold (1520) but failed to secure an English alliance.

- He was captured at Pavia, transferred to Madrid as a prisoner and only gained his release when he arranged for his two sons to be imprisoned in his place.
- He invaded Savoy and won control of Nice (1538), but defeats against superior Spanish, English and German troops (1542–46) led to the loss of Boulogne at the Treaty of Ardres (1546) and the invasion of France.
- He agreed to let the Turkish fleet winter at Toulon in 1543–44, to the amazement of Christian Europe.

4.3 Henry II, 1547–59

Aims

Henry II's aims were to:
- avenge his 3-year imprisonment in Madrid at the hands of Charles V
- gain Milan and Naples
- recover Boulogne

Problems

- Henry II did not know how to raise enough money to fund armies in Italy, the empire and France.
- War against Charles V could well result in war against England, and vice versa.
- Henry's willingness to ally with German Lutherans and Turkish Muslims (in 1552) was condemned by the Pope and most Catholics.

Achievements and failures

- Henry recovered Boulogne (1550) and Calais (1558) from England.
- He gained the imperial bishoprics of Metz, Toul and Verdun from Charles V.
- He ended the expensive Italian wars at Cateau-Cambrésis (1559): Spain kept Milan and Naples but France held three Italian towns (Turin, Pinerolo and Saluzzo), which reduced the threat of encirclement.
- War had bankrupted the Crown: debts and interest payments went unpaid in 1557–59.

EXAMINER'S TIP

This topic appears at AS in the OCR specification. You might be asked: 'How do you explain France's lack of success in Italy in the period 1521–29?' You should consider a range of explanations, which may include the financial strain of fighting, the nature of Italian politics and relations with the papacy, diplomatic issues and military defeats at the hands of Spanish and imperial troops. Wherever possible, demonstrate links between these reasons.

KEY QUESTIONS

(1) What were the origins of the French wars of religion?
(2) How important were individuals and ideas in the wars?
(3) How far did Henry IV solve his domestic problems, 1589–1610?
(4) How successful was Henry IV's foreign policy, 1589–1610?

1 What were the origins of the French wars of religion?

1.1 Background

In 1562 civil war began in France and lasted until 1598. Though later called the 'wars of religion', religion was only one of several issues that divided the French people. Indeed, political and economic factors contributed significantly to the outbreak of the wars.

1.2 Strengths and weaknesses of the monarchy, 1547–62

The monarchs

Between 1547 and 1562 France had three kings: Henry II, Francis II and Charles IX. The expected role of the monarch was to protect and lead his subjects in peace and war, to be the source of justice and patronage, and to symbolise the nation's unity. Henry II (1547–59) fulfilled these criteria. He protected his people from Protestant heresy and he waged successful campaigns to recover Boulogne and Calais from England and gain Metz, Toul and Verdun from the empire.

In 1559 Henry died, leaving behind his 15-year-old son, Francis, and the queen mother, Catherine de Medici. Francis was physically weak and sickly, and a year later he died from an abscess in his ear. His 10-year-old brother, Charles IX, became king but Catherine soon assumed the role of regent. Resented on account of her Italian origin and her determination to play a central part in government, she never gained the respect or trust necessary to keep France united and at peace.

Royal finances

Henry II inherited financial problems in 1547, which worsened in the course of his reign. A corrupt administration, expensive wars, rising inflation, increasing numbers of state pensions, and the Estates-General refusing to reform the tax system all contributed to a state debt estimated in 1559 at 41 million livres. As long as the Crown had a financial weakness, it would command less respect, increasingly come to rely on loans from the aristocracy and have its policies compromised by financial deals.

1.3 The nobility and growth of faction

In the course of Henry II's reign, noble families vied for political and military power. War in Italy and Flanders gave them the opportunity to gain lands, titles and rewards from the Crown. The three main families were as follows.

Montmorency

Constable Anne de Montmorency was the king's chief adviser, who dominated the court as grand master and chaired council meetings. He also controlled the royal army but suffered the indignity of being captured at the battle of St Quentin (1557). Though he

was strongly Catholic, his three nephews (Coligny, d'Andelot and Odet), whom he promoted to state and Church offices, were Huguenot (Calvinist).

Guise

Francis, Duke of Guise was France's most celebrated soldier. He had victories in Italy, Metz and Calais to his name, and in 1562 controlled the royal ordnance. His brothers, Charles and Louis, monopolised ecclesiastical patronage and were fierce defenders of the Catholic faith. Upon the death of Henry II, Guise assumed an increasing role in central government. Francis II was married to his niece.

Bourbon

Anthony, Duke of Bourbon was also King of Navarre and the senior prince of the blood. His brother, Louis, Prince of Condé, was an avowed Huguenot who had some 500 armed retainers at his command. The Bourbons were still feeling the effects of the treasonous behaviour of a former duke in 1523 but Condé was ambitious for power.

Factions

Each family expected to gain during the regency. Robert Harding, an American historian, has claimed that competition for royal patronage quickly turned into aristocratic rivalry, feuds and vendettas. The absence of foreign war also left many nobles idle and with armed troops on their lands. As royal control declined, nobles became more independent. Governors appointed their own clients to offices within their jurisdiction and in return built up provincial power blocs. Thus, Montmorency-Damville effectively controlled the political affairs of Languedoc, Condé ruled Berry and Guise governed Brittany.

The lesser nobility also felt aggrieved at the changing political conditions. Many had loaned money to the Crown but received no interest repayments after 1556. They were barred from trading as a profession, left unemployed when the Italian wars ended and, as land rents fell and prices rose, were forced to become clients of wealthier lords. Many nobles, in particular women, had turned to Huguenotism, possibly due to their children's Protestant tutors but also due to the influence of Margaret, sister of Francis I (see Unit 12, 3.2).

1.4 The growth of Huguenotism

(See also Unit 12 for more details on Huguenotism.)

Huguenotism (Calvinism) constituted no more than 10 % of the French population in 1562 but it had the support of several leading nobles, who protected their tenants and clients. Since 1555 Calvinism had increased in numbers as French missionaries returned from Geneva and converted the lower clergy and townspeople. By 1559 district, provincial and national synods had been established. Nobles and their retainers brought a military organisation to Calvinism: individual religious communities were led by captains and the provincial colloquies by colonels.

Calvinism, however, was an unlawful faith. The Edict of Compiègne (1557) reminded *parlements* that the death penalty must be imposed on heretics and, though some *parlements* did persecute Huguenots, most did not. In 1560 a second national synod took place at Poitiers and some of the more reckless nobles plotted to take control of the king.

1.5 Crisis, 1559–62

In the 17 months of Francis II's reign (1559–60) his uncle, the Duke of Guise, took control of affairs and stepped up religious persecution. At the same time many nobles converted to Huguenotism, attracted by the economic incentives of controlling Church lands and clerical taxation.

The Tumult of Amboise, 1560

Condé, La Renaudie and several Huguenot nobles planned to kidnap the king, assassinate the Duke of Guise and his brother, the Cardinal of Lorraine, and make Anthony of Navarre the principal adviser to the Crown. The plot, however, known as the 'Tumult of Amboise', failed. The Guises took revenge and, with the consent of the Crown, executed 57 Huguenot conspirators. As a result:

- the Huguenots became targets of the Guise faction
- Condé was arrested and charged with treason (he was only saved by the sudden death of the king in December 1560)
- Catherine convened a meeting of Huguenots and Catholics at Fontainebleau, where it was decided an Estates-General should be called; but when it met it failed to raise money or solve the religious crisis

The Colloquy of Poissy, 1561

As riots broke out and both Catholics and Huguenots armed themselves, Catherine decided to act. She invited the royal family, princes, councillors, bishops, cardinals and lawyers to Poissy and told them that she would:

- release Huguenot prisoners
- begin to reform the Church
- try to reconcile the differences between Catholics and Huguenots

The Edict of January 1562

In January the Estates-General was persuaded to grant concessions to the Huguenots. These included:

- full legal status
- the right to worship outside towns
- the right to hold meetings and assemblies

The Massacre of Vassy, 1562

As Catherine tried to find a middle way the religious groups became more resolute. Leading Catholics, fearing that the French Church might become Protestant, forgot their personal rivalry, formed a triumvirate (the Guise, Montmorency and St André families) and elicited promises of help from Spain and the papacy. The Huguenots, on the other hand, grew in confidence. They openly celebrated their faith, took over churches and destroyed Catholic images. In March 1562 the Duke of Guise and his retainers came across some Huguenots worshipping in a barn in the town of Vassy. Technically the Huguenots were breaking the law so he attacked them, killing 30 and wounding 120 of them. Guise went on to Paris, the royal family retreated to the country and Condé issued a formal declaration of war on behalf of the Huguenots.

EXAMINER'S TIP

This topic appears at AS and at A2 in the AQA (Alternative B) specification. At AS you might get this question: 'What factors contributed to the weakening of the French Crown in the period 1547–62?' While many candidates will run through a list of factors (e.g. ambitious nobles, weak royal finances, Italian wars, the rise of Huguenotism), the best answers should discuss the effects of each of these factors, prioritise them and show how they were interrelated.

2 How important were individuals and ideas in the wars?

2.1 The significance of individuals

Louis, Prince of Condé

Louis led the Huguenot movement in the 1560s, though more for political than religious reasons. In 1562–63 he negotiated with Elizabeth of England to recover Calais if she would send him troops but he was captured at Dreux (1562) and English troops were forced to evacuate Le Havre (1563). Louis accepted limited toleration for Huguenots at the Peace of Amboise (1567) but saw it dissolve in 1568. He was killed at the Battle of Jarnac (1569).

Gaspard de Coligny

Gaspard de Coligny assumed command of the Huguenot army after Condé's death. The Guises were convinced he was responsible for the murder of Duke Francis in 1563 and pursued him thereafter. He accepted the terms offered by Catherine at the Peace of St Germain (1570), by which the Huguenots gained religious toleration and a measure of political security. In 1571–72 Coligny drew closer to Charles IX and persuaded him to send help to the Dutch rebels against Spain. As he rose in power his enemies plotted his death, which was accomplished at the St Bartholomew's Day massacre (1572).

Henry of Navarre

In 1572, 4 days before the St Bartholomew's Day massacre, Henry married Margaret of Valois and became Huguenot leader following the death of Coligny. As King of Navarre he had a claim to the French throne and in 1584 became heir presumptive when Alençon died. A very capable soldier, immensely likeable and honest, he became king in 1589 but only secured Paris once he had converted to Catholicism, in 1593. Many questioned the sincerity of his conversion.

Charles, Cardinal of Lorraine

Charles, brother of Francis of Guise, held numerous ecclesiastical titles, 24 abbeys and lands worth 300,000 livres. Arrogant and outspoken, he represented the Catholics at the Colloquy of Poissy and consistently opposed the Crown in its attempt to reach a compromise with the Huguenots in the 1560s. He may have been responsible for the attempted arrest of their leaders in 1568. He died in 1574.

Henry of Guise

In 1576 the eldest son of Francis, Henry, founded the Catholic League, backed by Spain, to oppose any toleration towards Huguenots. When Alençon died (1584), Henry supported the claim of the Cardinal of Bourbon to the throne to prevent Henry of Navarre from succeeding, and declared war on him. Between 1585 and 1588 Guise gained control of most towns in northern and central France and entered Paris at the head of his own army. Confronted with barricades (May 1588), the king fled to Blois but got his revenge in December when his guards murdered Henry and his brother.

Francis of Alençon

Intelligent, unscrupulous and very ambitious, Francis of Alençon was bitterly jealous of his brother, Henry III. In the 1570s he joined the ***politiques***, was suggested by his mother as a possible husband for Queen Elizabeth of England, and led armies in the Netherlands against Spain. Catherine de Medici was always wary of his unpredictability: in 1574 she arrested him in case he attempted to stop his brother from becoming king. Upon his release, Francis joined up with Montmorency-Damville and Navarre to secure a very

favourable treaty for the Huguenots (the Peace of Monsieur, 1576). Involved in various plots and scandals, Francis fought for and against the Huguenots, reopened marriage talks with Elizabeth (1578) and took an army into the Netherlands in 1582–83. He achieved little in France, however, and even less in the Netherlands and England. He died of tuberculosis in 1584.

Catherine de Medici

Anxious to protect her sons and retain her own political influence, Catherine tried to hold the balance between conflicting noble and religious factions. She believed that a religious compromise was attainable and declared an amnesty and toleration of Huguenots (1561), but neither Catholics nor Huguenots wanted this. Initially the *politiques* gained her support, but the rising influence of Coligny upon the king had to be removed and she probably orchestrated his murder in 1572. Most contemporaries and many historians have held her responsible for the ensuing Massacre of St Bartholomew's Day, when 3,000 Huguenots in Paris and some 12,000 in other cities were murdered. Henry of Navarre later commented that, given her universal unpopularity and persistent meddling, he was surprised 'she never did worse'. She died in 1589.

Charles IX, 1560–74

For much of the 1560s Charles IX was dominated by his mother, Catherine de Medici. She moved her bed into his room and in 1564–66 they progressed together around France. In 1571 Charles took over the reins of government and befriended Coligny, though he never really endorsed Coligny's plan to invade the Netherlands. Historians have held Charles responsible for approving the St Bartholomew's Day massacre.

Henry III, 1574–89

Shrewd, intelligent, effeminate and eccentric, Henry III surrounded himself with his male courtiers (known as 'mignons'). Following the death of Montmorency (1567), he led royal armies from 1567 to 1573, winning battles at Jarnac and Moncontour. As king he became more independent of the queen mother but was unable to break free from the Guises, who grew in power in the 1580s and even prevented him from entering Paris in 1588. Henry plotted the deaths of the Duke of Guise and his brother but in 1589 was himself assassinated by a Dominican friar.

2.2 The role of ideas

Huguenot theories of resistance

For most of his life Calvin preached obedience to the ruling magistrate, a view he modified in the early 1560s when violence broke out in France. He suggested that if a ruler governed in a way contrary to the good of his people, then inferior magistrates had the right to resist; but individual people did not. Initially, however, Huguenots pinned their hopes on Catherine de Medici, who campaigned on their behalf as she tried to find a compromise solution. Claims that the French government was breaking the constitution first appeared in 1567–68, when Huguenots argued that the monarchy and the government were not inseparable. It was the St Bartholomew's Day massacre, however, that led Huguenot writers to reappraise the relationship between the monarch and his or her subjects.

Francis Hotman

Hotman believed that the Estates-General and the aristocracy had the power to control the monarchy. In his *Francogallia* (1573) he stated that the king, according to the ancient constitution, was originally elected by the people and the people could in theory remove him.

Theodore Beza

In *The Right of Magistrates over Subjects* (1574) Beza argued that any resistance to a ruler must be expressed through magistrates and not through the Estates-General. Common people must only act through their superior magistrates, whom he identified as upper nobles and locally-elected politicians. Resistance, nevertheless, was justified if the king failed to fulfil his political and religious duties.

Philippe du Plessis-Mornay

The *Vindiciae Contra Tyrannos*, a pamphlet written in 1579 and attributed to du Plessis-Mornay, was the most radical Huguenot theory of resistance. The king, it was averred, had pledged to honour two contracts at his coronation: one with God and one with his people. The people must obey the king provided he gave them good government. If he did not, then they had a duty to God to oppose him.

Views of the Catholic League

The Catholic League traditionally supported a strong monarchy and the Catholic faith. Fears that the monarchy might seek to compromise with the Huguenots (e.g. at the Peace of Monsieur, 1576), however, led Catholic writers to claim that there were certain 'fundamental laws' that the monarchy must apply (e.g. the king should always be Catholic). If these were broken the people could oppose the king. After 1584 the Catholic League realigned its objective to prevent a Huguenot from ascending the throne. In the Manifesto of Péronne (1585) the league championed the Cardinal of Bourbon, Navarre's uncle, as heir presumptive and denounced Huguenots. Following the assassination of Henry of Guise and his brother (1588), the league proclaimed the king to be a tyrant and released French subjects from having to obey him. The Sorbonne concurred in 1589. Later Jean Boucher, the priest of St Benoît, Paris, wrote that Henry III must be deposed because he had broken his coronation oath. Following the accession of Henry of Navarre, Catholic propaganda justified Cardinal Bourbon's claim to the throne and, after his death (1590), calls for an election by the Estates-General increased until Navarre's conversion to the Catholic faith in 1593.

Theories of monarchy

Early sixteenth-century writers, such as Seyssel and Budé, had offered contrasting theories of the monarchy — that royal power was limited (Seyssel) or that it was absolute (Budé). Most French people accepted that the king held his authority from God and that subjects had a duty to be obedient. This theory was eloquently expressed by Jean Bodin in his *Six Books of the Commonwealth* (1576). As the French wars continued, however, theories of resistance were developed, first by Huguenots and then by Catholics.

In the 1560s an alternative to sectarianism emerged in the shape of the *politiques*. They argued that the only way to solve France's problems was to allow two Churches to coexist. They sought 'peace without God rather than war with him'. St Bartholomew's Day, however, was a turning-point in the wars. Huguenotism ceased to be so popular but existing converts were even more determined to defend their faith. Moderate Catholics were equally horrified at the rising tide of murders but saw little reason to trust the Huguenots. Both sects looked to the monarch to uphold the true Church.

This topic appears at AS and at A2 in the AQA (Alternative B) specifications. You could be asked: 'How important were individuals in prolonging the wars of religion?' Evaluative questions require assessments, so avoid writing a narrative of the events. Instead, the role of leading individuals (e.g. the Valois monarchs, Catherine de Medici, the Guises) should be examined and key turning-points (such as the Massacre of St Bartholomew's Day and the formation of Catholic Leagues) considered. Were individuals or ideas more responsible for prolonging the war?

3 How far did Henry IV solve his domestic problems, 1589–1610?

3.1 Henry IV's personality

Henry IV was:

- amiable, populist, persuasive and a self-publicist
- coarse and ill-mannered
- a womaniser; married to Margaret of Valois and then to Marie de Medici, he had 56 mistresses and eight illegitimate children
- a pragmatic politician and a successful soldier

3.2 Religious problems

Henry was a Catholic until 1572, a Calvinist from 1572 to 1593 and then a Catholic again. Neither the Huguenots nor the Catholics entirely trusted him yet each group relied on the king to preserve their faith. Henry knew the Huguenots were too numerous and entrenched to be ignored, converted or removed, and so a compromise had to be reached.

The Edict of Nantes, 1598

- Huguenots received full civil rights, protected by the *parlements*.
- Huguenots could hold any office of state and enter any school, university or profession.
- Law courts were to comprise an equal number of Huguenot and Catholic judges.
- Huguenots received religious freedom in two places in every **bailliage** or wherever Huguenotism had been practised in 1596–97.
- A hundred towns (but not Paris) were garrisoned and some paid for by the state.
- Provincial synods were allowed to meet regularly and a national assembly could meet with the king's permission.
- The terms of the edict were 'by the grace of the king' and could be revoked.

Reaction to Nantes

- There was initial opposition from Huguenots, who felt they could have done better; they were not equal to Catholics, only tolerated by them, and were not permitted inside cathedral cities.
- Some Huguenot towns banned Catholic worship (e.g. La Rochelle, Nîmes).
- There was strong opposition from the Paris *parlement* and other *parlements*; only in 1609 did Rouen register the edict.

Conclusion

Religious peace was maintained but toleration was not popular. Jesuits, banished in 1595, returned in 1603 and St Francis de Sales, Bishop of Geneva, who believed nuns

should be able to play an active part in the Counter-Reformation, arrived from Savoy in 1602; convents were founded amid a Catholic revival.

3.3 Political problems

Henry IV's political aims were to restore the power of the Crown and to curtail the political power of the nobility but allow them their social and economic privileges.

Nobles

- In the 1590s Henry bribed the nobles to ensure that they did not oppose him (e.g. the Duke of Mercoeur received the governorship of Brittany and 4 million livres).
- To compensate the nobles for no longer holding central political offices, Henry handed out pensions and titles, at a cost of 30 million livres.
- He encouraged the nobles to enlist in the army, which became more permanent and national.
- He enlarged the '*noblesse de la robe*' (new hereditary nobility) to counter the influence of the '*noblesse d'épée*' (old aristocracy).
- He only called one Assembly of Notables (1596) and never convened an Estates-General.
- He appointed 'intendants' to oversee the work of provincial noble governors.

Government

- Henry took all decisions; he introduced few governmental changes.
- An inner council of five or six councillors advised Henry — mainly *noblesse de la robe*, lawyers and merchants — led by Bellièvre, Villeroy and Sully.
- In the provinces Henry increased the number of officiers (new professional administrators) and intendants to break the aristocratic patronage and **venality** among many governors and local office-holders, but members of the Catholic League remained very powerful.

Parlement

To weaken the influence of *parlements* and nobles, Henry created the Paulette tax (1604). Purchasers of judicial and administrative offices could pass on their posts on retirement; henceforth, they owed their loyalty to the Crown rather than to the *parlements*.

Conclusion

Restoring the authority of the Crown was a slow process. Treasonous activity from the aristocracy was dealt with firmly. Marshal Biron (1602), Governor of Burgundy, who plotted with the Duke of Bouillon, Spain and Savoy to overthrow Henry with one of his illegitimate sons, was executed and Bouillon was exiled. By a judicious blend of persuasion and force Henry brought peace to his kingdom.

3.4 Economic problems

As superintendent of finances, minister of public buildings and director of communications, Maximilien de Béthune, Duke of Sully, became Henry's principal adviser in economic affairs.

The main problems were:
- a debt of 350 million livres
- the fact that expenditure exceeded revenue by 50%

- financial corruption at every level of administration
- the disruptive effect of the wars on trade, industry and agriculture
- the fact that the majority of taxation fell on the peasantry

Finances

No changes were introduced to the administration but indirect taxes were handled more efficiently.

To cut expenditure:
- court costs were reduced
- tax farming was investigated (1597)
- the Crown defaulted on debt repayments to foreign allies and on back payments of government bonds

To raise revenue:
- salt tax was increased
- crown lands were recovered
- patents of nobility dating back to 1578 were cancelled
- claims for tax exemption were examined and reduced by 40,000
- the Paulette was introduced
- feudal customs were resumed
- the clergy offered a '*don gratuit*' (donation)

As a result, the debt was reduced by 125 million livres, revenue rose by 70% and the Treasury had a surplus of 12–15 million livres by 1610.

Agriculture

- The development of new crops and drainage techniques was encouraged.
- Nobles were forbidden from riding over arable land and vineyards, but without success.
- Olivier de Serres and Barthélemy Laffemas promoted the growing of mulberry trees for silkworms.

Trade

- Commercial treaties were signed with England and Spain.
- Transport was improved: roads were repaired and new canals dug linking the Seine and the Loire, and the Saône and the Loire.
- Overseas settlements were founded by private companies (e.g. in 1604 the Port Royal company traded with Nova Scotia; in 1608 the New France company traded with Quebec). There was no state investment, however, mainly due to the absence of a royal navy, which would have been necessary to protect overseas trade.

Industry

- Laffemas, as controller-general of commerce, forced every worker to join a guild and made strikes illegal.
- Henry supported luxury industries (e.g. glass, carpets, silk, tapestries).

Conclusion

There was little economic progress due to a lack of investment by the nobility, Sully's prejudices against manufacturing, the ineptitude of Laffemas, and excessive burden put upon the peasantry. Crown finances and domestic communications, however, did show signs of improvement.

GLOSSARY

baillage: a district of town.

venality: the sale of public offices.

EXAMINER'S TIP

This topic appears at AS in the OCR specification and at A2 in the AQA (Alternative B) specification. You might be asked: 'How far was Sully rather than Henry IV responsible for the recovery of France between 1589 and 1610?' The instruction 'how far' requires you to evaluate the individual roles of Henry and Sully in terms of their subsequent achievements and limitations. In assessing both men you could consider the problems of differentiating between their contributions.

4 How successful was Henry IV's foreign policy, 1589–1610?

4.1 Aims: a 'Grand Design'?

In his memoirs, written after the death of Henry IV, Sully claimed that the king had a 'Grand Design', which was intended to eliminate war from Europe. To achieve this:

- the power and ambition of the Spanish and Austrian Habsburgs had to be reduced
- the Turks and Russians would be expelled from Europe
- each country would have a new constitution
- a Council of Europe would be established, with 66 members
- there would be a multinational army to keep peace
- all states would be disarmed
- three religions would coexist: Catholicism, Lutheranism and Calvinism

Historians, however, do not regard Sully's memoirs as an accurate account of Henry's aims and policies. Indeed, it is likely that Henry's main aims were more pragmatic, i.e. to:

- expel Spanish troops from France
- end Habsburg encirclement of France
- probe the Spanish empire's lines of communications, especially in north Italy
- keep peace in Europe

4.2 Main events

Spain

Between 1589 and 1598 Spanish troops occupied parts of France. First Henry fought to secure his throne, and after 1595 to expel Spanish troops from Burgundy, Brittany and Normandy. At the Treaty of Vervins (1598) Spain withdrew from all French territories.

Savoy

In 1601 French troops occupied Chambéry, the capital of Savoy, when its duke failed to restore Saluzzo to France. At the Treaty of Lyons (1601) France gained the provinces of Bresse, Gex and Bugey to the southwest of Franche-Comté.

Valtelline

Henry IV allied with the Grisons (1601), inhabitants of the Valtelline, and built up good relations ready to counter any Spanish threat from nearby Milan. He also signed treaties with Venice, Switzerland, Florence and Savoy to isolate the Milanese.

The Netherlands

Henry allied with the Dutch and assisted in negotiating their truce with Spain in 1609.

Cleves-Julich

The death of the Duke of Cleves-Julich (1609) led to a contested succession between two Protestant German claimants. Emperor Rudolf invaded the duchy and installed his own Catholic candidate. Henry IV agreed to support the Protestant claimant, backed by German princes in the Evangelical Union (1610), and prepared for war. Only Henry's unexpected death kept France out of war.

4.3 Successes and failures

- Spanish troops were expelled from France and a favourable treaty was negotiated at Vervins.
- Towns in Savoy were acquired, which would enable troops to advance into north Italy should the opportunity arise.
- War was avoided between 1598 and 1610.
- By joining the Evangelical Union Henry nearly took France to war against Spain and Austria. It angered Catholics, one of whom assassinated him.

EXAMINER'S TIP

This topic appears at AS in the OCR specification and at A2 in the AQA (Alternative B) specification. If you are asked: 'How successful was Henry IV in his foreign affairs by 1610?', use the events to assess Henry's aims and strategies. Consider Sully's Grand Design but do so critically. Set Henry's aims and achievements in the context of the years 1589–1610 as well as future developments.

KEY QUESTIONS

(1) What was the condition of the Roman Catholic Church in 1500?
(2) What was the role of the papacy in the Catholic Reformation?
(3) What was the importance of the new orders to the Catholic Church in the sixteenth century?
(4) What did the Council of Trent achieve by 1600?
(5) How effective were the Inquisition and the Index?
(6) Was there a Catholic or a Counter-Reformation?

1 *What was the condition of the Roman Catholic Church in 1500?*

1.1 Background

The Roman Catholic Church exercised considerable power in western Europe in the later Middle Ages. It was also generally felt that the Church could be improved. Indeed, there were many examples of reforms in the years preceding Luther's attack on indulgences (see Unit 9) but, in the opinion of many, these changes had not gone far enough.

1.2 Criticisms of the Church

The main criticisms of the Catholic Church at the beginning of the sixteenth century were as follows:

- The papacy consistently abused its authority and set a poor example to the laity and clergy. Simony and nepotism were rife in the **Curia** (e.g. Leo X sold over 2,000 offices); popes led armies into battle (e.g. Sixtus IV), built up their lands in Italy (e.g. Alexander VI), and spent much of their wealth on Renaissance art (e.g. Julius II).
- Many secular clerics were corrupt and incompetent. Some held several offices (pluralism) and neglected their duties for long periods of time (absenteeism); many were poorly educated or had little knowledge of Church doctrine and the Scriptures.
- The regular clergy (monks and nuns) were greedy landowners who seemed more interested in managing their estates than serving their community.
- The Church had lost its way in teaching, pastoral care and standards of morality. Rules governing monastic orders had been relaxed and the papacy showed little interest in reform.
- Church fees and taxes were high, arbitrary and frequently the source of legal disputes.
- Clergy in holy orders enjoyed unfair privileges over laypeople (e.g. they were tried by canon law and punishments were less severe than sentences given in the common-law courts).

1.3 The critics

Most criticisms were voiced by a small, literate and professional group of people — lawyers, merchants, town councillors, academics and clergymen. Among the best-known critics were:

- Desiderius Erasmus (see Unit 9) — a Dutch scholar who condemned monastic abuses, ignorant priests and papal corruption, in works such as *In Praise of Folly* and

Julius Exclusus
- Jacob Wimpfeling — professor of poetry at Heidelberg and a fierce critic of clerical abuses
- John Colet — Dean of St Paul's, London, who in a sermon preached before the king in 1512 identified covetousness, immorality and material ambition as the most serious of abuses
- Giles Viterbo — an Italian cardinal who urged Leo X to end corruption in the Roman Church

1.4 Heresy

Heresy was not a serious problem in 1500. The main heretical groups which had challenged orthodox beliefs and papal authority had been contained and their leaders condemned. Inquisitions operated in Spain and Portugal, and in France and England suspects were sentenced by the Church and executed by the state. The main continental heretical groups were:
- Waldensians — located in southeast France and northwest Italy, they questioned the doctrine of purgatory and papal authority
- Hussites — confined to Bohemia, they took the Scriptures as their sole authority, used a vernacular Bible and gave the laity both bread and wine at communion

1.5 Evidence of revival

The Catholic Church was not a static institution, incapable of change; indeed, there was much evidence of reform in the late fifteenth and early sixteenth centuries:
- Observant orders — 'observant' monastic houses turned away from 'conventual' practices, restored stricter rules and, as a result, attracted many patrons and novices.
- New orders — the Bridgettine order of nuns was based on meditation, piety and self-denial; the Oratory of Divine Love was dedicated to charitable work; the Brethren of the Common Life practised the '*devotio moderna*' (a belief that spiritual perfection could be achieved through prayer, charity and poverty).
- Mysticism — works such as *The Imitation of Christ* encouraged the laity to communicate with God through meditation and private prayer.
- Popular piety — endowments in cash and goods to local churches for chantries, fraternities, relics and ornaments continued; as the half-millennium approached, fear of the **Apocalypse** and imminent death increased.
- Humanism — scholars (e.g. Erasmus, Colet, Ximenes and Lefèvre) revealed the differences between original Greek and Hebrew texts and the Latin translations favoured by the Church. Thus biblical humanists challenged several orthodox beliefs, even if most scholars held back from questioning the papacy.
- Secular rulers — Queen Isabella of Castile encouraged Cardinal Ximenes, Archbishop of Toledo, to reform the Spanish Church. He wrote devotional works, produced a new liturgy for the clergy, tried to enforce clerical residence and founded Alcala University to educate priests.

1.6 Conclusion

It is extremely difficult, if not impossible, to judge accurately the condition of the Church in 1500. Its critics proclaimed its faults and weaknesses but there were many examples of good Christian practices, and the lower clergy in particular appear to have met the needs of most people. Lay piety and Christian humanism demonstrated the strength of popular devotion, and both Church and state initiated reforms in the late fifteenth and early sixteenth centuries.

Apocalypse: the end of the world; it was widely predicted that this would happen at the half-millennium (1500).
Curia: the council of administration at the Vatican.

This topic appears at AS in the AQA (Alternative B) specification and at A2 in the OCR specification. You might be asked: 'How serious were the problems facing the Catholic Church in 1500?' In assessing the condition of the Church, consider the motives of the complainants and the nature of their criticisms. Put the problems in a rank order and evaluate rather than describe them.

2 What was the role of the papacy in the Catholic Reformation?

2.1 Background

Since 1471 all papal candidates had sworn that, if elected, they would call a general council of the Church within 2 years. None had. Popes feared that **conciliarism** would resurface and undermine their authority; but the papacy was also concerned that state churches would act independently if it did not put its own house in order.

2.2 The role of the papacy before 1534

Most popes between 1500 and 1534 were more interested in Italian politics and the welfare of their own families than attending to papal duties:

- Julius II (1503–13) was keen to increase his estates in central Italy and was prepared to wage war to achieve it.
- Leo X (1513–21) concluded a Lateran Council in 1517, which condemned clerical abuses but failed to root out corruption in the *Curia*.
- Adrian VI (1521–23) was aware of the need to combat Luther in Germany and unite Christian princes against the advancing Turks, but he accomplished neither.
- Clement VII (1523–34) was too lethargic to implement reforms. He distrusted general councils, and even the Sack of Rome (1527) left him unmoved.

Moreover, these popes received little support from Charles V and Francis I. Both rulers talked about the need to reform the Church but they seemed more interested in scoring points off each other as they fought for control of Italy. Italian popes and cardinals had good reason to distrust foreign princes, whose armies ravaged their lands.

2.3 Paul III (1534–49)

The accession of Paul III saw the first sign of papal-led reforms. Supported by bishops and cardinals (e.g. Giberti, Cajetan, Caraffa), who were equally, if not more determined to implement reform, much was achieved:

- a report was commissioned on clerical abuses (1536)
- the Jesuits were licensed as a new order (1540)
- Contarini was sent to Regensburg to try to heal the schism with the Lutherans (1541)

- a Roman inquisition was established (1542)
- the first session of a general council began at Trent (1545–49)

2.4 The papacy, 1549–1600

- Julius III (1550–55) revived the Council of Trent (1551–52) but little progress was made.
- Paul IV (1556–59) introduced the first Roman Index (1559), ordered Jews to be confined to ghettos and encouraged the Roman Inquisition to arrest and sentence heretics.
- Pius IV (1559–65) presided over the final session of the Council of Trent (1562–63) and commissioned a Catholic catechism.
- Pius V (1565–72) led a life of humility and asceticism. He visited the poor, treated lepers, oversaw reforms to the **Breviary** and **Missal**, and tried to enforce clerical residence among Italian bishops.
- Gregory XIII (1572–85) reformed Rome to eliminate its decadent buildings and behaviour, removed prostitutes and sorcerers, and supported Jesuit missions to Protestant countries (e.g. England).
- Sixtus V (1585–90) reformed the *Curia*, established 15 'congregations' to administer papal affairs (1588) and continued to rebuild Rome. St Peter's had a new dome, statues of saints were placed on top of ancient columns and a new library was opened.
- Clement VIII (1592–1605) revised the Vulgate (1592) and issued a new Index (1596).

2.5 Conclusion

Between 1545 and 1600 Rome and the papacy underwent a remarkable transformation. The city was cleansed, its buildings modernised and numerous colleges founded. The papacy, whose prestige was considerably enhanced by the Council of Trent (see section 4 of this unit), re-established its reputation as the moral and spiritual leader of the Catholic Church.

EXAMINER'S TIP

This topic appears at AS in the OCR, AQA (Alternative B) and Edexcel specifications, and at A2 in the OCR specification. At A2 you might be asked: 'Assess the role of the papacy in the development of the Catholic Church during the sixteenth century.' At least half of your answer should be focused on the work of the papacy throughout the century, but remember that 'assess' requires you to set its contribution alongside other factors (see sections 3, 4 and 5).

3 What was the importance of the new orders to the Catholic Church in the sixteenth century?

3.1 Background

Many of the long-established monastic orders introduced reforms in the fifteenth century. The Dominicans and Franciscans encouraged missionaries; some Augustinians

introduced the *devotio moderna*; and the Carthusians developed mystical ideas. But monasticism was still concerned with institutional improvements and remained remote from most people's lives. A distinctive feature of the sixteenth-century Catholic Reformation was the emergence of new religious orders that were mainly concerned with spiritual renewal.

3.2 The new orders

The aim of these orders was to pray, fast and serve God and their communities. They were first set up in Italy to meet the social and ecclesiastical needs of the people whose living conditions had worsened as armies destroyed much of the country in the 1520s. They were not founded to counter Protestantism.

The Oratory of Divine Love (1497)

A lay order, established in Genoa, that was based on the ideas of St Augustine and performed religious exercises (prayers) and charitable work. Similar brotherhoods were started in Rome, Naples and Bologna.

The Theatines (1524)

Cardinals Caraffa and Cajetan started this order. Bound by monastic vows, they worked, preached and prayed in hospitals in Rome.

The Capuchins (1528)

These were Franciscan friars in Ancona who were dedicated to a life of poverty and preaching. By 1574 there were over 3,500 members in 300 Italian convents; by 1600 the order had spread to France, Spain, Germany and the Netherlands.

The Somaschi (1530)

A small organisation, often known as the 'Society of Servants of the Poor', they were dedicated to working among prostitutes, orphans and the poor in Venice, Verona and Milan.

The Barnabites (1533)

Founded in Milan, they worked in prisons and hospitals and cared for the poor and homeless.

The Ursulines (1535)

An order of nuns founded by Angela Merici in Brescia, they looked after orphans, assisted in hospitals and educated girls in the Christian faith.

3.3 The Jesuits

The Jesuits (Society of Jesus) were founded by Ignatius Loyola of Spain in 1540.

Aims

Loyola's aims were to:
- defend and propagate the Christian faith by preaching and lecturing
- educate children
- hear confessions and administer the sacraments
- perform charitable work

Training

To help individuals decide whether they were capable of becoming Jesuits, Loyola devised a series of meditative prayers, questions and commentaries, known as 'spiritual exercises'. This 4-week programme of self-evaluation enabled the student to compare his own experiences with those of Loyola and then with those of Christ. Vows of honesty, chastity and obedience were then taken. There followed a 10-year period of studying theology, philosophy, reasoning, logic and humanism, together with charitable work experience. Finally, for the few who completed their training, a fourth vow was taken: to serve the papacy.

Achievements by 1600

- **Seminaries** were founded in Italy, Spain and Portugal in the 1540s, and in Germany in the 1550s, to educate boys from all social backgrounds. By 1600 there were 230 colleges across Europe; 155 were in Germany.
- University departments of theology were often dominated by Jesuits (e.g. Munich and Würzburg in Germany).
- Missionaries went to Protestant countries (e.g. Campion and Parsons travelled to England).
- Natives were converted to Christianity (e.g. 10,000 in India, 200,000 in Japan and 650,000 in the Philippines). Xavier went to Africa, India, Malaysia and Japan; Ricci went to China.
- They instructed rural communities in Italy, Spain, Germany and France and established 'Marian congregations' to maintain Christian fellowship.

Conclusion

Although the Jesuits are the best known of the new orders and their contribution to the development of the Catholic Reformation was considerable, the work of other orders in Italy and elsewhere in Europe should not be underestimated.

GLOSSARY

seminaries: training colleges for priests.

EXAMINER'S TIP

This topic appears at AS in the OCR, AQA (Alternative B) and Edexcel specifications, and at A2 in the OCR specification. You might be asked at AS: 'How important were the Jesuits to the revival of the Catholic Church in the sixteenth century?' Such a question can easily elicit a narrative response, and this should be avoided. Consider the achievements of the Jesuits in the context of other contributors to the Catholic revival. The key phrase in this question is 'How important…to the revival', not simply 'the Jesuits'.

4 What did the Council of Trent achieve by 1600?

4.1 The council's aims

When Paul III convened a general council of the Church at Trent (in northern Italy) in 1545 he had three main aims:

- to protect his own authority as head of the Catholic Church
- to remove clerical abuses
- to define Catholic doctrine and defend it from Protestants

Charles V hoped to find a compromise solution to prevent a permanent religious schism in Germany, and was supported by like-minded bishops known as the 'spirituali'.

Opposed to any form of compromise were the *zelati*, mainly Italian bishops and cardinals. In fact, Lutheran representatives only attended the second of three sessions (1551–52) and the *zelati* triumphed. Charles also wanted abuses discussed before Church doctrine but the papacy and Italian cardinals (who formed the majority) objected. Doctrine and abuses were therefore discussed alternately.

4.2 The Tridentine Decrees

After 25 sessions spanning 18 years (1545–49, 1551–52, 1562–63), the Tridentine (Latin for Trent) Decrees were published in 1564. The Catholic faith was defined according to orthodox teaching:

- The seven sacraments were to be treated equally.
- The Mass was declared a sacrificial act, sung in Latin and celebrated with bread only.
- Transubstantiation was confirmed as the only interpretation of the Eucharist.
- The Scriptures and unwritten 'traditions' were declared of equal validity and the Vulgate was free from dogmatic error.
- Chantries, purgatory, saints, images and pilgrimages were all endorsed.

The decrees also addressed clerical abuses:

- Seminaries were to be set up in every diocese to educate the clergy.
- Absenteeism and pluralism were condemned and indulgences abolished.
- Parish clergy were told to preach every Sunday and on feast days; they would be supervised by bishops and were warned about socialising with their parishioners.
- The clergy were not allowed to marry.
- Bishops were required to preach, administer the sacraments, hold regular visitations and synods, be resident, of mature age and well-qualified.
- All female orders were to be **cloistered** and brought under monastic rule.

4.3 The significance of Trent

- Papal authority emerged as supreme; only the Pope had the right to interpret the decrees.
- The role of the clergy as the intermediary between God and commoners was emphasised.
- Bishops were given greater authority to oversee pastoral and teaching duties and to eliminate clerical abuses.
- By 1600 seminaries were established in Spain (20), Italy (11) and Portugal (7) but there were only a handful in Germany and none in France.
- The Catholic Church redefined its faith whereby it united its followers and embraced popular customs and beliefs.
- No compromise was made with Protestants. Instead, all Lutheran and Calvinist notions of justification by faith alone were rejected.
- Nothing was said about the *Curia*, and little mention was made of the role of the monastic orders, the Inquisition and the Index (see section 5 below).

4.4 Conclusion

As a result of the Tridentine Decrees the Church became more assured and positive; it no longer felt the need to react to the challenge of Protestantism. The effective implementation of the decrees rested with future popes, churchmen and secular rulers, however, and progress varied from country to country. Philip of Spain, for instance, endorsed the decrees in 1564 and encouraged reform; France, on the other hand, was beset with civil war and only in the late seventeenth century were the decrees registered and reforms begun.

GLOSSARY

cloistered: confined to a convent.

EXAMINER'S TIP

This topic appears at AS in the OCR, AQA (Alternative B) and Edexcel specifications, and at A2 in the OCR specification. At AS you might be asked: 'To what extent did the Council of Trent strengthen the power of the papacy by 1600?' It is important that you contrast the condition and status of the papacy before 1545 with that of 1600. Trent was a turning-point in the history of the papacy and helped to galvanise the pontiffs between 1563 and 1600 to lead by example.

5 How effective were the Inquisition and the Index?

5.1 The Inquisition

The Inquisition was an ecclesiastical court set up to investigate and prosecute heretics. Established in Germany, Italy, Spain and Portugal in the Middle Ages, most tribunals had fallen into abeyance in the fourteenth century and only Castile and Aragon set up permanent courts in the late fifteenth century.

The Spanish Inquisition

At first the Spanish Inquisition investigated *conversos* (see Unit 7, section 2) but by the 1520s it was targeting Erasmians, Illuminists (mystics) and Lutherans. Few were found. In 1559–62, however, it was very active, putting some 77 alleged Protestants to death. Most of these cases were heard by inquisitors in Barcelona, Saragossa and Seville but Protestantism never became a serious problem. Thereafter, the Inquisition was more concerned with lapsed *conversos* and *moriscos*, and with investigating acts of immorality by Spanish Christians. Although less than 2% of those arrested were burned at the stake, the secrecy that surrounded investigations and the stigma attached to being a suspect led most penitents to confess and adhere to the orthodox teaching of the Church.

The Roman Inquisition

The aim of the Roman Inquisition, formed in 1542, was to set up a network of tribunals throughout Catholic Europe. In practice, most countries acted independently of the Roman court: Spain and Portugal (established in 1547) had their own organisations, and France and Germany were unwilling to defer to the papacy when dealing with heresy. Regional tribunals were established in Milan, Lucca, Florence, Naples and Venice, which prevented Protestantism from taking hold. In fact, much of the Inquisition's time was spent investigating cases of immorality and witchcraft, and few executions occurred.

5.2 The Index

The censorship and licensing of literature formed an important part of the Inquisition's work. In the early sixteenth century university faculties of theology and city councils

produced their own lists of prohibited reading — the Sorbonne (Paris) in 1543 and Venice in 1549, for instance.

The Spanish Index

- Charles V granted the Spanish Inquisition the right to censor books in 1545 and further revisions occurred in 1551.
- Valdes, the inquisitor-general, expanded the Index in 1559 and listed some 670 works.
- In 1583 the Index was extended to 2,375 titles.

The Roman Index

- Begun by Paul IV in 1559, it banned over 500 authors, including Erasmus, Machiavelli and 50 vernacular Bibles.
- The Tridentine Index (1564) compiled a more select list (although Erasmus was still proscribed).

Conclusion

Historians have argued whether these indices successfully protected Catholics from 'harmful' publications and, if they did, whether Spain in particular became culturally isolated from the rest of Europe. Recent research suggests that though the volume of Protestant literature entering Catholic countries remained small, forbidden works still circulated, sometimes as a result of false titles going undetected but more usually on account of smuggling.

EXAMINER'S TIP

This topic appears at AS in the OCR, AQA (Alternative B) and Edexcel specifications. You might be asked: 'How important was the role of the Inquisition and Index in the Catholic revival between 1545 and 1600?' You can reasonably be expected to write more on the Inquisition than on the Index but part of your answer (perhaps one third) should be directed to an assessment of their importance in relation to other factors (e.g. the new orders and the Council of Trent).

 6

Was there a Catholic or a Counter-Reformation?

6.1 The debate

For a number of years historians have debated whether the origin of the sixteenth-century Catholic revival lay in medieval precedents or in its response to the Lutheran movement. Protestant historians have often claimed the latter (implying that the Catholic Church was incapable of innovation and, when forced into reform, borrowed many of its ideas from Protestantism).

Catholic historians have naturally resented such allegations and instead have taken the view that the reformation owed very little, if anything, to the Protestant movement.

Arguments in favour of a Counter-Reformation

- The papacy led the Catholic revival, which only became apparent after the pontificate of Paul III (1534–49).
- The Jesuits (1540), Inquisition (1542) and Index (1559) were focused on combating heresy.
- Only the double challenge of Lutheranism and Calvinism forced the Church to call a general council at Trent (1545–63).

Arguments in favour of a Catholic Reformation

- Most of the main features of the Catholic revival had medieval precedents (e.g. 'new' orders, a general council, inquisitions).
- Evidence of a resurgence in spirituality was apparent well before 1517 (e.g. biblical humanism, mysticism, personal piety).
- While the sixteenth-century Catholic Reformation was in part focused on how to respond to the Protestant challenge, the Catholic Church was really concerned with reforming its own spiritual and institutional condition.

Conclusion

Most historians no longer accept the traditional view that the Catholic movement was essentially a 'counter-reformation' (e.g. the judgement of H. Evennett). Some historians (e.g. R. Po-Chia Hsia) prefer to use the phrase 'Catholic renewal' or 'Early Modern Catholicism' (R. Bireley). The majority, however, agree with A. G. Dickens that the revival owed something both to medieval precedents and to sixteenth-century Protestantism.

6.2 Successes of the reformation by 1600

- Traditional Catholic states (e.g. Bavaria, Spain, Italy) were strengthened.
- States in danger of turning Calvinist remained Catholic (e.g. Poland, Hungary, Austria).
- Several Lutheran states became Catholic again (e.g. Bohemia, Styria, Swabia).
- Most of France and the Netherlands stayed Catholic.
- The papacy became a far stronger institution: reformed, respected and unchallenged.
- Trent defined Catholic doctrine clearly and unequivocally, and initiated important reforms for the future (e.g. seminaries).
- The quality of clerical teaching and preaching improved.
- The Jesuits, both as teachers and as missionaries, energised the Catholic Church.

6.3 Limitations of the reformation

- Catholic reform had little impact on northern and central Germany, England, Scotland, Scandinavia and much of Switzerland.
- The Tridentine Decrees were not implemented in every Catholic state (e.g. Austria) and often only patchily (e.g. Germany).
- Most rural areas held firmly to traditional beliefs and resisted change.
- Few seminaries were set up by 1600 due to the cost.
- Nepotism, pluralism, absenteeism and low clerical salaries remained a problem.
- The intrusive activity of the Inquisition cast a shadow over Catholic societies.

EXAMINER'S TIP

This topic appears at AS in the OCR and AQA (Alternative B) specifications, and at A2 in the OCR specification. You might be asked at AS: 'Assess the reasons why efforts to reform the Catholic Church gathered pace in the sixteenth century.' An explanation is required but the key phrase in this question is 'gathered pace'. At A2 a consideration of changes and developments in the Catholic Church throughout the sixteenth century is an integral part of the synoptic module. A typical question is: 'How far was the Catholic Reformation during the sixteenth century simply a reaction to the Protestant Reformation?' Arguments claiming that the Catholic renewal was mainly a reaction to the Protestant movement need to be balanced with the view that the revival preceded the emergence of Luther in 1517.